QUESTIONS & ANSWERS: Family Law

Multiple Choice and Short Answer Questions and Answers

By

Mark Strasser
Trustees Professor of Law
Capital University Law School

ISBN#: 0820556696

Editorial Offices
744 Broad Street, Newark, NJ 07102 (973) 820-2000
201 Mission St., San Francisco, CA 94105-1831 (415) 908-3200
701 East Water Street, Charlottesville, VA 22902-7587 (804) 972-7600
www.lexis.com

(Pub.3183)

DEDICATION

To my family
George, Emma, and Nathan

ABOUT THE AUTHOR

Mark Strasser has a B.A. from Harvard College, an M.A. and Ph.D. from the University of Chicago, and a J.D. from Stanford Law School. He is the Trustees Professor of Law at Capital University Law School in Columbus, Ohio, where he teaches Family Law, Constitutional Law, and Sexual Diversity and the Law. He has written extensively in Family Law, Constitutional Law, Tort, and Law and Sexual Minorities.

PREFACE

Traditionally, family law is a matter of state rather than federal concern and it would be a mistake to believe that family law is uniform across the states. Nonetheless, the states treat a variety of matters in similar ways whether because of federal constitutional or statutory law or because states have adopted various uniform laws or simply because the states have learned from each other. The law represented here does not focus on that of a particular jurisdiction but instead involves a sampling from a variety of states.

There are two types of questions in this volume—short answer and multiple choice. Often, the questions will involve fact scenarios in invented jurisdictions, an approach that emphasizes (1) the overlap and differences among the states, and (2) the importance of examining the background laws of the jurisdictions in which the events occur. Because this has become an increasingly mobile society in which attorneys must not only consider the substantive law but also which courts should be deciding the relevant issues, some of the questions here will focus on jurisdictional rather than substantive issues.

This book covers a variety of areas discussed in family law courses. As a general matter, federal and state statutes and case law will be used as supporting authority. The aims of this book are two-fold: (1) to improve test-taking skills, and (2) to help students understand the substantive material by highlighting some of the obvious and not so obvious points that are important in resolving some of the kinds of difficulties that arise in family law.

Professor Mark Strasser

mstrasser@law.capital.edu

Columbus, Ohio

September, 2003

TABLE OF CONTENTS

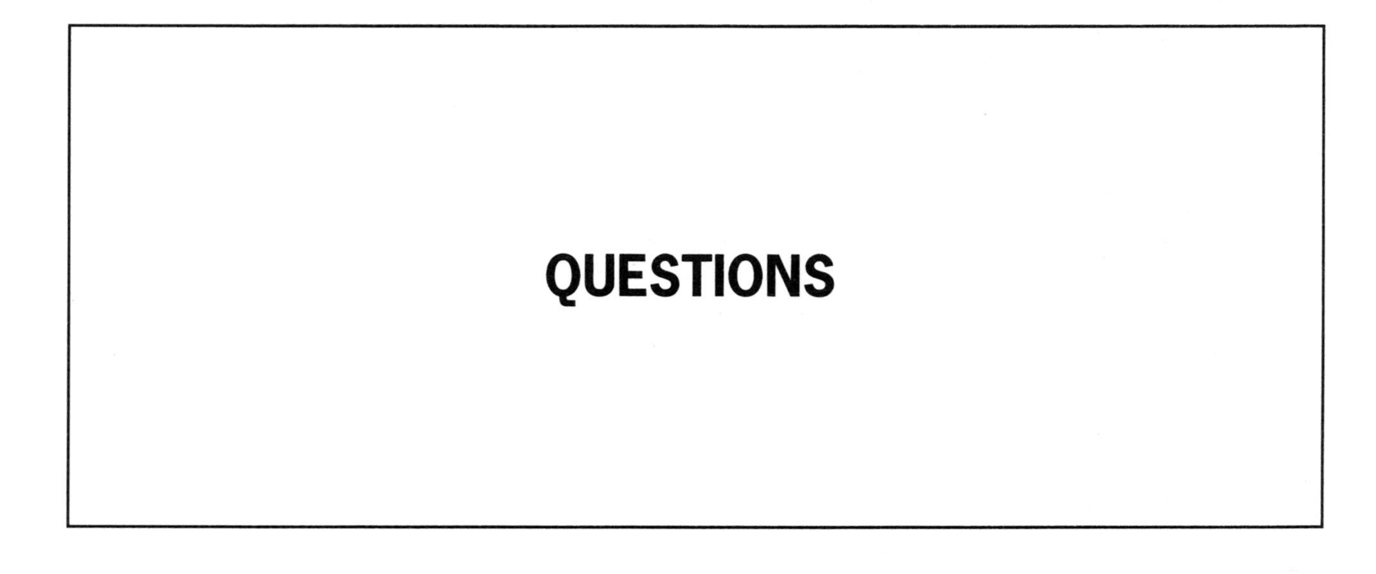
QUESTIONS

TOPIC 1: MINOR MARRIAGES

QUESTIONS

Andrew Adams, 19, and Bonnie Bellington, 17, wish to marry. However, their state does not permit individuals under the age of 18 to marry without their parents' permission. Because Bonnie's parents have said that they will not consent to the marriage, Andrew and Bonnie decide that Bonnie will simply lie about her age to the Justice of the Peace. They live together for a few months in a basement apartment in Andrew's parents' home, but they then split up before Bonnie reaches her 18th birthday. A year later, Andrew meets someone new whom he wishes to marry. He consults an attorney to find out whether he must seek an annulment or divorce before he can marry his new love.

1. The attorney should say:

   (A) Because Andrew and Bonnie split up before Bonnie reached 18 years of age, the marriage was not valid and thus there is no need for Andrew to have the marriage annulled.

   (B) If minor marriages are voidable rather than void in the jurisdiction in which Andrew and Bonnie live, Andrew must seek an annulment or divorce if he wishes to marry his new sweetheart.

   (C) If minor marriages are void rather than voidable in the jurisdiction in which Andrew and Bonnie live, Andrew must have his marriage to Bonnie annulled if he wishes to marry his new sweetheart.

   (D) Because Bonnie's parents did not give their permission for Bonnie to marry at the time of the marriage's celebration, there is no need to have the marriage annulled if her parents never gave their blessing to the union once it had been celebrated.

Assume the facts as stated in Question 1 and that the jurisdiction treats minor marriages as voidable. However, also assume that Andrew and Bonnie lived together for more than a year in the basement apartment, well after Bonnie had reached her 18th birthday. Then they split up, and Andrew meets someone new whom he wishes to marry. He consults with an attorney to establish the status of his marriage with Bonnie.

2. The attorney should say:

   (A) Because Andrew and Bonnie had married without her parents' permission and before she had reached 18 years of age, the marriage was not valid and thus cannot be legally recognized.

   (B) Because Andrew and Bonnie lived together as husband and wife after they both were of legal age, the marriage has been ratified and is now valid.

   (C) The marriage is now valid if and only if the jurisdiction recognizes common law marriages.

(D) Because Andrew and Bonnie no longer love each other and are not living together, their marriage does not exist and each is free to marry someone else.

John Jones has given his permission for his to 12-year-old daughter, Joanna, to marry Samuel Smith. Joanna and Samuel take part in a religious marriage ceremony. Samuel is charged with corrupting a minor. Samuel pleads his marriage to Joanna as a defense.

3. What result?

(A) Because John gave permission for his daughter to marry, the marriage is valid, since a child can marry at any age if the parent gives permission.

(B) Because Joanna was a minor, she could not marry even with parental consent.

(C) If Samuel did not show Joanna any pornographic materials, he cannot be charged with corrupting a minor, regardless of the validity of the marriage.

(D) Although states permit minors to marry with parental consent, they tend not to allow someone as young as Joanna to marry even with that consent, so the marriage will likely be treated as invalid and not a defense.

Paul Perry and Roberta Roberts are both 17 and hence minors, unable to marry in their home state of Califington without parental consent. They are married by a Justice of the Peace, after they lie about their age. They tell no one about the marriage, waiting for an auspicious time to tell their parents.

Tragically, about a week later, Paul dies in a car accident. When Paul's mother, Penelope, finds out that Paul and Roberta had married, she seeks to have the marriage annulled.

4. Will Penelope be successful?

(A) Because neither Paul nor Roberta had reached their 18th birthday, Paul's mother will be permitted to annul the marriage if Paul and Roberta had not had sexual relations after the ceremony had been performed.

(B) Because Paul and Roberta had not told anyone about the marriage, they were not known in the community to be married and hence the marriage may still be annulled.

(C) If the marriage between Paul and Roberta was voidable rather than void, it cannot be challenged after the death of one of the parties.

(D) Because Penelope never gave Roberta a chance to establish her love for Paul, Penelope will be precluded from challenging the marriage now.

Cindy is a senior in high school and Don is in his first year of college. They have been dating for several years and want to get married, although their parents say that they are too young. Their domicile, New Vermshire, makes marriages involving an individual between 16 and 18 years voidable if celebrated without parental permission.

One day, Don and Cindy go to the neighboring state of East Massmont, where they are old enough to marry without parental permission. They do so and return to New Vermshire without telling anyone what they have done.

A few days after returning, Cindy finds out that she has been accepted at Prestigious College that is 1,000 miles away. She and Don fight about whether she should go, and she eventually tells him that she is going to go whether he likes it or not. He says that if she goes she can forget about having any relationship with him. They talk no more about it that spring and see each other only occasionally over the summer.

Cindy in fact goes to school at Prestigious College, confident that Don will change his mind. Cindy celebrates her 18th birthday at school and then hears from a girlfriend that Don has started dating someone else. She decides that he is much less mature than she had thought and that she could do much better.

Cindy does not go back home until the following summer and, to her surprise, finds out that Don has married someone else. Cindy decides to mention to the district attorney that Don has committed bigamy.

5. Does Don face potential criminal liability?

ANSWER:

Carol Connolly, 16, and David Duncan, 17, wish to marry soon because Carol is pregnant and they want to be married before their child is born. However, both Carol's and David's parents are inalterably opposed to the marriage.

6. If Carol and David wish to marry legally, do they have any options or must they simply wait until both are at least 18 years of age?

ANSWER:

TOPIC 2: BIGAMOUS/POLYGAMOUS MARRIAGES

QUESTIONS

Sara Samuelson, 30 years old, and Tim Tomasson, 65 years old, have married in their home state of New Orrington, notwithstanding the great age difference between them and the strong objections of Tim's children from a previous marriage. A few years into the marriage, Tim has a heart attack and dies intestate. Discovering that Sara was not legally divorced from her first husband until a year after her marriage to Tim, Tim's children seek to establish the invalidity of the marriage between Sara and Tim, and thus that she should not inherit anything from the estate. Sara argues that the once the impediment to her marriage was removed, the marriage became valid and that, in any event, the marriage can no longer be challenged now that Tim has died. New Orrington refuses to recognize common law marriages.

7. What result?

(A) As a general matter, the states will treat the marriage between Sara and Tim as valid once her divorce from her first husband becomes final. Absent a statute to the contrary, Tim's children's claim should be dismissed on the merits and Sara is entitled to her share of the estate as surviving spouse.

(B) Because Tim had died, the validity of the marriage could no longer be challenged and the marriage will be treated as valid, even if it would have been found invalid had it been challenged while Tim was still alive. Sara is entitled to her share of the estate as surviving spouse.

(C) Because Sara had a husband living at the time she married Tim, her ceremonial marriage with Tim will likely be treated as void and of no effect.

(D) Regardless of whether Sara and Tim's marriage was valid, void, or voidable, Tim's children will be successful in precluding Sara from inheriting if they can establish that Tim would not have wanted her to inherit had he known about her first marriage.

A few days after Georgina and Herbert celebrated their 20th wedding anniversary, Herbert had a heart attack and died. Shortly thereafter, Georgina heard from Herbert's first wife, Frankie, who claimed to be Herbert's widow. Georgina did not take this particularly seriously because she knew Frankie and Herbert had gotten a divorce 25 years ago and that there was no record of their ever having remarried. Georgina nonetheless consulted an attorney about her rights.

8. What possible bases might Frankie have for claiming to be Herbert's lawful widow?

ANSWER:

TOPIC 3: INCESTUOUS MARRIAGES — QUESTIONS

John, 30, has fallen in love with Sarah, 20, his elder brother's eldest daughter. They marry. A year later, John is in a fatal accident at work. Sarah will receive benefits from John's employer if and only if she can establish that she was legally married to John.

9. Will she receive the benefits?

   (A) Because John has died, Sarah's marriage to John can no longer be challenged and must be recognized as valid.

   (B) If uncle-niece marriages are incestuous and void *ab initio*, the marriage will not be recognized and Sarah will not receive the benefits.

   (C) Because John's brother gave his permission for Sarah and John to marry, the marriage is valid.

   (D) If the Town Clerk has a record of the marriage, the marriage will be considered valid and Sarah will receive the benefits.

Albert marries Betty, who is 15 years his senior. He thus becomes the stepfather of Carol, who is only five years his junior. From the moment that they met, the attraction between Albert and Carol was very strong, although they both chose to ignore it at first. Eventually, however, they realized that they could not continue to resist it. Albert divorces Betty and starts to date Carol, with whom he has a child. Eventually, Albert and Carol marry. Betty, who was invited to the wedding, sends her regrets.

10. Will the marriage between Albert and Carol be recognized?

ANSWER:

Wally and Mira have been living together without benefit of marriage in the state of Pennio, which does not recognize common law marriage. Wally has been helping Mira raise her daughter, Soni, who is a beautiful young woman. When Soni goes away to college, Wally realizes just how much he misses her and that his feelings for her are not strictly paternal. Wally and Soni start to date and eventually marry.

11. What difficulties, if any, are posed for the validity of the marriage?

ANSWER:

TOPIC 4: SEXUAL RELATIONS AND MARRIAGE — QUESTIONS

Eddie and Ethel Edwards have been trying to have children for years with no success. They have timed their sexual relations as their infertility doctor suggested and still have had no luck. Eventually, they both are tested and Eddie discovers that he is unable to father children. Ethel, who very much wants to have children, files for divorce on the basis of impotency.

12. What result?

    (A) Ethel will not be able to get a divorce on this ground. While impotency can be a ground for divorce, that has been interpreted to mean the inability to have sexual relations rather than the inability to have children.

    (B) The divorce will be granted if Eddie's inability to father children is permanent rather than temporary.

    (C) The divorce will be granted only if Ethel is not also sterile. If she is, then no harm will have been done to her by Eddie's impotency and the divorce will not be granted.

    (D) Once Eddie and Ethel have had sexual relations, they will only be able to divorce if one of them has sexual relations with a party outside of the marriage.

Marjorie and Malcolm love each other and want to marry, even though they both know that they will not be able to engage in marital relations. They marry. After several years, Marjorie decides that she no longer wishes to be married to Malcolm. She seeks an annulment, arguing that the marriage was never consummated.

13. What result?

    (A) Because they never had sexual relations, the marriage was never consummated and each state will permit Marjorie to have the marriage annulled.

    (B) If she is not be estopped from seeking the annulment because she knew at the time of the marriage that they would have no marital relations, Marjorie will be granted the annulment on this basis.

    (C) Marjorie may well be precluded from having the marriage annulled both because she knew at the time of the marriage that they would not be having marital relations and because she waited so long to press her claim in any event.

    (D) Because marriage is sacred, Marjorie and Malcolm will not be able to have their marriage annulled under any conditions.

Bob and Betty Billings have been married for 15 years. While they had sexual relations a few times in the beginning of their marriage, they have not had relations since, notwithstanding Bob's frequent requests for such relations. Bob now seeks to annul the marriage, claiming that his wife is impotent.

14. What result?

ANSWER:

TOPIC 5: MARRIAGE AND COMPETECNY

QUESTIONS

To bolster his courage, Yevgeny Younger has several drinks before marrying Olga Older. Regrettably, Yevgeny discovers that his initial reservations about marrying Olga were justified and he seeks to have the marriage declared void. Yevgeny argues that he was drunk at the time of the marriage and thus was unable to give the proper weight to the benefits and drawbacks of marrying Olga. Olga claims that Yevgeny was not too drunk to know that he was marrying her, and thus that the marriage is valid. Olga is suing Yevgeny for divorce, alleging that he has abandoned her.

15. What result?

    (A) Because marriage is a serious venture involving weighty responsibilities, a ceremony in which one of the parties is inebriated is invalid. Yevgeny will be successful in having the marriage annulled.

    (B) Because marriage is a serious venture involving weighty responsibilities, a ceremony in which one of the parties is drunk will be considered valid if the drunk party understood what he or she was doing and the nature of the ceremony. Olga will be successful in securing a divorce and Yevgeny will be unsuccessful in having the marriage annulled.

    (C) This will depend upon whether the state treats marriages entered into where one of the parties is inebriated as void or as voidable. If the former, then Yevgeny wins. If the latter, then Olga wins.

    (D) The marriage will be considered valid and Olga will be successful if she can establish that he understood what he was doing at the time of the marriage and that Yevgeny has left the marital home without lawful cause and has constantly refused to return.

Assume the facts in Question 15 except that witnesses testify that Yevgeny seemed so drunk that he did not seem to know where he was or what he was doing during the ceremony.

16. What result?

    (A) Because Yevgeny did not have the requisite *compos mentis*, he did not validly enter into the marriage contract and thus the marriage will be void.

    (B) Even if Yevgeny did not know the effect of what he was doing during the ceremony, that likely will merely have made the marriage voidable, and his subsequent actions will likely be construed as condoning or ratifying the marriage, thus making it valid. Olga will be successful if she can establish that he left the marital home without cause and has consistently refused to return.

    (C) Marriage involves such an important matter that whether Yevgeny was slightly or extremely drunk, his having uttered the correct words at the correct time makes the marriage valid. Olga will be successful if she can establish that Yevgeny abandoned her.

(D) Marriage involves such an important matter that whether Yevgeny was slightly or extremely drunk, his having uttered the correct words at the correct time is irrelevant and the marriage is invalid.

Jillian Jameson marries Marty Martinson. One year later, Jillian dies. Jillian's daughter from a former marriage, Nancy, challenges the marriage, claiming that her mother was insane when she married Marty and that Jillian had never regained her sanity before her death. Nancy further argues that Marty should not inherit anything from Jillian and that instead Nancy should receive everything, since she is her mother's sole living relative.

17. Will Nancy be permitted to challenge the marriage?

(A) Marriages can never be challenged once one of the parties to the marriage has died, and thus Nancy will be precluded from challenging the marriage and the marriage will be treated as valid by the state.

(B) If the state treats marriages by individuals who are insane as void, then Nancy will be permitted to challenge the marriage. However, if the state treats marriages involving the insane as merely voidable, then Nancy will be precluded from challenging the marriage because, absent statutory specification to the contrary, voidable marriages cannot be challenged once one of the parties has died.

(C) Whether the marriage is void or voidable, Nancy will be permitted to challenge the marriage.

(D) If the marriage is treated as voidable then Nancy will be permitted to challenge it. However, if the marriage is treated as void, then there will be nothing for Nancy to challenge, so Nancy will be barred from challenging the marriage.

Sarah and Thomas have been drinking heavily. Suddenly, Thomas suggests that they get married. Sarah, who is feeling very good after having had several drinks, agrees that this would be a great idea. Sarah and Thomas drive to the house of a Justice of the Peace, wake him up, and insist that he marry them. He does so, his wife acting as a witness.

The next day, Sarah and Thomas awake in a strange hotel room and vaguely remember what had happened the night before. They decide to try to make their marriage work, although it is doubtful that they would have married if they had not both had so much to drink.

Regrettably, it becomes clear after a while that the marriage simply will not work. The no-fault divorce provision in local law requires them to live separate and apart for a year before they can get a divorce. Thomas seeks to have the marriage annulled.

18. What result?

ANSWER:

TOPIC 6: COHABITATION, PRENUPTIAL, AND POSTNUPTIAL AGREEMENTS

QUESTIONS

Frank and Frieda Frederickson have been married for a few years. They are having marital difficulties and Frieda suggests that if they are to stay together they should sign a postnuptial agreement. Frank agrees and signs a postnuptial agreement that treats Frieda very favorably. Regrettably, after a few months, Frank and Frieda divorce anyway. Frank argues that the postnuptial agreement is unenforceable.

19. Is Frank correct?

    (A) Frank is correct. In fact, there is no such thing as a postnuptial agreement that is made in contemplation of the marriage continuing, although it is of course true that separation agreements are made in anticipation of divorce.

    (B) Frank is incorrect. Postnuptial agreements are enforceable if they are informed, voluntary, and not unconscionable.

    (C) Frank is correct because the threat that the marriage would be ended unless the agreement was signed constitutes duress or coercion.

    (D) Frank is incorrect. In fact, postnuptial agreements must be enforced unless duress or coercion can be established.

Karl and Karen Kelinsky have been having marital difficulties. Karl makes clear both that he will move out immediately and divorce Karen unless they sign a postnuptial agreement and that if they sign one he will try very hard to make the marriage work. They both sign the agreement. Within a few days, Karl moves out of the house, admitting that he was intending to divorce Karen all along and that he had just wanted to get her to sign the agreement so that he could get a more favorable distribution when they divorced. When Karl files for divorce, Karen challenges the validity of the postnuptial agreement.

20. Will Karen's challenge be successful?

    (A) Because Karen voluntarily signed the agreement, it is valid and enforceable.

    (B) Because Karl proposed that they have a postnuptial agreement and because Karl is filing for divorce, the agreement is invalid and unenforceable.

    (C) Because Karl defrauded Karen when promising that he would try to make the marriage work if she signed the agreement, the agreement will likely be treated as invalid and unenforceable.

    (D) Because Karl would have moved out immediately and divorced Karen had she not signed the agreement and because he at least stayed a few extra days because they made the agreement, Karen cannot claim that there was no consideration for the agreement and the agreement will be enforceable.

Wayne and Wanda Williams have signed a postnuptial agreement which specifies that in the event of a divorce: (1) any child born of the marriage will be in the custody of the parent who is of the same sex as is the child, and (2) neither parent shall be required to pay child support should he or she be the non-custodial parent. Wayne and Wanda signed the agreement voluntarily and with a full understanding of the implications of the agreement. After signing the agreement, they have two children, a boy and a girl. Eventually, they divorce. Wanda seeks custody of both children and seeks child support from Wayne. Wayne wants the postnuptial agreement enforced—he wants custody of his son but not his daughter and does not want to pay or receive child support.

21. What part of the agreement, if any, will be enforced?

(A) Because Wayne and Wanda signed the agreement voluntarily and with a complete understanding of its implications, the agreement will be enforced in its entirety.

(B) Because it would violate public policy to decide which parent would have custody without considering which parent's having custody would promote the best interests of the child, this provision of the agreement will be struck. However, because support merely involves money, this provision will be upheld.

(C) The provision specifying no child support will be struck down as violating public policy but the provision specifying which parent would have custody will be seen as an attempt to promote the best interests of the child and will be upheld.

(D) Both provisions will be struck down as violations of public policy. Custody will be awarded after a consideration of which parent's having custody would promote the best interests of the child and support will be decided in light of the applicable child support guidelines.

Fred and Gertrude have been living together for several years. Fred desperately wants to marry Gertrude because his family is constantly pressuring him to get married. Gertrude is quite satisfied not being married, especially because her first marriage ended in a bitter divorce. Gertrude says that she is willing to go through the ceremony with Fred but only if he will sign a statement making clear that they are only going through the ceremony to satisfy Fred's parents and that in their own eyes they are not really married. Fred signs the statement, which Gertrude places in a safe-deposit box. A few years after their marriage, Fred and Gertrude decide to split up. Fred makes some suggestions about how they might divide some of the property acquired during the marriage and Gertrude points out that they were never really married, so that they will not have to worry about how to distribute that property. She reminds him of the signed statement that she still has in her safe-deposit box. The trial court finds that they are indeed married. On appeal, the question before the court is whether the marriage should be recognized.

22. Will the court uphold the existence of the marriage?

(A) The marriage will not be recognized because one or both of the parties did not subjectively intend for the marriage to be legally recognized.

(B) The marriage will be recognized because they met all of the formal requirements of marriage, even if one or both of the parties did not subjectively intend for the marriage to be legally recognized.

(C) The marriage will not be recognized because their agreement is, basically, a prenuptial agreement, and such agreements have been held enforceable by the courts.

(D) The marriage will be recognized because once a couple lives together as a married couple for more than a year, the validity of the marriage can no longer be challenged.

Mary Mahoney and Nicholas Nickleby are deciding whether to marry each other. They each have children from a prior marriage and each had a less than amicable divorce in which the custody of the children was a major sticking point. They decide to enter into a prenuptial agreement specifying property division and who would have custody of any children born of the marriage so that these issues would be settled were they ever to divorce. They marry and two children are born of the marriage. Regrettably, they divorce after several years and the validity of the prenuptial agreement is contested.

23. What part, if any, the agreement will be upheld?

(A) The agreement will likely be found unenforceable in its entirety because agreements in anticipation of divorce undermine the family and hence are contrary to good public policy.

(B) The property provision will likely be unenforceable because it would have been impossible to know how much property would be acquired during the marriage and subject to distributionHowever, their parenting abilities would already have been established so the custody provision would likely be enforceable.

(C) Both provisions will be enforceable, absent fraud, duress, coercion, or unconscionability.

(D) Absent fraud, duress, coercion, or unconscionability, the support provision will likely be upheld because this is the kind of matter that prenuptial agreements are meant to address, but the custody provision will not be enforceable because it was made without giving adequate consideration to what would best promote the interests of the children born of the marriage.

Zelda Zelinski and Yogi Youngwood are considering marriage. They decide to enter into a prenuptial agreement which specifies that in the event of divorce Zelda will not have to make any spousal support payments to Yogi. Further, they each would keep their separate property (of which Zelda has much and Yogi has little) and any increase in value in that property would also be considered separate. They marry. A few years later, Zelda and Yogi divorced. Yogi challenges the prenuptial agreement in court, suggesting that it is void because it was made under duress. Zelda suggests that it is valid and enforceable.

24. Is the prenuptial agreement enforceable?

(A) Precisely because Zelda made Yogi's signing the prenuptial a condition of their marriage, Yogi was under duress when signing it and thus it is not enforceable.

(B) The agreement is enforceable because it represents the intentions of the parties prior to the marriage.

(C) Because the distribution is obviously not equitable, the prenuptial agreement is not enforceable.

(D) The agreement will be enforceable, absent additional evidence of lack of informed consent or voluntariness.

Sandra Stevenson and Thomas Thompson are considering marriage. They have decided to create a prenuptial agreement specifying that neither party will pay spousal support to the other party in the event of a divorce. However, included within the agreement is a provision that the no-support provision will be void should the marriage end because one of the parties had committed adultery.

Sandra and Thomas sign the agreement and marry. Five years later, Sandra files for divorce after discovering that Thomas is having an affair. Thomas argues that the no-support provision is void and that therefore Sandra should be ordered to pay him spousal support as would be required by statute absent an enforceable prenuptial agreement. Sandra argues that the no-support provision should be enforced because the failure to enforce it would encourage adultery and thus violate public policy.

25. What result?

ANSWER:

Mohammed al Farabi and Mary Nazareth are considering whether to marry. They are in love but are of different faiths and are afraid that this would become a problem should they ever divorce. After much discussion, they decide to write a prenuptial agreement specifying that there would be no spousal support in the event of a divorce, that Mary would have custody of the children, and that the children would be raised in the Islamic faith. Mohammed and Mary marry and have two children. Ten years later, they divorce. Each now wants some of the conditions of the premarital agreement to be enforced but wants other conditions to be held unenforceable.

26. Which conditions are enforceable and which are not?

(A) Either all of these conditions are enforceable or none of them are, because it would be impossible to tell whether the agreement would have been made if any one of the conditions had not been included.

(B) A custody provision is not enforceable because it has been made without a consideration of the best interests of the children. However, the other two are both enforceable, since they were made voluntarily by informed parties.

(C) The religion condition is unenforceable because it violates First Amendment guarantees, but the others may be enforced.

(D) Even if the agreement was voluntarily made by informed parties, only the spousal support condition is enforceable. The others either ignore the best interests of the child or implicate First Amendment guarantees.

Don and Darla Davis separate. They reach an agreement regarding the distribution of assets, although neither consulted an attorney. The agreement is reduced to writing. Shortly before the agreement is to be incorporated within the final judgment granting the divorce, Darla happens to be talking to an attorney about another matter and realizes that she could have gotten much more in the property settlement, especially because Don had committed adultery. When Don wants the agreement incorporated into the final decree, she challenges the agreement, claiming that it is void.

27. What result?

(A) Darla will likely be successful if the decree in fact is unwise and unfair.

(B) Darla will likely be unsuccessful because once made the agreement cannot be undone.

(C) Darla will be successful only if she can establish fraud, duress, concealment, or overreaching.

(D) Darla will be unsuccessful unless she can establish that her husband implicitly or explicitly suggested that there had been no need for her to consult an attorney.

Robert Richardson and Paul Purdue enter into a written agreement to combine their efforts and earnings and share equally in the property accumulated as a result of their individual and combined efforts. After a while, Paul and Robert agree in writing that Paul will give up his lucrative career as a singer and entertainer to be a full-time companion, homemaker, housekeeper, and cook in exchange for financial support for the rest of his life. A few years later, Robert and Paul split up. Robert pays support payments for about a year and then stops making them. Paul sues to force Robert to continue making the payments.

28. Will Paul be successful?

(A) Paul will likely be unsuccessful because there is no basis upon which a claim could be made given that they were not married.

(B) Paul will likely be successful because each understood and voluntarily signed the agreements.

(C) Paul will likely be unsuccessful because Robert has already paid some support and that is more than Paul could reasonably have expected in the first place.

(D) Paul will likely be successful if he can establish that this was not an agreement that was inseparably based upon consideration of sexual services.

Ethel and Frederick Goosetree are having marital difficulties. Frederick is tempted to seek a divorce, but Ethel wants to work to keep the marriage together. Frederick agrees to try but only if Ethel will sign a postnuptial agreement that gives Frederick a very favorable distribution of the marital assets. Ethel signs the agreement. Ethel and Frederick stay together for another several months but Frederick ultimately decides that he wants a divorce. When they appear before the court, Ethel does not contest the divorce but argues that the postnuptial agreement is unenforceable and that she is entitled to a more equitable distribution of the assets.

29. What result?

ANSWER:

Karen Kowalski and Liam Lincoln are going to get married. About an hour before the wedding, Liam presents Karen with a prenuptial agreement that he wants her to sign. He attempts to reassure her by pointing out that his attorney has prepared it and then suggests that if she does not trust him enough to sign it then they should probably cancel the wedding anyway. Karen signs the prenuptial agreement.

Three years later, Karen and Liam are going through a divorce. Karen claims that the prenuptial agreement is unenforceable.

30. What result?

ANSWER:

TOPIC 7: MARRIAGE AND FRAUD

QUESTIONS

When asking her to marry him, Bobby mentioned to Billie Joe that he had been a star football player in college. Billie Joe, who had always wanted to marry a football player, agreed to marry Bobby. Years later, after they had had three children together, Billie Joe found out that the only sport Bobby had played in college was foosball, and that he had never been very good at it. She immediately left him and went to court to have the marriage declared null and void.

31. Which of the following is true?

(A) Billie had no need to go to court to have the marriage declared void, since it was void from the beginning because it was based on a lie.

(B) Billie will probably be successful because the majority of states will allow an individual to have a marriage declared void if the partner knowingly made a material misrepresentation that resulted in the celebration of the marriage in the first place.

(C) Billie will probably be unsuccessful because it is unlikely that the court would find that this misrepresentation went to one of the essentials of marriage.

(D) Billie will be unsuccessful because marriages cannot be declared void once children are born to the marriage.

John was raised with traditional values and he wants to marry someone who has never had sexual relations before. He believes that he has found the perfect woman, Mathilda. In fact, he is so attracted to her and so much wants her to be his wife that he has sexual relations with her before their marriage. They marry and all is well until John discovers that Mathilda had indeed had sexual relations with someone prior to the time that he and she had started dating. He files for divorce, claiming fraud.

32. What result?

(A) Most states would not permit the marriage to be annulled on this basis, especially given that John and Mathilda had had intercourse before the marriage.

(B) Because this was important to John and because he had made its importance clear to Mathilda, the annulment will be granted in most states.

(C) John would have been granted the annulment if Mathilda's sexual relationship with someone else had occurred after they had started dating but not if it had occurred before they had first met.

(D) John would have been granted the annulment if Mathilda's sexual relationship with someone else had occurred before they had started dating but not if it had occurred only after John and Mathilda had started dating.

Adam has proposed marriage to Eve. She makes clear that she has no wish to have or raise children and that she does not wish to marry Adam unless he feels the same way about not having children. Adam claims to share her attitude towards children but secretly wishes to have a large family. Adam and Eve marry and Adam immediately starts pressuring Eve to have children.Once it became clear that they were each firmly and inalterably committed to their respective positions on having children, Eve sought to have the marriage annulled.

33. What result?

    (A) The court will likely grant the annulment because Eve had made quite clear before the marriage that this was important to her, Adam lied to her, and Eve relied to her detriment on Adam's misrepresentation.

    (B) If the state permits no-fault divorce, the court will not grant the annulment because the parties have a different way to end their marriage which would not impose too great of a burden on either of them.

    (C) The court may well grant the annulment if it reasons that, just as the misrepresentation that one wanted children would go to the essentials of marriage and thus provide the basis for an annulment, the misrepresentation that one did not want children might also be thought to go to the essentials of marriage.

    (D) The court will not grant the annulment because everyone knows that individuals lie to induce reluctant potential spouses to marry.

34. The putative spouse doctrine is a doctrine

    (A) to help determine who is falsely claiming to be another individual's spouse.

    (B) establishing that individuals need not go through a ceremonial marriage to establish a marriage, e.g., if they have met the requirements of a common law marriage.

    (C) that protects an individual believing in good faith that he or she is married, even if there is an impediment to the validity of that marriage.

    (D) that establishes quasi-spouse status for individuals until the validity of their marriage can be determined by a court of law.

35. The last-in-time marriage presumption suggests

    (A) a bride or groom arriving shortly before the ceremony is scheduled to begin has probably had second thoughts and the marriage might be presumed unlikely to last for very long.

    (B) a marriage celebrated in accord with the domicile's requirements will thereby invalidate any marriages previously celebrated.

    (C) a subsequent marriage creates the strong presumption that any previous marriages were ended either by death, divorce, or annulment.

    (D) a marriage celebrated long ago will not have as strong a presumption of validity as a marriage celebrated relatively recently, because of the possibility of the loss of records or death of witnesses.

Abby and Bill have been dating and are considering marriage. However, Abby very much wants to have children and Bill does not. To convince her to marry him, however, Bill claims to want to have children as much as Abby does. They marry. Only then does Abby find out that Bill does not want to have children. By this time, Abby and Bill have each had a change of heart—Abby has decided that she does not want to have children and Bill has decided that he does not want to be married to Abby. Bill seeks to have the marriage declared void because it had been entered into based on a misrepresentation going to the essentials of marriage.

36. What result?

ANSWER:

TOPIC 8: COMMON LAW MARRIAGES

QUESTIONS

Wayne Wainwright and Yolanda Younger are domiciled in the state of Pennio, which does not recognize common law marriages with one exception—Pennio will recognize a common law marriage that is established in another domicile. Wayne and Yolanda have never formally married, notwithstanding the lack of a legal impediment to their doing so. However, they treat each other as husband and wife and hold themselves out as married. Wayne and Yolanda frequently vacation in the state of Texahoma, which does recognize common law marriage. After several years, Wayne and Yolanda decide to separate, and it is important to establish whether they are validly married. Wayne seeks a declaratory judgment that there is no marriage.

37. Do Wayne and Yolanda have a valid common law marriage?

    (A) The court is likely to hold that Wayne and Yolanda have a valid common law marriage because they have met all of the requirements for establishing such a marriage in Pennio.

    (B) The court is likely to hold that Wayne and Yolanda do not have a valid common law marriage because the state of Pennio has made clear that such marriages violate public policy.

    (C) The court is likely to hold that Wayne and Yolanda have a valid common law marriage because they have spent a considerable amount of time vacationing in a state that recognizes such marriages and they met all of the requirements for establishing such a marriage while in a state recognizing such unions.

    (D) The court is likely to hold that Wayne and Yolanda do not have a valid common law marriage, notwithstanding having spent a considerable amount of time vacationing in a state that recognizes such marriages, because they never met all of the requirements for establishing such a marriage while domiciled in a state recognizing such unions.

After having been beaten yet again by her husband, Robert, Sally summons up the courage to leave him. She moves to Texahoma, a state that recognizes common law marriages, to start a new life. Eventually she meets Thomas with whom she starts to live. They live together for several years, treating each other as wife and husband. Indeed, they are thought by everyone in the community to be a married couple. Sally and Thomas move to Pennio because of a job opportunity. Pennio does not recognize common law marriages with one exception—Pennio will recognize a common law marriage that is established in another domicile. Two months after their move, Sally hears on the national news that Robert is one of the many passengers who has died in a plane crash. Sally feels a little sad but thinks no more about it. Another two months pass. While in a pedestrian walk, Thomas is run over by a drunk driver. Sally's ability to collect damages is dependent upon her having been validly married to Thomas.

38. Did Sally and Thomas have a valid marriage?

(A) Because Sally and Thomas had a valid common law marriage in their former domicile of Texahoma, they had a valid marriage in Pennio.

(B) Sally and Thomas did not have a valid marriage in Pennio because there had been a legal impediment to establishing a common law marriage in Texahoma, assuming that neither Sally nor Robert ever got an ex parte divorce.

(C) Sally and Thomas had a legal impediment to establishing a common law marriage, but once Robert died there was no impediment, and thus their common law marriage was established.

(D) Sally and Thomas did not have a valid common law marriage in Pennio because only ceremonial marriages need be recognized by the different states.

Illiana does not recognize common law marriages. However, a common law marriage recognized in another jurisdiction will be recognized in Illiana. Lyle Lincoln and Mary Masters are domiciled in Illiana. They frequently vacation in Minnegan, which does recognize common law marriages. Lincoln and Mary consider themselves husband and wife and are reputed in the community to be husband and wife. While they are not legally prohibited from marrying, they have never bothered to do so.

Lincoln dies intestate and Lincoln's brother claims that Mary is not entitled to any of the estate. Mary goes to court to establish her rights, if any.

39. What result?

(A) Illiana does not recognize common law marriages. Knowing that, Mary and Lincoln could have married but chose not to, and Mary cannot now avail herself of one of the benefits of marriage. Mary will not receive anything.

(B) Because Mary and Lincoln treated each other as husband and wife, were reputed in the community to be husband and wife, were not prohibited from marrying, and spent time in a jurisdiction recognizing common law marriages, they had a common law marriage.

(C) Because Mary and Lincoln were not domiciled in the jurisdiction recognizing common law marriage they could not establish a common law marriage, and thus were never married.

(D) If Minnegan law permits non-domiciliaries to establish a common law marriage if they meet the relevant requirements and in addition spend a certain amount of time in the state, and if Mary and Lincoln did meet those requirements, including having spent the requisite amount of time in Minnegan to establish a common law marriage, then they did have a common law marriage which should be recognized by Illiana and Mary is entitled to the benefits of a wife whose spouse dies intestate. Otherwise, she will not be entitled to those benefits.

Virginia Vernwood and Walter Winston live in New Caledonia, a jurisdiction that has recently begun to recognize common law marriages. Virginia and Walter treat each other as husband

and wife and are viewed by the community as married. However, Walter is still married to Zena. Virginia knows about Zena but also knows that the marriage between Walter and Zena died long ago even if neither Walter nor Zena ever bothered to secure a divorce.

Walter is killed in an industrial accident at work. Virginia consults Audra Attny, an attorney, to find out if she is entitled to workers' compensation benefits. Audra discovers that Zena had died two months before Walter, although neither Walter nor Virginia had learned of Zena's death.

40. What should Audra tell Virginia?

    (A) Audra should say that Virginia is entitled to the benefits due a spouse. Once Zena died, the impediment to the common law marriage disappeared and in all jurisdictions recognizing common law marriage, once the impediment to the marriage is removed, the marriage is recognized if the parties have been treating each other as married and have been viewed by the community as if they were married.

    (B) Audra should explain that Virginia is not entitled to the benefits due a spouse. While Virginia and Walter had treated each other as husband and wife, they had known that Walter was still married to someone else and thus could not contract a common law marriage even once the impediment to the marriage had been removed.

    (C) Audra should explain that Virginia will likely win if New Caledonia follows the practice of some of the states recognizing common law marriage, namely, that if the other conditions have been met, the common law marriage will be recognized once the impediment to its existence have been removed. However, Audra should explain that Virginia is unlikely to win if New Caledonia follows the practice of some of the other states recognizing common law marriage, namely, that even if the other conditions have been met, a common law marriage will not be recognized unless the parties do something to indicate that they understand that their status has changed because of the removal of the impediment to their marrying.

    (D) Audra should tell Virginia that because of the important state interest in recognizing the existence of a marriage whenever possible, the state would have recognized the common law marriage of Walter and Virginia whether or not Zena was still living, if both Zena and Walter had recognized that the marriage between them was no longer viable.

Abigail and Bernard have been living together for years without benefit of marriage. They consider and treat each other as husband and wife, and they are believed by all who know them to be husband and wife. However, Abigail's husband had still been alive until about a year ago. The jurisdiction in which they live, Marylania, recognizes common law marriage, and it is now important to establish whether or not Abigail and Bernard are married.

41. What result?

ANSWER:

Morris Markham and Nancy Newsome have been living together for several years in the state of West Marriagelandia. Morris and Nancy consider themselves married and hold themselves out as married to all who know them, notwithstanding that Nancy never divorced or received a divorce from her first husband, Oscar. West Marriagelandia recognizes common law marriages.

One day, Nancy reads in the local newspaper that her first husband, Oscar, was executed by the state of West Marriagelandia for various crimes that he committed years ago. Nancy goes out, purchases a ring for Morris, and places it on his ring finger that night, explaining that now that Oscar is dead they really can call each other husband and wife.

A year later, Morris dies. The insurance company, There When You Need Us, refuses to distribute the death benefits due Morris's lawful spouse, claiming that Morris and Nancy were not legally married. Nancy sues for the benefits.

42. What result?

ANSWER:

TOPIC 9: CIVIL UNIONS — QUESTIONS

43. A civil union is

    (A) a separate status reserved for same-sex couples that has the rights and responsibilities of marriage but not its name.

    (B) a marriage that has been performed by a justice of the peace but was never celebrated in a religious ceremony.

    (C) a marriage that is marked by an unusual lack of discord.

    (D) another name for a common law marriage.

John Jones and Greg Gunderson have entered into a civil union in accord with local law. Several years later, John realizes that he is no longer in love with Greg and wants to end the union. In front of several of their friends, John tells Greg that, as far as he is concerned, the union is over.

44. What effect, if any, will this pronouncement have on the continuing existence of their union?

    (A) Because at least one of the parties no longer wishes to be a member of the union, it will no longer be recognized.

    (B) No effect. The union will continue to exist until it is formally dissolved.

    (C) Because John made a public pronouncement that their union was over, John and Greg no longer have a reputation in the community as being joined in a civil union, and thus the law will not recognize their having that status.

    (D) While they technically would still be in a civil union until the Town Clerk had been notified, the continuation of that status would have no legally significant ramifications.

TOPIC 10: DIVORCE

QUESTIONS

Arthur and Alice Adams have been married for several years in the state of Puninia. They have two children. Since shortly after the birth of their second daughter who is now eight years old, Arthur has been abusive, sometimes physically threatening. After one particular episode in which Arthur had drunkenly threatened to harm Alice and the girls, Alice moved out, taking the girls with her. Arthur and Alice have lived separate and apart for 12 months. Alice has filed for divorce, arguing constructive desertion. Arthur also seeks a divorce, arguing actual desertion. According to Puninia law, a finding of marital fault can be taken into account when determining custody and when dividing the marital assets.

45. The court hearing this case is likely to

    (A) refuse to grant the parties a divorce, since both parties are obviously at fault.

    (B) grant the divorce, finding Arthur responsible for the break-up of the marriage if his conduct is found to have made it dangerous for Alice and the children to have remained in the home.

    (C) grant the divorce, finding Alice at fault, because she left the marital home. Because Arthur stayed in the home he obviously cannot be found to have committed actual or constructive desertion.

    (D) grant the divorce, finding both parents unfit because they both are obviously bad influences on their children.

46. To establish that a spouse has committed adultery, many states require

    (A) that the innocent spouse witnesses the spouse committing the adulterous act.

    (B) that the accused spouse admit his or her wrongdoing.

    (C) that the act be witnessed and that it be corroborated.

    (D) that there be both opportunity and the disposition to commit the act.

Jack and Jill Johnson have fallen out of love with each other and have reached the conclusion that their marriage is over. They cannot afford to maintain separate residences so they live in the same house. They alternate where they will sleep—sometimes Jill sleeps in the bed and Jack sleeps on the couch, and sometimes Jack sleeps in the bed and Jill sleeps on the couch. They have not had marital relations for at least 15 months and want to get a no-fault divorce based on their living "separate and apart" for a year, which is the amount of time required by state law.

47. Which of the following statements accurately reflects whether they will be able to divorce?

(A) Jurisdictions vary as to whether couples who wish to meet the "separate and apart" requirement can live under the same roof so it is unclear whether their living together is a bar to their making use of this ground to get a divorce.

(B) Because they share the same address, they will be unable to secure a divorce on this ground.

(C) If they can convince the court that they in fact have not had marital relations for the required period of time, they will be able to secure a divorce on this ground.

(D) Living separate and apart is a criterion involving the mental attitudes of the parties, so their mailing address is irrelevant.

Monty and Marla Michaelson are married. However, they have maintained separate residences for the past year and a half and have finally decided to end their marriage. They now realize that all they have in common is that they enjoy having sexual relations with each other and, indeed, have been enjoying their relations even more now that they are no longer living in the same house. However, they each reached the conclusion that they can continue to have sexual relations even if they are not married to each other and that if they are divorced they can date other people without feeling guilty about doing so.

48. If the statute requires couples to live separate and apart for 18 months, will the Michaelsons be able to divorce on this basis?

(A) Yes, because they have more than met the statutory requirement of maintaining different residences for a year and a half.

(B) They may well not be granted a divorce, because continuing their sexual relationship means that they will not have lived separate and apart in the relevant sense.

(C) Yes, if they will stop having sexual relations once their divorce is final.

(D) No, to meet this ground they will have to live separate and apart for 18 months without ever having sexual relations.

49. A no-fault divorce can be obtained

(A) whenever both parties agree that the marriage is no longer viable.

(B) only when neither party has committed a marital fault.

(C) when, e.g., the parties have lived separate and apart for the amount of time required by statute.

(D) only when neither party blames the other for the breakdown of the marriage.

50. A divorce from bed and board is

(A) a legal separation where the couple is still married in the eyes of the law.

(B) a legal directive to a spouse or child that he or she should stop just eating and sleeping all the time and instead look for a job.

(C) a special kind of divorce that allows the couple to divorce but bars the spouse at fault from marrying until the innocent spouse dies.

(D) simply another term for a marital dissolution where each of the parties is now free to marry someone else.

51. The concept of a divisible divorce

(A) underlies what makes legal separations possible.

(B) recognizes that one issue involves the marriage itself and another involves the property rights and the obligations of the parties.

(C) recognizes that for purposes of the law one of the parties might be recognized in the law as still married while the other party (the innocent spouse) will be permitted to marry someone else.

(D) permits any court dissolving a marriage to determine whether spousal support is owed and, if so, how much.

Oscar and Olga Smith are legally separated. Oscar has started to see Elizabeth and has in fact been spending several nights a week at her house. Olga, who has evidence of Oscar's affair, files for divorce, claiming adultery. Oscar admits that he is having an affair but argues that because he and Olga are legally separated and because they are going to divorce anyway, his relationship with Elizabeth cannot be held against him legally.

52. Can Oscar's affair be held against him?

(A) Because Oscar's relationship with Elizabeth caused no harm, it cannot be used either as a basis of divorce or as a basis upon which to justify a more favorable support award or distribution of marital assets for Olga.

(B) Because Olga would have done the same thing if she had met someone with whom she wanted to establish a relationship, Olga will be estopped from asserting Oscar's adultery as a basis for their divorce.

(C) Because Olga and Oscar are still married in the eyes of the law, Oscar's relationship with Elizabeth is adulterous and may well be the ground upon which the divorce will be based.

(D) While Olga cannot use Oscar's adultery as a divorce ground, she can now start a relationship with someone else without fear of its being used against her.

Sarah and Sonny Singlebury are married and living in Illigan. Unfortunately, they are having difficulties and, with Sarah's consent, Sonny moves to and becomes domiciled in Pennio. They live separate and apart for a year. However, Illigan requires its domiciliaries to be apart for two years before they can get a divorce on those grounds. During her extended summer vacation, Sarah moves to Pennio, meeting that state's residency requirement, and files for divorce. Sonny contests the divorce, arguing that because Sarah is still domiciled in Illigan, the separate and apart criterion of that state has not been met and the Pennio court cannot grant the divorce. In addition, Sonny argues that because Sarah is not domiciled in Pennio, she cannot file for divorce there. Sarah admits that she is an Illigan domiciliary but argues that the divorce can nonetheless be granted.

53. What result?

(A) Because Sarah is an Illigan domiciliary, she cannot file for divorce in Pennio, so the divorce cannot be granted.

(B) Although Sarah can file for divorce in Pennio because Sonny is domiciled there, the Pennio court must use the Illigan divorce grounds, so the divorce cannot be granted.

(C) Absent contrary statute, because at least one of the parties has met the residency requirement and one of the parties (Sonny) has met the domiciliary requirement, the divorce can be granted if one of the Pennio grounds for divorce can be established.

(D) Because there is personal jurisdiction over both of the parties, the divorce can be granted.

Alice and Andrew Adamson have been married for three years and are living in Hawifornia. However, they are having difficulties and they both agree that it might be better if Alice goes to live with her sister in the neighboring state of Washegon. They live separate and apart for a year, meeting one of the Hawifornia grounds for getting a no-fault divorce. Andrew publishes a notice in the local paper to give Alice constructive knowledge of the divorce. She does not appear. He is awarded the divorce. There are no children of the marriage and there is no marital property to distribute.

Andrew meets Betina. They have a whirlwind courtship and marry within a few months. However, their happiness is cut short when Andrew has a horrible, fatal accident at work. The only consolation is that Andrew's spouse will receive insurance proceeds totaling about one million dollars. Alice happens to hear of Andrew's death and claims that she is entitled to the insurance proceeds.

54. What result?

(A) Because Alice received all that she was entitled to in the divorce (there was nothing to distribute), she is not entitled to the insurance proceeds and they will go to Betina.

(B) Because Washegon requires that couples be apart for two years, the divorce between Alice and Andrew is invalid and Alice is entitled to the proceeds.

(C) Because Alice would have known of the marriage if only she had subscribed to the local paper in Hawifornia and because Andrew and Alice had in fact lived separate and apart for the requisite amount of time, the divorce is valid and Betina will be recognized as the widow.

(D) Because Andrew knew where Alice was living, his published notice in the local paper did not meet the requirements for constructive notice and the divorce will not be considered valid. Alice is Andrew's widow in the eyes of the law.

55. Assuming the facts of Question 54, is there any way that Betina will be entitled to any of the insurance proceeds?

    (A) Yes, if Betina can establish that Alice committed adultery while she and Andrew were living apart, since that would provide a ground for divorce even if Alice and Andrew had not been living apart for the requisite period of time.

    (B) No, because Alice's due process rights were violated since she was not given notice of the proceeding.

    (C) Yes, if Hawifornia recognizes the putative spouse rule and Betina had in good faith not known that Andrew was still legally married to Alice.

    (D) No, because Betina and Andrew had not had any children together.

Suppose that Andrew had gotten a divorce from Alice in the way described in Question 54. Suppose further that Alice learned what Andrew had done one year later when she somehow learned that Andrew had married Betina. However, Alice did nothing. Twenty-four years later, Andrew dies and Betina stands to get one million dollars in insurance proceeds. At this point, Alice asserts her rights. Betina, who had known nothing about Alice, pleads laches in defense.

56. What result?

    (A) Betina will lose because she never validly married Andrew.

    (B) Betina's defense of laches may well be upheld and Alice's rights not recognized because Alice did not assert those rights in a timely manner.

    (C) Betina may only get something as a putative spouse if local law permits that, and she should be thankful that she can get some of the insurance proceeds since she never had a valid marriage with Andrew.

    (D) Betina will win because she lived with Andrew for a longer period than Alice did.

Jurisdictions vary with respect to the effect of a finding that one of the parties has committed adultery. Suppose that Wanda Wife wishes to divorce Harvey Husband because she believes that he has committed adultery. Suppose further that a court finds that she is correct and, in addition, that she is blameless.

57. How, if at all, might such a finding affect custody, spousal support and the distribution of marital assets?

    (A) Husband's adultery might make his having custody of the children less likely but could not affect either spousal support or the division of marital property.

    (B) Husband's adultery might make his having custody of the children less likely and might affect spousal support and might affect the division of marital property.

    (C) Husband's adultery might make his having custody of the children less likely and might affect the division of marital property but could not affect spousal support.

(D) Husband's adultery could affect the division of property or the amount of spousal support but could not affect his having custody since that is determined by examining the best interests of the child.

Kim, a post-operative male-to-female transsexual, marries a man named John in Blissfulvania, where they live. However, after a few years, Kim seeks a divorce. John argues that they were never legally married because Blissfulvania treats same-sex marriages as void *ab initio*.

58. Will the marriage between Kim and John be recognized?

(A) Regardless of how the state defines an individual's sex, the court will likely hold that the marriage is valid if John knew all along that Kim was a post-operative transsexual.

(B) The court will likely hold the marriage void because states prohibiting same-sex marriages will not permit a post-operative male-to-female transsexual to marry someone who also has XY chromosomes.

(C) The court may recognize the marriage if, e.g., the state classifies post-operative transsexuals in terms of their self-identified, rather than their chromosomal, sex.

(D) The court will hold the marriage void because transsexuals are not permitted to marry anyone.

Jill and Karl have been married for several years. However, they have been having marital difficulties for the past several months and decide to get a legal separation. During their separation, they sometimes get together for dinner and spend the night together.

The morning after they had last spent the night together, they realized that they have been legally separated for the period required by law to get a divorce on the ground of living separate and apart for six months. They come to the conclusion that they will never be able to live together as a married couple and file for divorce based on their living separate and apart for the requisite period.

59. What result?

ANSWER:

Richard and Sally Thomas wish to get a divorce. While much of their married life was spent in the state of Utoo, Richard is now temporarily living in Coloda and Sally is temporarily living in the neighboring state of New Canada. They both have received business assignments in their respective states and both plan to leave their respective states once the assignments have ended.

Because neither Richard nor Sally is domiciled in the current state of residence, Richard decides to file in the state in which they both are domiciled—Utoo. Sally appears, contesting the divorce, claiming that Richard does not meet the residency requirement. Richard responds that because he has met the domicile requirement he has, of course, met the residency requirement as well.

60. What result?

ANSWER:

Olga and Oscar Oppenheimer are domiciled in Marriageforeverland and are spending the summer in the state of Lasnevania. To his surprise, Oscar is served notice that Olga is divorcing him. Oscar decides not to challenge the divorce while in Lasnevania and will instead wait until they get back to Marriageforeverland to contest the divorce. Olga is awarded the divorce.

When they return to Marriageland, Olga seeks to have the marital assets distributed now that she has been awarded a divorce. Oscar challenges the divorce, arguing that Olga was not domiciled in Lasnevania, and thus that the Lasnevania court did not have jurisdiction to grant the divorce.

61. What result?

ANSWER:

TOPIC 11: DIVORCE DEFENSES

QUESTIONS

Beth and Carl Carlson wish to end their marriage quickly. However, their domicile, Marriageland, permits no-fault divorce only if the couple has lived separate and apart for two years. They do not wish to wait two years and decide to claim that one of them has been unfaithful so that they can divorce earlier. They flip a coin and Beth loses. Beth admits to an imaginary affair with someone else. Carl is awarded a fault-based divorce.

62. The scenario described above is an example of:

    (A) Collusion.

    (B) Condonation.

    (C) Contract, because the parties made a voluntary, informed agreement and they should expect this agreement to be enforceable in court.

    (D) Recrimination.

Olga and Oscar Overton are having marital difficulties and, in fact, Olga desperately wants a divorce. However, she is unwilling to break her marriage vows and believes that the required period for living separate and apart seems very long indeed. After one of their more heated arguments, Oscar says that unless Olga is willing to give him marital comfort whenever he wants, he is going to seek comfort elsewhere. Without uttering a word, Olga opens up the telephone directory, locates the number for an escort service, dials it, and hands the phone to Oscar. Oscar makes a date and, in fact, has sexual relations with someone other than his wife. As soon as he admits what he has done, Olga packs some belongings and moves in with her sister. Soon thereafter, she files for divorce, claiming that Oscar has committed adultery.

63. What is Oscar's best argument if he wishes to contest the divorce?

    (A) Oscar should claim laches because Olga has wanted to get a divorce for a long time and is only now filing for one.

    (B) Oscar should claim condonation because Olga clearly wanted him to do something to provide a ground for divorce.

    (C) Oscar should claim connivance because Olga implicitly if not explicitly encouraged him to make use of the escort service and should not be allowed to complain when he did what she encouraged him to do.

    (D) Oscar should claim recrimination, because Olga has been constantly criticizing him over the past several years.

Mr. Jones seeks a fault-based divorce from Mrs. Jones. Mrs. Jones asserts a defense of recrimination.

64. In other words, Mrs. Jones is asserting:

(A) Mr. Jones has also committed a marital fault that could serve as the basis of divorce.

(B) While Mrs. Jones was once at fault, she never repeated her error and thus was not guilty of recrimination.

(C) What Mrs. Jones did was not a criminal offense.

(D) The offending act must be committed on at least two separate occasions in order for it to be a ground for divorce.

65. What effect, if any, will a successful defense of recrimination have?

(A) It precludes the parties from ever getting a divorce.

(B) It will preclude the parties from getting a divorce on the ground asserted but would not bar a divorce on a different ground, e.g., irreconcilable differences. However, the benefits that would have accrued to the "innocent" spouse had there been no defense of recrimination, e.g., a more favorable distribution of marital assets, might no longer be available were the basis now a no-fault ground.

(C) The public prosecutor will now be able to charge both spouses.

(D) No effect, now that no-fault divorces are recognized.

Ken and Kathy Kranston have been married for years. Kathy has had a few affairs during the marriage. After each of the first two affairs had ended, Kathy told Ken that she had had an affair, that she was dreadfully sorry, and that she would never have an affair again. Each time, Ken forgave her and they resumed having marital relations. This time, however, Ken refused to forgive her. Although Ken and Kathy did have marital relations once after she had admitted her most recent affair, Ken said the very morning after they had slept together that he simply could not remain in the marriage. Thereafter, he slept on the couch. Ken has filed for divorce. Kathy contests the divorce, arguing condonation.

66. What result?

(A) Kathy's defense will likely be successful. Once Ken condoned her infidelity the first time and then condoned her second affair as well, he forever gave up the right to get a divorce on the ground of adultery.

(B) Kathy's defense will likely not be successful because regardless of what Ken said or did in the past he obviously does not want to remain in the marriage and he is the innocent spouse.

(C) Kathy's defense will likely be successful either because he implicitly agreed to permitting occasional affairs by his previous expressions of forgiveness or by his knowingly having sexual relations with her once he had learned of her most recent affair.

(D) Kathy's defense may well not be successful if the court finds that resumption of marital relations one time will not alone constitute condonation.

John and Katrina Meyer have been married for several years. Neither wants to remain married and both have paramours. However, their domicile, Punitania, imposes burdens on the marital partner found to be at fault for the end of the marriage so neither wants to admit being the guilty party. John finally decides that it is time to end the marriage and files for divorce, claiming that Katrina has engaged in adulterous behavior. Katrina admits that she has had an affair but argues that John has also committed adultery.

67. What result?

ANSWER:

Douglas and Melissa are married. Melissa has admitted having an affair but promises never to violate her vows ever again. Douglas says he forgives her and has marital relations with her, Melissa does all that she can to make amends but Douglas treats her so coldly as to make life intolerable for both of them. Melissa suggests that they should be legally separated. After they have been separate and apart for a year, Melissa seeks a no-fault divorce. Douglas cross-claims for a divorce based on Melissa's adultery.

68. What result?

ANSWER:

TOPIC 12: RECOGNITION OF FOREIGN MARRIAGES AND DIVORCES — QUESTIONS

William and Wanda White are married and live in Ohio. William goes to Nevada, meets that state's residence requirement, gives his wife actual notice that he is going to secure a divorce, and then is granted a divorce in accord with local law. William then goes back to Ohio, marries his long-time girlfriend, Wilhelmina, and then returns to his former job from which he had taken a brief leave of absence. Wanda goes to court in Ohio challenging the Nevada divorce.

69. Her best argument is:

    (A) William should have been denied a divorce in Nevada because both he and she had committed adultery.

    (B) William should have been denied a divorce in Nevada because he was the party at fault and she was innocent.

    (C) William should have been denied a divorce in Nevada because the Nevada court did not have personal jurisdiction over her.

    (D) William should have been denied a divorce in Nevada because William had never established domicile in Nevada.

Paul and Penny Pennington live in Illinois. They are having marital difficulties. Eventually, Penny decides that she cannot stand being married to Paul any longer. She goes to Nevada, meets the residence requirement, and files for divorce. Paul, who had actual notice that Penny was going to file for divorce in Nevada, went to Nevada to contest the divorce. Paul argues that Penny is not domiciled in Nevada. The Nevada court finds that Penny is domiciled in Nevada and has met the residence requirement. The court grants the divorce. Paul believes that the Nevada court is mistaken and challenges the divorce decree in Illinois. Penny brings the Nevada decree to the attention of the Illinois court.

70. The Illinois court should

    (A) perform an independent assessment of whether Penny had established domicile in Nevada at the time the decree had been issued.

    (B) give the Nevada decree full faith and credit.

    (C) look at the Illinois residency requirement to determine if Penny was in Nevada for a long enough period to establish residence.

    (D) see where Penny is now domiciled to determine whether the Nevada court had jurisdiction to grant the divorce.

Carl and Carol Cartwright decide to get a divorce. They go to Dominica, a foreign country, meet the residency requirement, and get a divorce. Their marital property is divided equitably in accordance with the agreement that they had reached. No children were born of the marriage. They return to their home state of New Lousico and marry their respective paramours. Carl's remarriage does not work out. To avoid having to divide marital property with his second "spouse," Carl claims in a New Lousico court that his second marriage was void because he had never been validly divorced from Carol.

71. The New Lousico court

(A) is required by the Full Faith and Credit Clause to recognize the Dominica divorce.

(B) is required by considerations of comity to recognize the first divorce.

(C) must recognize the divorce because Carol has happily remarried and, in fact, has had children with her second husband.

(D) could estop Carl from challenging the validity of his first divorce but could also refuse to recognize that divorce because the Cartwrights had never been domiciled in Dominica and thus the Dominica court had not had jurisdiction to grant the divorce.

Bubba and Betty Lou Armstrong entered into a covenant marriage in Lorsiona. However, Betty Lou discovers that she really cannot stand Bubba and she wants to get a divorce. She and Bubba agree that it might be a good idea for her to live with her sister in Texarkana while they sort things out. Betty Lou has established domicile in Texarkana and has lived there for six months, which meets the local "separate and apart" requirement for getting a divorce as well as the relevant residency requirement. Betty Lou files for divorce. Bubba contests the divorce, arguing that their covenant marriage imposes stricter requirements than those posed by Texarkana law and thus that the divorce cannot be granted.

72. What result?

(A) Because the Armstrongs married in Lorsiona, Lorsiona law applies to the divorce and the Armstrongs cannot get divorced unless they meet one of the Lorsiona requirements for a dissolution of a covenant marriage.

(B) Absent contrary statute, because Betty Lou is now domiciled in Texarkana, the court cannot even consider that the Armstrongs entered into a covenant marriage in Lorsiona and must grant the divorce if the local requirements have been met.

(C) The Texarkana court must look to Lorsiona law to see what it says about foreign dissolutions of covenant marriages that had been contracted in Lorsiona.

(D) The Texarkana court can grant the divorce. However, it might also estop Betty Lou from seeking a divorce because of the vows she took when entering into a covenant marriage.

Carrie Carrollson and Donald Davidson live in Caloregon. They want to get married but Donald is still married to Donna, who is unwilling to get a divorce. Donald and Carrie do not want to wait until the state's "living separate and apart for a year" ground has been met. Donald, who will have to spend a few months in Nevada on business anyway, decides to divorce his wife while he is there.

Donna is given actual notice of Donald's intention to divorce her, but she does not go to Nevada to stop him. Instead, she decides to wait until he returns from his business trip.

Donald meets the Nevada residency requirement and gets a divorce. Carrie flies out to Nevada, and she and Donald get married in a drive-through chapel. Carrie stays a few days and then returns home.

A few weeks later, Donald returns. Within one month of returning and living with Carrie in their new home, Donald has a massive heart attack and dies. Carrie and Donna each claim to be Donald's lawful widow, entitled to a share of his estate.

73. What result?

    (A) Assuming that the Caloregon court finds the Nevada divorce decree invalid, Carrie will have been precluded from marrying Donald because he still would have been married to Donna. Carrie's marriage to Donald will be treated as null and void because bigamous. Donna rather than Carrie will be treated as Donald's widow and entitled to a share of his estate.

    (B) Because Donna refused to challenge the divorce in Nevada and instead decided to wait, she will be precluded from challenging the divorce and subsequent marriage now. Carrie, and not Donna, will be treated as Donald's widow.

    (C) Because Carrie and Donald ratified their marriage by living together in the state of Caloregon, their marriage will be recognized as valid and Carrie will be treated as his widow. If Donald had had a heart attack while he was still in Nevada, however, he and Carrie would never have ratified the marriage within the state and then Donna rather than Carrie would have been recognized as Donald's lawful widow.

    (D) Donna rather than Carrie will be recognized as Donald's lawful widow because Donald and Carrie did not live together as a married couple in the state for at least six months.

John and Mary are first cousins who are domiciled in West Kentucky. Because their home state precludes them from marrying each other, they slip over the border, marry in East Kentucky where they are permitted to marry, and then return home claiming to be validly married.

74. Were the marriage challenged in court in West Kentucky,

    (A) West Kentucky would have to recognize it because of the Full Faith and Credit Clause.

    (B) West Kentucky could not recognize it because such a marriage could not validly be performed within the state.

(C) West Kentucky might recognize it depending upon whether such marriages were obnoxious to an important public policy of the state.

(D) West Kentucky would have to recognize it because a marriage valid where celebrated is valid everywhere.

Wendy and Walter Wexler are married and living in the state of Intucky. Wendy and Walter have been having marital difficulties and Wendy decides that she has had enough and wants a divorce. Wendy decides that she will take the necessary steps during her 10-week summer vacation in the state of Tennio, which is about 1,000 miles away from Intucky. Then, when she comes back to her job in the fall, she will be a free woman.

That summer, Wendy more than meets Tennio's six-week residency requirement for divorce. She files for divorce, claiming irreconcileable differences. Walter has actual notice of the divorce proceeding but chooses not to come 1,000 miles and make an appearance. The divorce is granted.

Wendy goes back to Intucky once her 10-week vacation has ended. She starts to date a co-worker, Thomas. After the private detective that Walter hired discovered that Thomas and Wendy had spent the night together on several occasions, Walter files for divorce, claiming adultery. Wendy argues that her Tennio divorce must be given full faith and credit.

75. What result?

ANSWER:

Donna and David Downs live in Coloming with their one child, Morris. They decide that they would like to have a playmate for their son and eventually adopt a child, Margaret. The children get along wonderfully. After Morris and Margaret have each reached their 21st birthdays, they go to the neighboring state of Nezona, marry, and come back to Coloming to live.

76. Will their marriage be recognized?

ANSWER:

TOPIC 13: PROPERTY

QUESTIONS

77. Which of the following would be an example of dissipation of marital assets?

    (A) Marie buys a valuable painting with marital funds for investment purposes that she enjoys but her husband, Samuel, does not.

    (B) Lonnie buys an expensive gift for his mother-in-law to make her like him. She throws it away and tells him he is a good-for-nothing louse.

    (C) Winnie uses substantial marital assets to buy stock in a company that goes bankrupt after substantial accounting errors are made public.

    (D) Realizing that his marriage is on the rocks, Bobby spends thousands of dollars to buy cocaine for himself and his friends to make himself feel better.

Jack and Jill Kanterson live in the state of Caligonia. Jack has separate property in the neighboring state of Wyana. Jack and Jill agree to divorce. However, before they do so, Jack empties their common bank account and loses it at the racetrack. The court granting the divorce has very little marital property to distribute. The court awards it all to Jill but realizes that this hardly compensates Jill for all of the monies wasted by Jack.

78. What else, if anything, can the court do?

    (A) The court can award the Wyana property to Jill.

    (B) The court can order Jack to sell the Wyana property and give Jill a substantial part of the proceeds or, in the alternative, order Jack to transfer the property to Jill.

    (C) The court is without power to do anything else, because no jurisdiction permits a court to distribute separate property in the context of divorce.

    (D) The court can punish Jack by awarding custody of the children to Jill even if awarding custody to Jack would best promote the children's interests.

Norman and Josey Peterson are legally separated. Josey buys a lottery ticket and wins two million dollars. When Norman and Josey finally divorce, Norman claims that the lottery winnings are marital income and subject to distribution.

79. What result?

    (A) Because Norman and Josey were still married when Josey bought the winning ticket, the winnings are marital property and subject to distribution.

    (B) Because Norman and Josey were legally separated when Josey bought the ticket and because they never got back together, the winnings must be treated as separate property.

(C) Only those winnings distributed before the divorce is final will be considered marital property.

(D) If they were separated as a result of Norman's marital fault, then the property will be treated as separate. Otherwise, it will be treated as marital.

John and Joanne Jones are married and have no children. John buys a new car with periodic payments coming out of his paycheck; only he drives that car. Joanne inherits a valuable painting from her great aunt. John hates the painting and he forces Joanne to keep it at her sister's house, where Joanne occasionally gets to look at it. John and Joanne divorce, at least in part, because John has such bad taste. They can agree about the division of all of the property except that they cannot agree about the appropriate characterization of the car and the painting.

80. How should the car and painting be characterized?

(A) Both the car and the painting are marital property because they were both acquired during the marriage.

(B) Both the car and the painting are separate property because only John uses the car and only Joanne views the painting.

(C) The car is separate property because only John uses it but the painting is marital property because it was acquired during the marriage, and thus John is entitled to half the fair market value of the painting.

(D) The car is marital property because it was bought with funds earned during the marriage but the painting is separate property because Joanne (alone) inherited it from her great aunt.

Giovanni and Maria have been married for fifteen years but are now getting ready to divorce. They can agree about all of the property except the couple's two cars, both of which were bought by Giovanni with marital funds. Giovanni argues that the car Maria drives is hers and that the car Giovanni drives is his. Maria argues that the car she drives is hers because it was a gift from Giovanni but that the car he drives is marital property. However, she would be willing to treat them both as marital property, since Giovanni's Ferrari is probably worth about $140,000 while her Accord is worth about $13,000. While Maria is not interested in getting the Ferrari or in forcing Giovanni to sell it, she argues that she should get a more favorable distribution of other assets to make up for the benefit that he receives by keeping the car. Giovanni disagrees, arguing that the cars should not enter the calculation regarding how the marital assets are distributed. They decide to ask an attorney who has the better argument.

81. The attorney should respond:

(A) This depends upon the intents of the parties. If Giovanni expressly or impliedly made the Accord a gift to Maria, then it is hers. If Maria neither expressly nor impliedly made the Ferrari a gift to Giovanni, then it is marital property, the value of which is subject to distribution.

(B) Because only Giovanni drives the Ferrari and only Maria drives the Accord, the cars should be treated as separate property and should not be considered when the distribution of marital assets is being discussed.

(C) Because Giovanni paid for both out of monies that he earned in his very lucrative profession, both cars are his and he should get an offset if Maria is going to keep the Accord.

(D) Because Maria never expressed any interest in driving the Ferrari, she is estopped from claiming any ownership share at this point.

Abigail and Arnold Adamson are married. They live in the house which Abigail owned before the Adamsons married. The Adamsons hope to have many children and have expanded the house considerably, the money to pay for these improvements coming out of a joint checking account. Both Abigail and Arnold have their paychecks directly deposited into that account. This account is also used to pay for repairs to the house.

After many years, the Adamsons discover, to their dismay, that they cannot have children. Arnold very much wants to adopt but Abigail is unwilling to do so. Their arguments over whether to adopt coupled with the years of frustration in unsuccessfully trying to have children eventually leads to the breakdown of the marriage.

When dividing up the property, Abigail argues that the house is hers and that the only property to be divided involves the retirement accounts, the cars, the amounts in the bank accounts, and some stock and bonds. Arnold disagrees, arguing that the house in addition to those other items must be divided.

82. Which of the following scenarios seems least likely?

(A) Abigail will get to have her house treated as separate property if she can establish that the contributions from Arnold were intended to be gifts to her.

(B) The house will be treated as marital property because marital funds were used to maintain and improve the house and because it is impossible to figure out how much Arnold should be credited for his contributions to the house.

(C) While Abigail will get to keep the house, Arnold will be credited for all of his contributions to its maintenance and improvement and thus will get a larger share of the other assets than he otherwise would have.

(D) Because Arnold wanted to adopt and Abigail did not, and because the house was expanded to make room for children, the house will be held to have been gifted to the individual who in fact wanted to have children live in it, namely, Arnold.

Beatrice Bottoms and Bradley Binghamton meet at a party for apartment owners in an upscale section of the town of Swankyville in the state of Iowisota. They start to date and eventually marry, living in a house owned by Bradley. Beatrice, who works as an attorney, pays someone to manage and maintain her apartment buildings out of the rents from the buildings. Monies earned from Beatrice's attorney fees are used for household expenses, family trips, etc.

Bradley does not have another job. Instead, he collects his own rents and maintains his own buildings. Monies from Bradley's rents are used for household expenses, family trips, etc. After ten years, Beatrice and Bradley decide to divorce when Beatrice discovers that Bradley is having an affair with one of his tenants.

Beatrice argues that Bradley's apartment buildings are marital property and that her apartment buildings are separate property or, in the alternative, that Beatrice deserves to be credited for the marital time and money that went into the upkeep and improvements on the buildings. Bradley argues that if his apartments are marital property, then Beatrice's apartment buildings are marital property, and that if hers are not then his are not either. There are no children of the marriage, neither party seeks spousal support, and Iowisota does not permit fault to be a consideration in the division of marital property.

83. What is the likely result?

    (A) Because Beatrice and Bradley both owned their apartment buildings before the marriage, both will be treated as separate property.

    (B) Because both Beatrice and Bradley are sophisticated individuals who should have known the importance of a prenuptial agreement, they deserve whatever happens. All properties will be treated as marital.

    (C) Because Beatrice kept the apartment buildings separate and neither spent time nor marital assets to maintain or improve those buildings, her apartment buildings will be treated as separate property. However, because Bradley spent time and marital assets to maintain and improve his buildings, they may well either be treated as marital property or Beatrice will get some credit for the time and marital assets which Bradley expended.

    (D) Because Beatrice and Bradley are both independently wealthy, the judge will simply treat the couple as if they had never married and direct her attentions to other cases before her.

Jason Johnson and Kristin Kowalski are both nurses working at Penniland State Hospital. They meet and start dating. Eventually, they marry. Kristin decides to quit her job and to go to law school. Kristin pays for law school by making use of scholarship funds and funds given to her by her parents. She does very well, securing a position on law review, a clerkship, and eventually a position at a prestigious firm. Jason continues working as a nurse. Jason's salary is used to pay household expenses and Jason does most of the cooking, cleaning, shopping, etc.

During Kristin's clerkship, Kristin spends a great deal of time with Larry, another clerk for the same judge. She eventually realizes that she and Jason do not have anything in common anymore and finds herself increasingly attracted to Larry. Kristin tells Jason she wants a divorce.

Jason and Kristin agree about how to divide most of the assets. However, they disagree about how the law degree should be treated. Jason argues that it is a marital asset and that he should receive a share of her future earnings, while Kristin argues that her law degree is hers alone and simply is not a marital asset.

84. While jurisdictions vary with respect to their treatment of professional degrees, which of the following scenarios is least likely to occur in any jurisdiction currently?

    (A) The court will treat the degree as marital property, assessing its worth in light of Kristin eventually being made partner, and then make an award accordingly.

    (B) The court will refuse to treat the degree as marital property but will nonetheless consider it when deciding how to divide up the marital assets.

    (C) The court will hold that the degree is not property but that Jason should be reimbursed for some of his financial contributions while Kristin was earning the degree.

    (D) The court will hold that because the degree is not a marital asset it simply cannot be included in the distribution.

Paul and Roberta Sudby have been married for 10 years. Paul works inside the home raising their children while Roberta is the primary wage earner for the family. Paul and Roberta have been having marital difficulties and have decided to divorce. They can agree about everything except for Roberta's vested pension benefits, which will not be available for Roberta for another 20 years.

85. How should those benefits be treated?

    (A) When Roberta starts receiving those benefits, a portion of them should go to Robert. Basically, that portion should correspond to the ratio of years worked at the company while they were married to total years worked.

    (B) Because it is not clear that Roberta will ever receive those benefits, they should not be considered in the distribution of marital assets.

    (C) When Roberta does start receiving those benefits, half should go to Paul and half to Roberta.

    (D) Because Roberta has been the primary wage earner and Paul has been saddled with the uncompensated duties involved in being the primary caretaker, Paul should get a greater share of Roberta's retirement benefits, e.g., 75%.

Ron and Rhonda Rocketfella were married in New York. After a few years, they decided to separate for a while, so that they could decide whether or not to stay together. Ron moved to Houston to help design a spaceship. Rhonda remained in New York where she had lived all of her life. After a year, Ron gave Rhonda the requisite notice that he was seeking a divorce. Ron secured a no-fault divorce in Houston, after establishing that he had met the relevant residence requirement. The Texas court awarded Rhonda the couple's jointly-held property in New York (a car and a sailboat). Rhonda no longer wishes to be married to Ron, but believes that the property division was unfair. She challenges the property division in New York.

86. Is Rhonda's challenge likely to be successful?

    (A) Rhonda will likely be unsuccessful because she had notice of the proceeding in Texas and could have gone there if she had been worried about how the property would be distributed.

(B) Rhonda will likely be successful because the Texas court did not have jurisdiction over her, and thus could not adjudicate her property rights.

(C) Rhonda will likely be unsuccessful because the Texas court had the power to grant the judgment of divorce and New York must give full faith and credit to that judgment.

(D) Rhonda will likely be successful because a judgment of divorce cannot be granted unless the court has jurisdiction over both parties.

87. Community property is

(A) the property owned by the town or village.

(B) property in a community property jurisdiction that is acquired during the marriage and does not meet one of the statutory exceptions making it separate rather than community property.

(C) property owned by the husband or by the wife separately which, because it was used by both husband and wife, is viewed by the law as jointly owned by both of them, i.e., is owned by the marital community.

(D) the property owned by a married couple which all members of the family use. This might include various rooms in a house, a car, etc.

88. Quasi-community property is

(A) something that belongs to the married couple in a community property state and is not quite property, such as frozen embryos that are neither persons nor property.

(B) separate property that has been improved as a result of the expenditure of marital funds.

(C) property which would be community property had it been acquired in a community property state. However, this property was acquired in a common law state and the couple is now divorcing in a community property state.

(D) property that is owned in a community property state by a couple that cannot quite have community property such as an affianced couple.

Thomas and Velina Underwood are married. They live in the house that Thomas owned before their marriage.However, as a gesture of his love for Velina, he put the house in both of their names. Mortgage payments came out of the paychecks of both Thomas and Velina as did the funds for any improvements to the house. Ten years later, Thomas and Velina divorce and the only contested issue is whether the house should be viewed as marital or separate property.

89. How should the house be classified?

ANSWER:

Julie and Ken Martinson have been married for 15 years but are now divorcing. They can agree about the distribution of all of their property with the exception of two items, each bought with marital funds. Julie gave Ken a painting worth $10,000 and Ken gave Julie a necklace worth about $10,000.

90. How should these different items be classified?

ANSWER:

TOPIC 14: CUSTODY/VISITATION — QUESTIONS

91. The best interest of the child standard involves several factors that determine

    (A) which parent is unfit.

    (B) which of two fit parents should be awarded custody.

    (C) how much child support must be paid by the noncustodial parent.

    (D) whether a parent's decision regarding what her child will be permitted to do may be overridden by the state.

92. The tender years presumption is a presumption that

    (A) parents of tender years, e.g., teenagers, could be deprived of child custody relatively easily.

    (B) children of tender years would have their preferences given great weight regarding which parent should be awarded custody.

    (C) mothers should be given custody of children below a certain age.

    (D) to promote the best interests of the child and to promote certainty and consistency, mothers will irrebuttably be given custody of children below a certain age.

93. Which of the following statements is false?

    (A) A parent's unwillingness to allow his or her child to have contact with the other parent may be viewed by a court as one factor among many to determine custody.

    (B) A parent's unwillingness to allow his or her child to have contact with the other parent may be viewed by a court as one factor among many to determine whether a change of custody would be appropriate.

    (C) A parent's unwillingness to allow his or her child to have contact with the other parent may be viewed by a court as a factor which in some cases will not detrimentally affect that parent's likelihood of having or continuing to have custody.

    (D) A parent's unwillingness to allow his or her child to have contact with the other parent may be viewed by a court as a factor in determining whether the withholding of child support by that latter parent was justified.

Zeus and Helen Agropolis live in the state of Georgama and are divorcing after fifteen years of marriage. Their fourteen-year-old child, Menelaus, has expressed a strong desire to live with his father. While no state statute explicitly deals with whether or how child preferences should be treated, Georgama follows the example set by other states in this area.

94. What weight, if any, will be given to the expressed wishes of Menelaus?

(A) Because Menelaus is a minor, his wishes will play no factor in determining which parent should have custody.

(B) If Menelaus has at least average intelligence and maturity for someone his age and respecting his wishes would not be contrary to his best interests, the court will likely give his expressed preference significant weight.

(C) Because Menelaus is the individual likely to be most affected by the custody decision, his preference is dispositive in this matter.

(D) Because Menelaus only has a few years before he reaches majority, his announced preferences will be given at most slight weight in the decision-making process.

Betty and Carl Anderson divorce, Betty being awarded custody of their two children. A year later, Carl files a petition requesting a modification of custody due to changed circumstances. Carl is now earning much more than he was the previous year and Betty has started living with David whom Carl thinks will have a bad influence on the children.

95. Will the request for a custody modification be granted?

(A) If Betty refuses to stop living with David, Carl may well be successful if the court views Betty's new living arrangement as involving a material change in the circumstances that is having an adverse effect on the children.

(B) Even if Betty's new living arrangement has an adverse effect on the children, Carl will be unsuccessful because changing custody would infringe upon the fundamental right to privacy.

(C) Regardless of whether Betty's living arrangement will have an adverse effect on the children, Carl will likely be successful because he can now be a better provider for the children than he was before.

(D) Carl will likely be unsuccessful because once a court has decreed that a particular parent has custody, the court will modify that award only if it can be established that the custodial parent is unfit.

Many states require a material change in the circumstances before one parent can seek a change in the child custody arrangements.

96. That standard involves

(A) whether one of the parents has had a significant negative or positive change in his or her income.

(B) whether there has been any change in particular enumerated factors which have been designated "material."

(C) important new facts that were unknown at the time of the prior custodial decree.

(D) a change in material matters, such as anytime the child changes residences.

97. When used in the legal context, parental alienation involves

(A) the condition of not wanting to be a parent, which may have been caused by having had an unhealthy relationship with one's own parents.

(B) the feeling that most parents have at one time or another when their children do something very upsetting.

(C) one parent causing his or her child to be distant or alienated from the child's other parent.

(D) a term describing the loss of feeling of one parent for the other parent in the context of a divorce.

Don and Doreen Davidson are married and live in Divorca. They have two children. They find that they have fallen out of love with each other. They divorce. Doreen is awarded legal and physical custody of the two children and Don is awarded liberal visitation rights. Doreen and the children remain in Divorca while Don moves to Newstartania. Both Newstartania and Divorca permit custody modifications two years after the initial decree.

Three years later, while the children have been visiting with Don for a month, Don goes to court in Newstartania, seeking physical and legal custody of the children, with Doreen being awarded liberal visitation rights. Doreen appears at the proceeding, making all of the appropriate arguments.

98. What result?

(A) Don will likely be unsuccessful because the Newstartania court must give full faith and credit to the Divorca court's final decree.

(B) Don will likely be successful if he can show a substantial change in circumstances.

(C) Don will likely be unsuccessful because the Parental Kidnaping Prevention Act and the Divorca version of the Uniform Child Custody Jurisdiction Act will likely establish that the Divorca court has jurisdiction of this matter.

(D) Don will likely be successful because Newstartania's version of the Uniform Interstate Family Support Act allows subsequent modifications.

Liana and Larry Langtree have been married and living in North Florilina for five years. They have two children, Mary, age four, and Michael, age two. Liana and Larry have been having marital difficulties and have decided to divorce. Liana will have primary custody of Mary and Michael, although the children will stay with their father over the summers.

Larry accepts a job in the state of Georgiana and moves there. Liana stays in North Florilina with the children. After a few years, Liana decides to accept a job in South Florilina. She gets permission from the court to relocate and moves there with her children. Eighteen months later, while the children are visiting their father in Georgiana, Larry files for a modification of custody in Georgiana, arguing that the South Florilina climate is bad for the children and thus constitutes a material change in the circumstances. Liana argues that the Georgiana court does not have jurisdiction to decide this issue.

99. Assuming no extenuating circumstances beyond the facts listed in the question, the Georgiana court should

(A) decline to hear this case because North Florilina has jurisdiction, having been the state in which custody was originally awarded.

(B) decline to hear this case because South Florilina is now the children's home state and thus has jurisdiction to decide modifications of custody, assuming the absence of unusual circumstances.

(C) hear this case because the children are in the jurisdiction pursuant to the original custody order.

(D) hear this case because Liana made an appearance and thus all personal jurisdiction requirements have been met.

Two years ago, Norman and Nancy Newman went through a bitter divorce in their home state of New Massashire, Nancy being awarded custody of the couple's two small children. Nancy has just received a fantastic job offer, although it would require moving to Wyana, 2000 miles away. Nancy seeks permission to relocate with the children. Norman seeks to prevent Nancy's moving with the children, because it would then be much more difficult for him to see them frequently.

100. What result?

(A) Because Nancy's moving so far away would in effect deprive Norman of the right to participate in the lives of his children, the United States Constitution precludes the court from permitting Nancy to do this absent some compelling justification.

(B) Because Nancy is the custodial parent, she can move with the children wherever she wants.

(C) Because Nancy's moving so far away would interfere with the children's relationship with their father and because it is important for children to maintain contact with both parents, Nancy's request will be denied, even if granting it would not violate constitutional guarantees.

(D) If the move would promote the best interests of the children and is not motivated by a desire to spite the other parent, permission will likely be granted.

When considering which parent should have custody of the children when one of the parents has committed a marital fault, states will sometimes use some form of a nexus test.

101. The nexus test would involve an examination of

(A) how closely connected in time was the discovery of the marital fault and the filing for divorce.

(B) whether the marital fault has some detrimental effect on the children.

(C) whether the marital fault arose because of something done by the children.

(D) whether punishing the parent for the commission of the marital fault would be connected to the promotion of an important public policy.

Victor and Winona are going to divorce because Winona has been having an affair with another man. The sole contested issue is who should have custody of their child, Teresa. Victor claims that because Winona committed adultery he should have custody of Teresa. However, testimony establishes that Winona has shielded Teresa from the affair and that the affair has had no adverse impact on Teresa. Testimony further establishes that Victor does not have a warm relationship with Teresa and that Winona does.

102. What result?

ANSWER:

John and Kaitlyn Madison are divorced. Kaitlyn has custody of their three-year-old child, Lawrence. Kaitlyn has started to date Matthew and John is worried that Matthew spends so much time with Lawrence that Lawrence is growing too close to Matthew. John files to modify custody or in the alternative to prevent Kaitlyn from having Matthew present when Lawrence is in the home.

103. What result?

ANSWER:

In *Parent v. Parent*, the New Mainland Supreme Court held that the tender years presumption violates equal protection guarantees of the federal and state constitution. Knowing this, Jon Johnson's attorney, Betty, presents evidence indicating that women are awarded custody of their children in divorces much more frequently than men are. Betty thereby seeks to establish that John Johnson's rights were violated when he was not awarded custody of his children. While the trial court made no comments suggesting bias, Betty argues that the statistics alone warrant a re-examination of the custody decision in light of *Parent*.

104. What result?

ANSWER:

Yolanda and Zeus Wainwright are married and living in West Carolandia with their child, Xerxes. One day, Yolanda comes home from work early and discovers Zeus in bed with Madeline.

Yolanda files for divorce and is awarded custody of Xerxes. Zeus is awarded visitation on alternate weekends and for a month during the summer, provided that no unrelated female is with him while Xerxes is visiting.

This arrangement continues for two years. In the third year, Zeus learns that Xerxes is having a great deal of difficulty getting along with the children of Hector, whom Yolanda has married. On several different occasions, Xerxes has mentioned that he would like to come to live with his father and Madeline, Zeus' wife. Zeus files for a modification of custody during Xerxes's summer visit.

105. What result?

ANSWER:

Assume the same facts as in Question 105 except that Zeus and Madeline have moved to the neighboring state of East Carolandia and that Zeus has filed in East Carolandia for a change in custody. Both East and West Carolandia have passed statutes mirroring the Uniform Child Custody Jurisdiction and Enforcement Act.

106. What result?

ANSWER:

Samantha Smith and Jean Jones are living together in West Monaho and raising Gina, a daughter born to Jean through artificial insemination. West Monaho permits second-parent adoptions for same-sex couples, although Samantha has not sought to adopt Gina. Samantha is Gina's primary caretaker.

After seven years, Samantha discovers that Jean is having an affair with another woman. Samantha and Jean decide to split up. Samantha still wants to have contact with Gina, however, which Jean opposes.Samantha files suit seeking custody of or visitation with Gina.

107. What result?

ANSWER:

Sandra and Tony Wainwright are a married couple living in New Arisey. They have had difficulty conceiving for a long time. They discover that Sandra is unable to have children and decide to hire a woman, Eva, to be artificially inseminated with Tony's sperm. The insemination is successful and Eva carries the child to term. When Eva gives birth to the child, Adam, she refuses to surrender him. Sandra and Tony sue to force her to surrender the child.

108. What result?

ANSWER:

Assume the facts Question 108. However, assume that the Wainwrights had gotten eggs donated, and then had made use of in vitro fertilization and a gestational surrogate.

109. How, if at all, might the change in facts affect the result?

ANSWER:

Olga and Paul Roberts have been divorced for two years, Olga having custody of their two children in West Wydaho. Olga has received a wonderful job offer from Major Corporation located 1,000 miles away in East Michsylvania, where her parents, brother, and his wife and children live. She seeks permission from the court to move. Paul opposes the move because he believes that it will interfere with his relationship with his children.

110. What result?

ANSWER:

John and Eileen are divorced, Eileen having been awarded custody of their two children. Eileen lives in Pennio and John lives in West Tennucky. Each summer, the children spend a month with John on his farm in West Tennucky. One summer, John decided that the children were enjoying themselves so much that it was clear that they should live with him rather than with their mother. He sought a modification of custody in the West Tennucky courts, claiming that the children would be much better off if he were to have custody. Eileen argues, inter alia, that the West Tennucky court does not have jurisdiction to decide this matter.

111. What result?

ANSWER:

TOPIC 15: SUPPORT

QUESTIONS

Fred Fingerlake and Freida Fineman wish to marry. Fred goes to Dominica, a foreign country, meets the residency requirement, and divorces his spouse. He then returns home to marry Frieda, a divorcee who was receiving monthly support from her ex-spouse. Frieda had no idea that Fred had ever married, much less that he had gone to Dominica to get a divorce.

Fred and Frieda marry, which pleases Frieda's former spouse, Edward, since he no longer has to pay support if Frieda remarries. Fred's first wife, Georgina, challenges the divorce, arguing that Fred was never domiciled in Dominica. The court finds that Fred was in fact never domiciled in Dominica, which means that the Dominica court did not have jurisdiction to grant the divorce, which means that Fred and Georgina are still married. Because Fred and Georgina were married at the time that Fred and Frieda (allegedly) celebrated their marriage, the marriage between Fred and Frieda is void.

Frieda now wishes that she had never met Fred and wants everything to go back to the way it was before, including her spousal support payments from Edward. Frieda claims that because she has never remarried (her "marriage" to Fred is void in the eyes of the law), Edward must continue to pay support. Edward claims that because, as far as he was concerned, Frieda had remarried, he should no longer be required to pay support.

112. A court hearing Frieda's motion to have the spousal support reinstated may well

  (A) distinguish between voidable and void marriages and then hold that Edward must resume his payments given that Frieda's marriage to Fred was void *ab initio*.

  (B) reject the distinction between void and voidable and follow the majority of states in holding that the payments must be reinstated whenever the second marriage is declared invalid.

  (C) suggest that Edward should not have to resume his payments if and only if he has incurred additional responsibilities such as another family.

  (D) suggest that none of this would have happened if only Georgina had let well enough alone, so Georgina should have to pay Edward for any payments that he is now forced to make to Frieda.

113. Rehabilitative spousal support involves

  (A) money given by one spouse to the other pursuant to a divorce decree so that the ex-spouse will undergo training to become a better person.

  (B) money given by one spouse to the other pursuant to a divorce decree to enable the latter to acquire or improve job skills so that he or she will be able to enter the job market.

(C) money given by one spouse to the other pursuant to a divorce decree so that the latter can have physical therapy and thereby make better use of arms, legs, or hands.

(D) money paid by one spouse or the other so that the couple can go to counseling sessions and thereby have a better chance of saving their marriage and avoiding a divorce.

114. Spousal support pendente lite is

(A) temporary alimony designed to give one of the spouses support while he or she gets training to be qualified to enter the job market.

(B) support for one of the spouses during the period in which the rights and responsibilities arising out of the divorce will be decided.

(C) support which is just enough for the recipient spouse to be able to survive on.

(D) support for the spouse that is held in abeyance until an important factual matter is resolved.

Jeri and Jerome Jones have been married for 35 years. Jeri has been the primary caretaker of the couple's six children and has not worked outside of the home since they married. Jerome has recently informed Jeri that he wants a divorce.

Jeri consults an attorney in a panic. She does not believe that she will be able to get back in the job market. Even if she can, she is confident that she will never be able to live in the style to which she has become accustomed. The attorney reassures Jeri, suggesting that the court will likely order Jerome to pay his soon-to-be ex-wife spousal support.

115. Which of the following factors is unlikely to play a role in determining the level of support that Jeri will eventually get?

(A) the length of the marriage.

(B) the likelihood that Jeri will be unable to enter the job market, even with training.

(C) the standard of living to which Jeri had become accustomed.

(D) Jeri's gender.

David and Danielle Douglass are getting a divorce. David says that he is going to seek custody of their two children unless Danielle agrees to his paying neither spousal nor child support. Danielle, who believes that David would be a terrible custodial parent, agrees because she wants to avoid the possibility that he will be given custody. Assume that the court awards Danielle custody, finding that her having custody would promote the best interests of the children.

116. What would the court say about their agreement regarding support?

(A) The court would approve neither the refusal of spousal support nor the refusal of child support, assuming that Danielle is not independently wealthy.

(B) The court would approve both the refusal to receive spousal support and the refusal to receive child support, assuming no evidence of fraud, duress, or coercion.

(C) Even assuming no evidence of fraud, duress, or coercion, the court would not approve the refusal of child support, since the children will need it and the child support is not Danielle's to bargain away. However, the court will approve Danielle's refusal of spousal support.

(D) While the court would not normally approve the refusal of child and spousal support, it will in this case because it is part of the deal that the two informed parents voluntarily made.

Cassius and Collandra Cassingham are divorced. They had agreed about everything: the property division, the custody issues, and that Cassius would pay for the twins' college tuition costs. However, Cassius had not anticipated that both children would get into and want to attend Prestigious Private College. While Cassius can afford to pay, his doing so would substantially limit the number and quality of the vacations that he could take during the next several years. Further, that would make it harder for him to buy free and clear that summer home on the lakefront that he had wanted to purchase. Cassius now says that he will pay only part of the cost of attending Large State University.

117. What result?

(A) Cassius' promise to pay will be viewed as aspirational. Many students have no help from their parents and the twins should be pleased to receive what Cassius is willing to offer, especially because Cassius cannot be forced to pay anything at all if he does not want to contribute.

(B) While Cassius can only be forced to pay the equivalent of the in-state tuition at the state university, the twins can still go to Prestigious Private College. However, they cannot force Cassius to pay more than he would have had to pay had they instead attended the state university.

(C) Because Cassius made an agreement to pay the tuition costs and did not specify that he would only pay the costs of a public institution, and because requiring him to pay would not impose an unreasonable burden, Cassius may well be required to pay the tuition at Prestigious Private College.

(D) Not only will Cassius be forced to pay the private college costs, but he will have to pay graduate school costs as well should the twins want to get postgraduate or professional training.

Abby and Arthur Anderson divorced years ago without specifying whether either would help to pay for their two children's college educations. Abby is helping to pay the college bills for both of the children and goes to court to force her ex-husband, Arthur, to share that burden. While Arthur can easily afford to pay, he refuses, figuring that his ex-wife is paying anyway.

118. What result?

(A) Had Arthur agreed to pay when the couple had divorced then he could be forced to pay now. However, absent such an agreement, he cannot be required to pay such support.

(B) Because of the importance of a college education, parents are required to pay their children's college education costs, assuming that would not impose too great a financial hardship. Arthur will be forced to pay his share.

(C) As to whether Arthur will have to pay, this will depend upon state law. Some states impose an obligation on divorced parents to pay their children's college education whereas others do not.

(D) Because college is a luxury rather than a necessity, no parent can be legally required to pay for his or her child's college education.

William and Wilhemina Washington have been trying to have a child for years. Eventually, they go to a physician who informs them that William is sterile. William and Wilhemina decide that Wilhemina should make use of artificial insemination. She does and in fact becomes pregnant, although she now mercilessly teases him about his inability to father a child.

In a moment of anger, she admits that she has been having an affair with someone else who, she has concluded with disgust, must also be sterile. William immediately consults an attorney about getting a divorce.

William and Wilhemina can agree about the distribution of marital assets. However, William wants nothing to do with the child born to Wilhemina. He claims that he should not be forced to support the child who, after all, has no genetic connection to him.

119. What result?

(A) Notwithstanding the lack of genetic connection, William will likely be estopped from challenging his support obligation, assuming that the child was a product of the artificial insemination

(B) Because there is no genetic connection between William and the child, he cannot be required to pay child support.

(C) William will be considered the father of the child regardless of who in fact is the biological father if and only if the child was born before the divorce was finalized.

(D) William will not be forced to pay child support if he is willing to forego any parental rights such as the right to have custody or visitation privileges.

Douglas and Danielle Davidson are married. Two children were born into the marriage. Quite by accident, Douglas discovers that Danielle is having an affair with Edward. Douglas asks Danielle for a divorce and she readily agrees.

Douglas and Danielle agree about the property division and that neither will receive spousal support. Douglas does not desire to have custody but wants reasonable visitation. To his surprise, Danielle announces that the children he has been helping to support for the past several years were fathered by Edward, whom Danielle plans to marry as soon as she is able to do so.

When they go to court, Danielle argues that Douglas should neither have support obligations nor visitation privileges.

120. A court hearing this case is likely to

(A) refuse to recognize that Douglas has any parental rights or responsibilities provided that Edward and Danielle marry, so Edward and Danielle can establish a nuclear family with their biological children.

(B) grant Douglas custody of the children, even though Danielle is fit and would be better able to promote the best interests of the children.

(C) recognize Douglas' paternity or in the alternative estop Danielle from denying Douglas' paternity, given that he has treated them as his own children for several years and wishes to have parental rights and responsibilities.

(D) deny that Douglas has any parental rights or responsibilities with respect to these children, but preclude Edward from being recognized as the legal parent of the children.

Isaac and Isabel Isherwood are divorcing. Isabel will have custody of their two children born during the marriage. The sole issue before the court hearing this case is whether Isaac can be forced to pay child support. He has recently learned that the two children he had been helping to support for the past several years are not biologically related to him and he wants nothing to do with them.

121. What result?

(A) No jurisdiction will require a man to continue to support children whom he has just discovered were fathered by someone else.

(B) All jurisdictions will require the husband to continue to support the children that he has been supporting, even if he suddenly discovers that they are not biologically related to him, because the children are innocent third parties whose interests would be promoted by that continued support.

(C) Whether he will be allowed to contest paternity may well depend upon whether he was on notice that he was not the father of the children.

(D) Isaac will be permitted not to support them if and only if the biological father is prepared to support them.

Steven and Nancy have been dating but have never had sexual relations, Nancy's requests notwithstanding. One might, Nancy again asks Steven whether he would like to have sex and Steven says that he would but that he really does not want to become a father. Nancy assures him that she is on the pill so that he need not worry about impregnating her. They have sexual relations.

A few months later, Nancy tells Steven that she is pregnant and that he is the father of the child she is carrying. Steven asks how that is possible and Nancy tells him that she had lied about being on the pill.

Nancy gives birth to a beautiful baby girl. Steven refuses to pay any support and Nancy goes to court to force him to pay his share.

122. What result?

(A) The court is likely to reason that because Nancy and Steven would never have had sexual relations if Nancy had not lied, Steven cannot be ordered to pay support.

(B) Because Steven knew that his having even protected sex might result in pregnancy and because the interests of an innocent third party, the child, are at stake, Steven will likely be forced to pay child support, intentional misrepresentation on Nancy's part notwithstanding.

(C) Steven will be forced to pay child support. However, he will be able to sue Nancy for intentional misrepresentation to recoup what he is paying in damages.

(D) Even if Steven will be forced to pay support, he can have Nancy's misrepresentation taken into account so that his support obligation is reduced.

Robert and Penny Quinley divorce. Penny is awarded custody of their child, Norman. Robert is ordered to pay $400 child support per month. Robert resents having to pay child support for a child that he does not ever plan on seeing anyway, so he quits his job and then seeks to have the support order modified because of a material change in circumstances. Penny contests the modification.

123. Will Robert's modification request be granted?

(A) Robert will likely not be successful because loss of a job is not a material change in circumstances.

(B) Robert will likely be successful because there is no point in ordering him to pay child support when he doesn't have the money to pay it.

(C) Robert will likely not be successful because his losing his job was a voluntary act on his part to avoid having to pay support.

(D) Robert will likely be successful because no support will be required of those who are willing not to exercise their visitation rights.

Larry and Lani Langdell are divorced. Lani has custody of their child, Montgomery. Larry has been ordered to pay child support at a certain level, which he has done faithfully. However, he now seeks a reduction in child support because there has been a change in circumstances, namely, he has remarried and now has another child to support. His salary has not kept pace with his increased obligations and the support payments are imposing a substantial burden on his new family.

124. What result?

(A) Because Larry make a voluntary decision to get into another relationship knowing all the while that he had existing child support payments, no jurisdiction would permit him to get a reduction in support because of his voluntary choice.

(B) Larry's new family obligations may be taken into consideration as a factor that might justify a reduction in support.

(C) Because the idea behind the child support obligations is to allow Montgomery to enjoy the standard of living that he would have if his parents had not divorced, Larry's decision to raise a new family cannot be used to justify reducing Montgomery's standard of living.

(D) Once Larry incurred new family obligations, any orders for support of his previous family were then automatically nullified in the eyes of the law.

George and Greta Green divorce. George is awarded custody of their child, Gregory. Greta is ordered to pay child support. A few years later, Greta becomes the president of a local company and receives a huge increase in pay. Gregory's needs are more than met by the existing support order and in fact have not materially changed since the original order. George's salary has increased over the past few years, but not substantially. George seeks to have the support order modified. Greta contests the modification.

125. Will George be successful in his attempt to have child support increased?

(A) Greta rather than George will likely be successful because Greg's needs are more than satisfied by the original order and the court will not be permitted to modify support unless the child's needs have changed.

(B) George will likely be successful unless Greta has not been taking full advantage of her visitation rights.

(C) George will likely be successful because Greta's salary has changed substantially and the station in life of a child should not be tied to the station of life enjoyed at the time of divorce.

(D) Greta rather than George will likely be successful because any other holding would make it less likely that non-custodial parents would try to work very hard and earn substantially higher salaries.

Andrew and Alice Abrams are married and live in Alaska, which has its own version of the Uniform Interstate Family Support Act mirroring the Model Act. They divorce. Andrew is awarded custody of Arby, their five-year-old who will eat nothing but roast beef sandwiches. Alice is required to pay child support. Alice moves for a new job to the state of Washington, whose version of the Uniform Interstate Family Support Act is identical to Alaska's. Andrew and Arby remain in Alaska. Because of a downturn in the market for airplanes, Alice is laid off at work. She goes to court in Washington to have her support obligation modified due to a material and substantial change in circumstances. The Washington court nullifies the terms of the original support order. Andrew, who does not care much for Alice who, after all, does not live there anymore, seeks enforcement of the original support order.

126. Will Andrew be successful in having the original support order enforced?

(A) Andrew will likely be successful because Alice, a capable person, will likely get a job again soon and she can borrow the money until that time.

(B) Andrew will likely be unsuccessful because the Washington court nullified the support order and the Washington court's judgment must be given full faith and credit.

(C) Andrew will likely be successful because the Washington court did not have jurisdiction to modify the order.

(D) Andrew will likely be unsuccessful because, as a matter of equity, Alice should not be forced to pay support when she does not have the money.

Assume the same facts as in Question 126. Also assume that Alice was ordered to pay Andrew spousal support. When Alice was laid off, she went to a Washington court to reduce her spousal support order, pointing out the change in circumstances.Andrew appears in Washington to contest the modification.

127. Will the support order be modified?

(A) Andrew will lose. Because the court has personal jurisdiction over Andrew, it is free to modify his spousal support.

(B) Andrew would have lost whether or not he had appeared. Alice obviously did not do anything in bad faith and this is a substantial change of circumstances.

(C) Andrew will win unless he is now making substantially more than he was before.

(D) Andrew is likely to win. If the Alaska court has continuing exclusive jurisdiction under local law, the Washington court will not have jurisdiction to modify the spousal support.

Oscar and Olga Othella marry in Oklahoma and continue to live there for a few years. Oscar is offered a job in New Mexico and the Othellas move there. Oscar and Olga start to have marital problems and Oscar sends Olga back to live with her mother in Oklahoma. After a year, Oscar informs Olga that he has started to see someone else and that he never wants to see Olga again. Olga files for divorce in Oklahoma after giving the requisite notice to Oscar. The Oklahoma court grants Olga a divorce and orders him to pay spousal support. Oscar challenges the divorce and the support order.

128. Will Oscar's challenge be successful?

(A) Oscar will likely be successful because the Oklahoma court did not have jurisdiction to grant the divorce, since it did not have jurisdiction over him.

(B) Oscar will likely be unsuccessful because the Oklahoma court did have jurisdiction to grant the divorce and support, notwithstanding its lack of jurisdiction over him.

(C) Oscar will likely be successful because even if the Oklahoma court had jurisdiction to grant the divorce it did not have the power to order support.

(D) Oscar will likely be unsuccessful assuming that the Oklahoma court had personal jurisdiction over him via the state's long-arm statute.

Edward Evanson has been ordered to pay child support until his daughter reaches 18 or until she is declared an emancipated minor. He believes that he should no longer pay support because he believes that she in fact is emancipated.

129. Which of the following would not help establish that she should be declared emancipated?

(A) She has married her junior high school sweetheart, Fred Fredrickson.

(B) She is self-supporting and, with parental permission, is living on her own.

(C) She has multiple sex partners, and hence is emancipated from existing (restrictive) societal conventions.

(D) She has joined the Army.

Madelyn McCarthy, 16, became an emancipated minor when she married her high school sweetheart John Jones. Madelyn's divorced father, Michael, was pleased by the marriage because it meant that he would no longer have to continue sending child support payments for her. However, the marriage between Madelyn and John has now been declared void by a court because Marilyn had married without the consent of either of her parents. This is fine with Marilyn who now hates John and wants to go back to living with her mother, Leticia, Michael's ex-wife. Leticia is more than willing to have Madelyn come live with her but wants the child support payments to begin again to help defray the expenses of raising Madelyn. Michael refuses and Leticia sues to have the payments reinstated.

130. What result?

(A) Because Madelyn's marriage was declared void, it never existed in the eyes of the law and thus Michael will not only be forced to start paying child support again but he will have to make up those payments that he withheld during Madelyn's purported marriage.

(B) Because Madelyn's marriage was declared void, the condition which once emancipated her no longer exists and she will again be treated as an unemancipated minor. While Michael may well be forced to again pay child support for Madelyn, he may well not have to pay the support that he withheld during Madelyn's purported marriage.

(C) The support payments which stopped when Madelyn became emancipated will not be reinstated, since no state will make a minor once emancipated become non-emancipated in the eyes of the law.

(D) The support payments will be reinstated only if there was a provision incorporated into the final divorce decree specifying that if the support payments were stopped as a result of minor emancipation they would be reinstated if, e.g., the minor marriage was later declared void.

131. Under the Uniform Interstate Family Support Act, which of the following will not give a state personal jurisdiction over a non-resident parent?

(A) The parent once resided with the child in the state.

(B) The child was conceived in the state.

(C) The parent is personally served while in the state.

(D) A letter is sent to the last-known address of the parent.

Wanda and William Wainwright have divorced. Wanda has agreed to pay William spousal support until he either dies or remarries. William has started cohabiting with Velina. Wanda believes that William living with someone else should relieve her of her continuing duty to pay spousal support, although William believes that if he does not marry Velina he is still entitled to support. Wanda consults an attorney to find out who is correct.

132. What should the attorney tell Wanda?

(A) States differ with respect to whether cohabitation will suffice to relieve a party of the duty to continue paying spousal support. Some states have made clear through their statutes or case law that support need not be paid under these conditions, while other states will require support to be paid until the spouse remarries or until the payor spouse can establish that the payee spouse's need has lessened.

(B) Because William and Velina are married for all practical purposes, all jurisdictions recognize that Wanda's support obligation has ended.

(C) Because Wanda could easily have included within the separation agreement that was incorporated in the final decree that support would end upon William remarrying or cohabiting and because Wanda nonetheless did not do so, Wanda will be forced to abide by the agreement.

(D) Regardless of the state in which they live, Wanda and William will simply have to testify about their intentions at the time of the divorce. This issue will be decided in light of whose claims seem more credible.

Barbara and Bill Bellington are divorced. Barbara has been ordered to pay support until Bill either dies or remarries. Bill has started cohabiting with Brian. Barbara argues that because the support would end were Bill cohabiting with a woman, the support should end now that Bill is cohabiting with a man.

133. Will Barbara have to continue paying support?

(A) This will vary by jurisdiction, some holding that even if cohabitation with a member of a different sex would end the requirement of paying spousal support, cohabitation with a member of the same sex will not, while others hold that this will end the requirement of support.

(B) Because no state currently permits same-sex couples to marry, no state will count cohabitation with a member of the same sex as justifying the cessation of spousal support.

(C) Because Bill and Brian would marry if they could and act as if they were married, all jurisdictions will permit the spousal support to end under these circumstances.

(D) Whether Barbara's duty of support will end will depend upon whether she is cohabiting with someone else. If she is, she will be estopped from claiming that this justifies stopping her support payments.

Quentin Roberts is a highly paid executive employed by a major corporation. He is tired of paying large sums in spousal and child support every month so he quits his job and instead gets one in which his salary is substantially lower. He then seeks to have his court-ordered support decreased because of a material change in circumstances.

134. What result?

ANSWER:

Mabel and Norman Overton have been married for several years. They have no children and Mabel is the primary wage earner. Mabel is ordered to pay Norman $1,000/month until he dies or remarries.

A year after the divorce, Mabel wins one million dollars in the lottery. Norman seeks an increase in his support.

135.What result?

ANSWER:

Assume the same facts as in Question 135. However, also assume that a child had been born of the marriage, that Norman had custody, and that Norman sought an increase in child support when Mabel won the lottery.

136. What result?

ANSWER:

Ethel and Frederick Goodman are married and living in Washegonia. They have one child, Hermione. Frederick stopped working outside of the home once Hermione was born so that he could take care of her. Unfortunately, Ethel and Frederick have been having marital difficulties and in fact decide to divorce.

The Washegonia court orders Ethel to pay Frederick $1,000/month in spousal support and $1,200/month in child support, retaining jurisdiction. After a few years, Ethel receives a wonderful job offer in Wydaho and decides to accept it. All is going well until the company for whom Ethel is working, Ensam, goes bankrupt. The generous salary that Ethel had received ceases and Ethel goes to court in Wydaho to reduce her support obligations. Both Washegonia and Wydaho have passed versions of Uniform Interstate Family Support Act which mirror each other and the Model Act. Frederick argues that the Wydaho court lacks jurisdiction to modify the support order.

137. What result?

ANSWER:

Cindy and David have been living together without benefit of marriage for several years and have been trying without success since the beginning of their relationship to have children. Cindy and David agree that Cindy should undergo artificial insemination and that they will each parent the child. Cindy is artificially inseminated and eventually has a child. However, during the pregnancy, Cindy and David grow increasingly distant.

Shortly before the child is born, David leaves. Cindy sues for child support. David claims that because he never married Cindy and because he has no biological connection to the child, he cannot be required to support the child.

138. What result?

ANSWER:

Myron and Mary Mouskowicz are divorced, Myron having custody of their child, Mildred. Mary has been ordered to pay child support to Myron. Mildred just learned that Myron has just won the lottery and she files to have her support payments reduced.

139. What result?

ANSWER:

Thomas and Terry Upton were married but have now divorced. Thomas has been ordered to pay Terry child support for the two children born of the marriage. After a few years, Thomas seeks to have his support obligation reduced because Terry is now earning much more than she was only a few years before. Terry argues that Thomas' support obligation should remain the same because the needs of the children have not at all diminished.

140. What result?

ANSWER:

Hilda and Isaac Jones are divorced, Isaac having custody of the two children born of the marriage. Hilda has been ordered to pay support in light of her salary as a mid-level manager in a large company. Hilda has remarried and now has an infant born of the second marriage. She has quit her job to take care of her young son and seeks to have her support obligation modified in light of her unemployment.

141. What result?

ANSWER:

Irwin Undertaker entered the hospital for emergency surgery. He signed agreements authorizing treatment and to pay for services rendered. While the surgery was successful, Irwin is unable to pay the bills and the hospital is now suing Irwin's wife, Ursula, to pay Irwin's bill. Ursula claims that because she neither authorized the surgery nor promised to pay she is not liable for Irwin's debts. The hospital pleads the doctrine of necessaries.

142. What result?

(A) Because Irwin rather than Ursula agreed to have the treatment and pay the bills, Irwin rather than Ursula is responsible. The doctrine of necessaries has nothing to do with this case and so will not help the hospital

(B) Because this case involves medical treatment rather than food or clothing, the doctrine does not apply.

(C) If the jurisdiction recognizes the common law doctrine of necessaries and has expanded it to make the wife responsible for the necessary expenses of her husband, Ursula can be held liable for the debts even if she did not authorize the procedure.

(D) Because Ursula thought the surgery a bad idea, she cannot now be held responsible for the costs of its performance, notwithstanding that everything turned out quite well and that it was necessary to save Irwin's life.

TOPIC 16: FAMILY PRIVACY AND THE CONSTITUTION — QUESTIONS

Andy and Susie have been dating for about a year. They are now having sexual relations less frequently than they were at the beginning of their relationship. Susie discovers that she is pregnant but decides not to tell Andy, because he now only calls her infrequently and they invariably fight when they do talk. When Susie gives birth, she puts the child up for adoption, claiming that she does not know who the father is. When Andy finds out what has happened, he seeks to establish his parental rights.

143. What result?

(A) Andy will likely be unsuccessful. Just as a man does not have the right to veto his wife's decision to abort, a man does not have the right to veto a woman's decision to put her child up for adoption.

(B) Andy will likely be successful because the father's right to the care and custody of his child is fundamental.

(C) Andy's challenge may be successful depending in part upon whether his assertion of paternity had been timely once he had learned what had happened.

(D) Andy will only be successful if he and Susie reconcile and she withdraws her consent to the adoption.

Carla and Denny have been living together for several years. Carla is pregnant with their first child and she and Denny have begun to argue quite frequently about what they will do when he is born. Carla eventually moves out, saying that she does not want her child to have to put up with having an inconsiderate and irrational idiot as a father. Carla moves in with her sister and neither contacts nor is contacted by Denny. She has a baby boy, Zachary, and Denny is listed as the father on the birth certificate. She eventually meets and marries Eddie who, after a year of marriage, would like to adopt Zachary. Denny is notified and objects to the adoption.

144. Will Denny be able to block the adoption?

(A) Denny will be able to block the adoption because *Stanley v. Illinois* establishes that an unwed biological father has a fundamental interest in the care and custody of his children which cannot be overridden by the state.

(B) Denny's objection will probably be unsuccessful because *Lehr v. Robertson* establishes that a state can refuse to recognize an unwed father's parental rights if the mother no longer wants to have any contact with the father.

(C) Denny will be able to block the adoption if he promises to be a better father to Zachary now.

(D) Denny's objection will probably be unsuccessful because he never paid any support for or established a relationship with his son.

Alice and Ben are married, although their marriage is somewhat rocky. Alice has started having an affair with Carl. Alice becomes pregnant and eventually gives birth to a little girl, Daniella, who bears a striking resemblance to Carl. By this time, however, Alice and Ben are getting along well. Alice is not interested in seeing Carl any longer and certainly does not want Carl to establish a relationship with Daniella.

145. As a matter of federal constitutional right, can Carl force Alice and Ben to permit him to establish a relationship with Daniella?

ANSWER:

Thomas and Tania are married. Tania, who is completing her third year of law school, has just discovered that she is pregnant. While she and Thomas want to have children some day, she does not want to have a child now. She decides that she wants to get an abortion. Thomas wants to be a father now and very much wants Tania to carry the fetus to term. When she refuses, Thomas seeks to enjoin her from getting an abortion.

146. What result?

(A) The court will issue the injunction. Just as a mother cannot put a child up for adoption without getting the consent of her husband (assuming that he has parental rights), a woman cannot get an abortion without the permission of her husband (assuming that he is the father).

(B) The court will not issue the injunction. A woman's right to get an abortion is absolute and cannot be limited by the state or by a spouse.

(C) The court will issue the injunction after balancing numerous interests: the couple wants to have a child eventually; Thomas wants to have a child now; the state has an interest in promoting life over non-life; Tania does not have a compelling reason to get an abortion now, e.g., that continuing the pregnancy would severely endanger her life or health. These interests weigh against permitting Tania to have the abortion.

(D) The court will not issue the injunction because the United States Constitution requires that the wife rather than the husband be allowed to make the ultimate decision in this kind of case.

Babette is a pregnant, unmarried minor. She wishes to get an abortion but state law does not permit her to get an abortion without parental permission. Her parents believe that abortion is wrong in all circumstances, and thus will not give their permission. Babette challenges the law as violating her constitutional rights.

147. What result?

(A) The law will be struck down as unconstitutional because the state cannot require that minors seeking to abort have parental permission unless the state also affords a judicial bypass option which would afford mature minors the possibility of aborting over the objections of their parents.

(B) The law will be upheld. The state has an interest in promoting life over non-life and is justified in presuming that parents will look out for the best interests of their children. The law merely promotes the state's interests in life and in the welfare of the pregnant minor.

(C) The law will be struck down as unconstitutional. If a young woman is old enough and mature enough to have sexual relations and to become pregnant, she is certainly old enough to decide whether or not to carry the fetus to term.

(D) The law will be upheld. Indeed, the law merely reflects the constitutional right of parents to the care and custody of their children.

Tara Thompson and Vince Verner are married and hoping to have children. They have discovered, however, that they can only have children if they make use of in vitro fertilization (IVF). They harvest several of Tara's eggs and fertilize them with Vince's sperm. They implant a few embryos and freeze the rest.

While the first implantation is unsuccessful, the second results in pregnancy. Regrettably, the pressures and disappointments connected with their difficulties in conceiving lead to the break-up of the marriage. They divorce, Tara being awarded custody of the newborn.

They can agree about all matters except the custody and disposition of the embryos. Tara wishes to have the embryos destroyed and Vince wishes to have them donated to a different, infertile couple.

148. Assuming no prior agreement specifying the appropriate disposition of the embryos, the court deciding this issue will likely

(A) award the embryos to Tara and allow them to be destroyed. Had the embryos been implanted in Tara, she would have had the right to abort, which establishes that she has ultimate say over the disposition of the embryos.

(B) award the embryos to Vince, thereby increasing the likelihood that they would eventually be implanted and lead to a live birth, since the state favors life over non-life.

(C) award the embryos to Tara, since the right not to be a parent outweighs the charitable desire to help others. The result might have been different if Vince had wished to use them himself and this would have been the only way that he could have been a biological father.

(D) award the embryos to Vince, since Tara would have no cognizable interest in their not being used if she could not be held legally responsible for them.

The state of South Georgialina has a law that criminalizes the knowing and voluntary ingestion of controlled substances during the third trimester of pregnancy. Sally Smith, who is addicted to cocaine, sniffs cocaine several times during the third trimester of her pregnancy. When she gives birth to her son, Sam, the presence of cocaine metabolites is discovered in his system. Sally is arrested and charged with violating the statute. Sally admits using cocaine during the third trimester but challenges the constitutionality of the statute.

149. Will Sally's challenge be successful?

(A) Sally's challenge to the statute will be successful because the statute is unconstitutional under *Roe v. Wade* and *Planned Parenthood of Southeastern Pennsylvania v. Casey.*

(B) Sally's challenge will be unsuccessful because the state in its role as *parens patriae* has a special interest in children and has plenary power with respect to all matters involving reproduction and children.

(C) Sally's challenge will be successful because such a statute violates the parent's fundamental right to autonomous decision-making with respect to the care and treatment of their children.

(D) Sally's challenge to the statute will be unsuccessful, notwithstanding that *Roe* and *Casey* still protect a woman's right to abort.

The West Kanbraska Legislature has made clear that partial birth abortions violate an important public policy of the state. The Legislature has imposed severe criminal penalties on any doctor who performs such an abortion, regardless of when or why. The partial birth abortion prohibition is challenged as a violation of constitutional guarantees.

150. What is the likely result?

ANSWER:

John G., a married man, and Jean H., an unmarried woman, were discovered in bed together in the master bedroom of the home that John shared with his wife. They each were charged with and convicted of adultery, a criminal offense in the state of Libertia. The convictions are challenged on federal constitutional grounds.

151. Will the challenge be successful?

(A) The challenge will likely be successful because, following *Eisenstadt*, if the right of privacy means anything, it is the right of the individual, married or single, to be free from unwarranted government intrusion into such fundamental matters.

(B) The challenge will likely be unsuccessful because the protection of adultery is neither implicit in the concept of ordered liberty nor deeply rooted in the traditions and collective conscience of the people.

(C) The challenge will likely be successful because, following *Griswold*, the "offense" occurred in the sacred precincts of the marital bedroom.

(D) The challenge will likely be unsuccessful because the Libertia Constitution offers a more expansive definition of the right to privacy than does the United States Constitution.

Joe and Jillian Johnson are sick of each other and ready to divorce. However, they have just become domiciled in Monowigan and the state requires one year of residency before a divorce can be granted. Joe and Jillian challenge the residency requirement, claiming that it unconstitutionally infringes on the fundamental right to marry, since the Johnsons will be precluded from marrying others until they divorce each other. They argue that their case is especially compelling because this would be an uncontested divorce.

152. What result?

(A) Because the right to marry is fundamental, Monowigan's residency requirement will be struck down as unconstitutional.

(B) Because the state has plenary power over the marital status of its domiciliaries, the statute's constitutionality will be upheld.

(C) Because the state is merely delaying rather than precluding their divorce and because the state has an important interest in preventing fraud, the constitutionality of the one-year residency requirement will be upheld.

(D) Because the divorce is uncontested and because the couple could simply establish domicile in another state which has a shorter residency requirement, the restriction will be held unconstitutional as an undue burden on the right to marry or the right to travel.

The town of Belleview has restricted land use to one-family dwellings. The town has defined a family as:

> One or more persons related by blood, adoption, or marriage, living/cooking together as a single housekeeping unit. A number of persons, not exceeding two, living/cooking together as a single housekeeping unit, though not related by blood, adoption, marriage shall be deemed to constitute a family.

Sarah Smith and her two children live with Bob Barnes. They have been told that they cannot live together in a house in the restricted area. They challenge the statute on federal constitutional grounds.

153. Will their challenge be successful?

(A) They likely will be successful because the statute violates their fundamental right to associate.

(B) They likely will be unsuccessful because they can marry if they want to live together in that neighborhood.

(C) They likely will be successful because they meet the functional definition of family and thus cannot be precluded from living together.

(D) They likely will be unsuccessful because such a statute will be upheld if it meets the rational basis test.

Jane Jones is 36½ weeks pregnant. Her doctors strongly advise her to have a caesarian performed for her own sake and for the sake of her fetus. She refuses because she strongly desires to have a natural childbirth. She is determined to be competent by independent tests. The doctors seek a court order requiring her to have a caesarian.

154.Will she be forced to have a caesarian?

(A) Jane will successfully avoid having a caesarian performed against her will only if she convinces the doctor that the fetus will not be harmed by her choice.

(B) Jane will not successfully avoid having a caesarian performed against her will unless she can get a doctor to state that she is not thereby increasing her own risk.

(C) Jane may well successfully avoid having a caesarian performed against her will, given that she is competent and that this is a very invasive procedure.

(D) Jane will likely not successfully avoid having a caesarian performed against her will because the viable fetus has as much right to live as she does.

Paul and Prunella Proudwright are sincere adherents of a religion that mandates that physicians and medicines are to be avoided. Their son, Absalom, is diagnosed with an illness that would generally be curable if treated with antibiotics. However, Paul and Prunella refuse to take Absalom to a doctor or a hospital and, regrettably, Absalom eventually dies. The state charges the Proudwrights with manslaughter and they argue that the manslaughter statute cannot be applied to them because of their constitutionally protected right to practice their religion. The state argues that while Paul and Prunella have the right to freedom from state interference with respect to their religious beliefs, they do not have similar latitude with respect to their religious practices.

155. What result?

(A) The First Amendment of the United States Constitution protects freedom of religion and that protection extends to the states through the Fourteenth Amendment. The court will suggest that the state cannot prosecute the Proudwrights in this case without violating constitutional guarantees.

(B) While a separate issue is whether the state statute contains an exception for those who contribute to the injury or death or their child in the sincere exercise of their religious beliefs, the court will likely hold that the United States Constitution does not bar prosecution in this instance because the constitutionally protected rights to freedom of belief are much more robust than are the constitutionally protected rights to freedom of religious practice.

(C) While individuals are free to hold a variety of religious beliefs, the state can always interfere in parenting practices because of its special interest in children.

(D) The Proudwrights can be prosecuted whenever they reject recommended treatment for their child.

Michelle McDonald is a beautiful 20-year-old who has the mental age of two. Her guardian seeks to have her sterilized fearing what would happen should she become pregnant.

156. The court will likely

   (A) refuse to allow Michelle to be sterilized unless the state has a compelling interest in having that procedure performed.

   (B) allow Michelle to be sterilized because the state otherwise might have to provide care for her offspring.

   (C) refuse to allow Michelle to be sterilized unless it could be established that such a refusal would be too burdensome for the parents.

   (D) allow Michelle to be sterilized if, e.g., it could be established that it would be in the best interests of Michelle to have such a procedure performed and she, if competent for a few minutes, would choose to have such a procedure performed for herself, given her incompetence.

Carl and Donna Chang are unable to have children because Donna has had a hysterectomy. However, Donna can produce eggs. The Changs hire Samantha Smith, a single woman, to be a gestational surrogate for them. An embryo created in a laboratory from genetic material produced by Donna and Carl is implanted in Samantha. When Samantha delivers the child, she finds herself unwilling to part with him. She goes to court seeking custody. All of this has taken place in the state of New California, which has a decision by its supreme court which mirrors *In re Baby M* and a different, more recent decision which mirrors *Johnson v. Calvert*.

157. When deciding *Smith v. Chang*, the state supreme court is most likely to hold that

   (A) Samantha is the mother, Carl is the father, and custody should be determined in light of who would promote the best interests of the child.

   (B) Samantha is the mother, Carl is the father, but the Changs should have custody because a child is always better off with a married couple than with a single mother.

   (C) Donna is the mother, Carl is the father, and the Changs should have custody because that was the intention of the parties when the agreement was made.

   (D) Donna is the mother, Carl is the father, and the Changs should have custody because they each have a genetic link to the child and Samantha has no genetic link to the child.

Julie Johnson is an informed, competent, 17-year-old who has leukemia. She refuses to consent to blood transfusions (a necessary part of treatment) because accepting blood would violate the personal religious convictions of the Jehovah Witness faith. Jill Johnson, Julie's mother, supports her decision wholeheartedly. With the treatment, Julie has a 25 percent (25%) likelihood of living at least five additional years. Without the treatment she will die within a month. A neglect petition has been filed by the State so that a guardian can be appointed to consent to medical care for Julie. Julie and her mother oppose the appointment of a guardian.

158. Will the court appoint a guardian to make Julie's medical care decisions?

(A) The court will not appoint a guardian, given that Julie and her mother both agree about the proper course of treatment. Either Julie's refusal is valid or the refusal of her mother (the person whom the state recognizes as the one to make decisions for Julie) is valid. Either way, no guardian is needed.

(B) The court will appoint a guardian because there is some chance that Julie will survive with treatment and no chance that she will survive without treatment.

(C) The court will not appoint a guardian because Julie is competent and has made an informed decision to refuse treatment.

(D) The court may appoint a guardian. The decision will likely depend, at least in part, upon whether the court believes that Julie is a sufficiently mature minor to make such a decision for herself.

159. Which of the following is not plausibly thought a partial explanation of the United States Supreme Court's decision in *DeShaney v. Winnebago County Dept. of Social Services?*

(A) Holding the County liable might have resulted in other counties' closing down their child protective services agencies for fear of potential crushing liability.

(B) The decision would likely reduce the number of cases in which children would have been permitted to remain in the home and continue to be subjected to further life-threatening abuse.

(C) A different result might have caused the state to be too willing to take children out of their homes in the first place or too reluctant to return the children to those homes once the children had been removed.

(D) The Court believed that Joshua was no worse off than he would have been had the state not acted at all.

Carl and Karen Montgomery have been married for years. They have been having problems recently and Karen has been less willing to have sexual relations than Carl would like. One day, in anger and desperation, Carl physically threatens Karen and forces her to have sex with him. Karen presses charges against Carl.

160. What result?

(A) Citing *Griswold v. Connecticut*, the court will say that the doctrine of marital privacy precludes the state from criminalizing this kind of behavior.

(B) Because no one has the right to force someone else to have sexual relations, all jurisdictions would simply treat this as an instance of forcible rape.

(C) Carl may well be subjected to criminal sanction, since most jurisdictions treat this as a crime, although even some of those treat a rape by a marital partner as a less serious offense than a rape by a stranger.

(D) Carl will be convicted unless Karen was unreasonably refusing to have sexual relations.

Assume the same facts as in Question 160. At trial, Carl seeks to preclude Karen from testifying against him, citing the privilege against testifying against a spouse.

161. What result?

(A) Until Karen divorces Carl, she will be precluded from testifying against him without his permission.

(B) Even were Karen to divorce Carl, she would be precluded from testifying about anything that happened during the marriage.

(C) This depends upon which spouse owns the testimonial privilege.

(D) Karen can be forced to testify, even if Carl and Karen have reconciled and neither she nor Carl wants her to do so.

The state of East Georgiana has passed a statute criminalizing exposure of a viable fetus to specified controlled substances. Sally Smith ingests cocaine during the eighth and ninth months of her pregnancy. When Sally gives birth to Samuel, Samuel is tested pursuant to law and it becomes clear that Samuel was exposed to cocaine during the pregnancy. Sally is tried and convicted of exposing Samuel to one of the specified controlled substances. Sally admits having voluntarily ingested the substance during her pregnancy but challenges the constitutionality of the statute, claiming that it violates her right to privacy as guaranteed by *Roe v. Wade* and *Planned Parenthood of Eastern Pennsylvania v. Casey*.

162. What result?

ANSWER:

Mickey and Minnie Meiselman have twin children, Thomas and Terry.Terry is in desperate need of a bone marrow transplant and the only known match is Thomas. There is relatively little long-term danger or pain associated with the procedure. Mickey and Minnie want the procedure performed.

163. What result?

ANSWER:

John and Mary Fienes have been married for several years. They are strict vegetarians and believe it an extremely important religious duty that their child not be exposed to milk or dairy products. Mary has given birth to a beautiful baby girl, Wilhemina. Mary is unable to breastfeed the child and is worried about some of the ingredients of commercial-based formulas. She and John decide to make their own formula.

Regrettably, Wilhemina does not get enough protein and suffers long-term difficulties because of her diet. The parental rights of John and Mary are terminated and Wilhemina is put in foster care. John and Mary challenge the termination of rights, claiming that their rights to privacy and religious freedom have been violated.

164. What result?

ANSWER:

The United States Supreme Court has repeatedly reaffirmed that the right to marry involves a fundamental interest that is protected by the Federal Constitution.

165. This means that

(A) states are precluded from restricting marriage.

(B) state restrictions of marriage must be supported by sufficiently important state interests and closely tailored to effectuate only those interests.

(C) a marriage that is recognized in one state must be recognized in every state.

(D) while states can restrict marriage in ways that they believe best promote public policy, Congress is severely limited in the restrictions that it can place on marriage.

John Jones and Katrina Katzen, domiciliaries of New Oklahodico, wish to marry in accord with their religious beliefs. Both are over 21 years of age. While John is already married, John and Katrina's religious beliefs permit men to have more than one wife. However, New Oklahodico prohibits plural marriages and does not have an exception for those that would be performed in accord with sincerely held religious beliefs. John and Katrina seek a declaratory judgment that the New Oklahodico marriage statute, at least as applied to them, is unconstitutional.

166. The court hearing the case will likely

(A) uphold the constitutionality of the statute, reasoning that marriage, by definition, cannot involve more than two persons.

(B) hold the statute unconstitutional, reasoning that *Loving v. Virginia* and *Reynolds v. United States* are controlling precedent.

(C) examine the statute to see whether it is reasonably related to a legitimate state interest and decide in light of that examination.

(D) examine the statute to see whether it is narrowly tailored to promote compelling state interests and decide in light of that examination.

The Winnigan State Legislature has found that in too many instances non-custodial parents are falling behind on their child support payments. The Legislature passes a statute precluding non-custodial parents from marrying if they are behind on their child support payments, although the statute includes an exception permitting such non-custodial parents to marry a parent of a child for whom they are responsible.

Bob Barnett wishes to marry Constance Cornett. However, he is behind on his child support payments for the child that he had with Darla Davenport, and he and Constance have not had any children together. When the town clerk refuses to issue a marriage license to Bob and Constance, Bob challenges the statute precluding his marriage to Constance on constitutional grounds.

167. What result?

ANSWER:

TOPIC 17: PARENTING RELATIONSHIPS

QUESTIONS

John Jones and Tawanda Meyer live together in Wisigan, a jurisdiction that does not recognize de facto parents. They plan on staying together for the rest of their lives, although they do not wish to marry each other. They decide that they want to raise a child together. However, because John has had a vasectomy, Tawanda goes to a licensed clinic where she is artificially inseminated with sperm from an anonymous donor (who has since died in a plane crash). Tawanda becomes pregnant and has a son whom she and John raise until the child is about six. At this point, Tawanda meets someone else with whom she falls in love. John and Tawanda decide to separate. Tawanda wishes to prevent John from having any contact with the child. John goes to court, arguing that he should have custody.

168. Will John be awarded custody?

(A) John may well not succeed. He would have been much more likely to have been awarded custody if he had adopted the child or had married Tawanda before the child's birth.

(B) John is likely to be awarded custodial rights if the child's best interests would thereby be promoted.

(C) John is likely to succeed because Tawanda has been unfaithful which establishes her *per se* unfitness in most states.

(D) John is unlikely to succeed because by having a vasectomy he gave up all future rights to fatherhood.

Paula, an unmarried woman, has decided that she wants to have a child. She contacts Peter, her neighbor, and explains that she wants to have a child. She says that she would like to use his sperm, making clear that conception would take place via artificial insemination. Peter agrees.

Eventually, a child is born to Paula whom she names Robert. To Paula's dismay, Peter wishes to develop a father-son relationship with Robert. Paula refuses to permit Peter to see Robert. Peter sues for visitation rights.

169. What result?

(A) Because Paula conceived via artificial insemination, Peter is not the father in the eyes of the law.

(B) Because Peter is the biological father regardless of how conception occurred, Peter has parental rights.

(C) It is unclear how this case will be decided. This may well depend on the explicit or implicit agreement that Paula and Peter had when conception occurred.

(D) Because Paula has the primary responsibility for Robert, this will be left up to her.

John and Jane Jones seek to adopt their foster child, Billy, who has been in their care for the past two years. In the same proceeding, the court holds (1) Billy's biological mother unfit and terminates her parental rights, and (2) that John and Jane can adopt Billy.

170. At least one legal difficulty posed by having the rights termination and the adoption performed in the same proceeding is that

(A) this would be a more efficient use of time.

(B) the court might be induced to compare the parenting skills of the interested parties rather than use an independent standard for unfitness.

(C) the biological parents might come to know who the foster parents are.

(D) the child might be too young to express a considered, mature preference.

171. An open adoption is

(A) one which is open in the sense that the biological parent still can challenge the judgment terminating his or her parental rights.

(B) one in which the biological parent is permitted to have continued contact with or information about the child whom he or she had put up for adoption.

(C) one in which the records detailing all of the important information are open to the public, *e.g.*, because of sunshine laws.

(D) one in which the biological and the adoptive parents are all recognized as the legal parents of the same child.

172. The "stepparent exception" permits

(A) the spouse of a biological/adoptive parent to adopt the latter parent's child without the latter parent being required to give up parental rights.

(B) a stepparent not to have child support obligations if he or she divorces a spouse who has children from a previous marriage.

(C) a stepparent to become a de facto parent, and thus to seek visitation privileges in the event of divorce.

(D) a stepparent to veto his or her spouse's suggestions with respect to how the spouse's child should be raised.

173. What kinds of fees, if any, may be paid by would-be adoptive parents to a biological mother placing her child in a private adoption?

(A) No fees whatsoever, since any exchange of money would amount to baby-selling.

(B) There is no limit on the fees that might be paid if the adoptive placement would in fact promote the best interests of the child.

(C) Medical and legal fees and, perhaps, some of the expenses of the mother.

(D) All costs plus whatever the going rate is for surrogacy arrangements.

174. What is an equitable adoption?

(A) One that is fair and equitable to all parties concerned, including the adoptive parents, birth mother, and child.

(B) One in which a child was not formally adopted but nonetheless will be recognized as entitled to some of the benefits that would have accrued from the adoption, e.g., should the would-be adoptive parent die.

(C) This is a requirement that when a couple wishes to adopt one child who has a sibling, the couple must adopt both or neither.

(D) This is a specific enforcement remedy which basically suggests that when one has consented to an adoption one will be estopped as a matter of equity from withdrawing that consent.

175. Which of the following is not one of the elements of an equitable adoption?

(A) Agreement to adopt, either express or implied.

(B) Reliance on the agreement.

(C) The child lived in the home of the adoptive parents.

(D) Money was given to the biological parents.

176. Which of the following factors will be considered irrelevant when considering whether a would-be adoptive parent will in fact be allowed to adopt?

(A) Marital status.

(B) Age.

(C) Economic status.

(D) Consent of other non-immediate family members, such as a grandmother.

177. A second parent adoption is

(A) an adoption of a child by a parent who has previously adopted a different child.

(B) a process whereby a child is allowed to establish a legal relation with his or her parent's new spouse.

(C) an adoption of a child by a parent's non-marital partner.

(D) an adoption of a child by one set of parents which follows the adoption of that same child by a different set of parents. This kind of case occurs when the initial adoption does not work out for some reason and the initial set of adopting parents returns the child to the placement agency.

178. An adult adoption is

(A) an adoption of one adult by another.

(B) an adoption of a child by an adult. The term "adult" is understood and thus not commonly stated expressly because almost all adoptions involve adults adopting children, but this is the term for adoption that is technically correct.

(C) an adoption of a specific kind of individual, namely, one who is an adult chronologically but not mentally.

(D) an adoption which is finalized after the child reaches majority even though the relationship between the two individuals started while the adoptee was still a minor.

Davinia Donaldson has two children, Ellie and Frederick. Ellie and Frederick have not seen their father, Gregory Grimes, in years, although he has sporadically sent Davinia child support and has occasionally sent cards to the children. Davinia wishes to have Gregory's parental rights terminated because she wants her new husband, David, to adopt the children. Davinia argues that Gregory has abandoned the children.

179. What result?

(A) Because Gregory has not maintained frequent contact with the children, he will be viewed as having abandoned his children. His parental rights will be terminated.

(B) Because Gregory never left his children in an unknown place without appropriate supervision, he will not be viewed as having abandoned them.

(C) As to whether Gregory will be viewed as having abandoned his children, this will depend upon the wording of the state statute, how long it has been since he last had contact with or sent support for his children, etc.

(D) Because abandonment requires a settled intention not to have further contact with his children, he could not be found to have abandoned them if he can establish that he had no such firm intention.

John and Mabel have been living together for years, raising Mabel's children from a previous marriage. The children consider John the father that they never had, since he does so much with and for them. Ken, the children's biological father, is alive and well. Ken has been sending occasional support and has been calling and writing the children periodically.

Mabel dies in a car accident. Ken and John each seek custody of the children.

180. What result?

(A) Because Ken is the children's father and John is not, no state will award custody to John, even if awarding custody to Ken would be detrimental to the children's interests.

(B) Notwithstanding that Ken is the children's father, all states would award custody to John if doing so would promote the best interests of the children.

(C) Because John has and Ken has not played a substantial parenting role in the children's lives, John may well be awarded custody if awarding custody to Ken would be detrimental to the children's interests.

(D) Because John and Ken each have parental relationships with the children, the court should simply use a best interest test to determine who should have custody.

Oscar marries Patty, who has two children from a previous marriage. They all live together for a few years until Oscar and Patty divorce. Patty seeks child support from Oscar for her two children.

181. What result?

(A) Because a stepparent is not the legal parent of his or her spouse's child, no state requires a stepparent to support the marital partner's child during the marriage, much less following their divorce.

(B) In many states, a stepparent will have a duty to support a martial partner's child if that child is a member of the household. However, that obligation will cease when the child is no longer living in the home or when the marriage ends, so it is likely that Oscar would not be required to support Parry's children, absent his having affirmatively done something to take on that responsibility even in the event of divorce.

(C) If Oscar knew about Patty's children before the marriage took place, he will be required to support them both during and after the marriage.

(D) Whether or not he knew about the children before the marriage, he will be required to support them both during and after the marriage, assuming that the state would otherwise be forced to take on that financial burden.

Samuel and Tania had a bitter divorce. They could agree about property issues, but vigorously disagreed about both who would have custody of the children and the religion in which the children would be raised. Eventually, they agreed that Tania would have custody and that the children would be raised as Catholics.

A few years after the divorce, Tania converted to Judaism and began to teach the children about Judaism. Samuel went to court to have Tania required to teach the children about Catholicism and to enjoin her from teaching them about Judaism.

182. The court is likely to

(A) require Tania to teach the children about Catholicism and enjoin her from teaching them about Judaism.

(B) require Tania to teach the children about Catholicism but refuse to enjoin her from teaching about Judaism.

(C) refuse to require her to teach the children about Catholicism but enjoin her from teaching the children about Judaism.

(D) refuse to require her to teach the children about Catholicism and refuse to enjoin her from teaching the children about Judaism.

Beth and Carl are of different religious faiths. They were married for several years and have now divorced. Beth, who is the custodial parent, seeks to enjoin Carl from saying frightening things to their children, *e.g.*, that they will burn in hell for eternity unless they believe as he does.

183. What is the court likely to do?

(A) The court will suggest that the custodial parent determines the religion of the children and thus will enjoin Carl from undermining the religious training that Beth is giving to the children.

(B) The court will suggest that the Constitution precludes the state from interfering in the religious upbringing of children.

(C) The court will interfere if it can be shown that the father is causing significant harm to his children by so instructing them.

(D) The court will decide based on whether it thinks that what the father is saying is accurate.

Robert and Sarah have been living together for a year in the state of New Formalonia, which does not recognize common law marriages. Robert and Sarah have a terrible fight, and Robert moves out. Sarah discovers that she is pregnant and calls Robert to tell him. Robert responds that he is probably one of 10 who might have fathered the child and that as far as he is concerned she should abort the child. Robert offers to help pay for the abortion, but Sarah says nothing in response.

Sarah decides not to abort. Several months later, she gives birth to a little girl whom she decides to put up for adoption. A few months after the adoption was finalized, Robert hears from a friend that Sarah had decided not to abort and instead had given birth to a little baby girl, whom she had put up for adoption. Robert decides that he wants to acknowledge his daughter after all and seeks to establish his parental results.

184. What result?

ANSWER:

John and Karen have been dating for several years. However, John has been putting in a great deal of time at work recently and Karen and John have not seen each other for several weeks. Karen has discovered that she is pregnant and has called John several times so that they can have some time together to discuss what to do. John has been unwilling to set aside a weekend, claiming that he is simply too busy to see Karen and that they will be able to get together once things at work become calmer.

Eventually, Karen stops calling. She decides that she will not even tell John about the pregnancy and she will decide what to do when the child is born.

John calls Karen a few times several months later but she says that she cannot find time to see him. John does not even know that Karen is pregnant.

When Karen gives birth to a little girl, she lists a friend of hers, Matthew, on the birth certificate as the father. She and Matthew both agree to permit the Adamsons to adopt the little girl.

Several months later, John learns from a mutual friend that Karen gave birth to a little girl and put the child up for adoption. When he confronts Karen, she admits that he is the father. John seeks to establish his parental rights.

185. What result?

ANSWER:

TOPIC 18: TORT ACTIONS

QUESTIONS

Romeo is married to Ethel in the state of Blissfulvania, which permits tort actions for criminal conversation and alienation of affection. Romeo meets Juliet and, after much begging, finally convinces her to go to Las Vegas for the weekend with him, where Juliet gambles for 48 hours straight, winning enough to pay for that camper that she has always dreamed about buying. Romeo, who loves a winner, divorces Ethel in the hopes that Juliet and he can go off into the sunset in that new camper. Ethel sues Juliet for criminal conversation and alienation of affection.

186. What result?

(A) Ethel will likely be successful in her suit for criminal conversation because Juliet and Romeo talked about going to Las Vegas for a weekend together when Juliet knew that Romeo was married to Ethel.

(B) Ethel will likely be unsuccessful in her suit for criminal conversation because there is no evidence that Romeo and Juliet talked about committing adultery.

(C) Ethel will likely be unsuccessful in her suit for alienation of affection if, several months before Romeo had even met Juliet, Romeo had lost all affection for Ethel and the marriage between Romeo and Ethel had been irretrievably broken.

(D) Ethel will likely be unsuccessful in her suit for alienation of affection because she will be unable to prove that Romeo and Juliet had sexual relations in Las Vegas.

John and Jill Johanssen are married and have two children, Hilde and Henrik. One day, as John is driving to work, he is hit by a driver, Carl Careless, who has run a red light. John has extensive brain damage and is no longer able to communicate with his family. Carl settles all claims except the children's claims for loss of consortium.

187. A court hearing this case will likely

(A) agree with all of the other states that children cannot bring a claim for loss of consortium with a parent even though a parent could bring a claim for loss of consortium with a child.

(B) permit the children to bring such a claim but also alert the District Attorney that John may well have been having sexual relations with his children.

(C) agree with all of the other states that children cannot bring a loss of consortium claim, since that claim is reserved for a spouse who has lost the services and companionship of his or her spouse.

(D) decide in light of whether that particular jurisdiction has joined the growing number of jurisdictions recognizing such a cause of action.

Mary Mahoney and Norman Nathanson are planning to get married in a year. Mary gives Norman a beautiful engagement ring. Six months before the wedding, Norman realizes that he is in love with Samantha Stevenson, his boss, and calls off the wedding. Mary asks Norman to return the ring. Norman refuses. Mary sues.

188. If Mary and Norman have not made any agreement with respect to how to resolve this issue, a court hearing this case is likely to hold that

(A) Norman can keep the ring because it was a gift. Mary will not be able to recover the cost of the ring.

(B) Norman must return the ring. However, had Mary and Norman mutually decided to call off the marriage, then he would have been able to keep the ring.

(C) Because there will be no marriage, the ring must be sold and the proceeds split between Mary and Norman.

(D) Norman must return the ring. However, had Mary been at fault, the jurisdictions would have been split with respect to whether he would have to return the ring.

Ulysses and Ursula Underwood have been told that they are each carriers of Tay-Sachs Disease and that any child that they had would have a 25% probability of having the disease. Ursula has a tubal ligation. However, due to her physician's negligence, the tubal ligation is not successful. Ursula eventually becomes pregnant and gives birth to a child, Rhonda, with Tay-Sachs. Ursula sues the physician for wrongful birth.

189. What result?

(A) Ursula may well be successful because she would never have been pregnant had the doctor not been negligent and she then would not have incurred all of the financial and emotional costs associated with having a Tay-Sachs child.

(B) Ursula is likely to be unsuccessful because she will be unable to establish harm, given that the doctor's negligence resulted in a live birth.

(C) Ursula is likely to be successful, although she should have sued for wrongful life rather than wrongful birth.

(D) Ursula is likely to be unsuccessful. However, Rhonda would have been much more likely to have successfully brought a claim.

Assume the same facts as in Question 189. Rhonda sues the physician for wrongful life.

190. What result?

(A) In those jurisdictions permitting the Underwoods to sue for wrongful birth, Rhonda will be permitted to sue for wrongful life. However, the court will be careful to make sure that there is no double-counting of the same harm.

(B) Very few jurisdictions recognize actions for wrongful life even if they recognize a cause of action for wrongful birth, so it is unlikely that Rhonda will be permitted to maintain this cause of action.

(C) Rhonda will be permitted to maintain this cause of action even if her parents cannot bring a wrongful birth claim because she, after all, is the person harmed by the physician's negligence.

(D) No jurisdiction recognizes wrongful life actions because life itself is a wonderful gift that can never be considered a harm.

Carl and Caroline Callandar have five children and do not wish to have any more. Carl has a vasectomy. However, the vasectomy is negligently performed. Caroline eventually becomes pregnant and gives birth to a healthy baby boy. Carl and Caroline sue the doctor for the expenses that they will incur in raising their newborn son to adulthood.

191. What result?

(A) In most jurisdictions, Carl and Caroline will be successful. But for the doctor's negligence, they would not have had all of the expenses associated with raising yet another child.

(B) In most jurisdictions, Carl and Caroline will not be successful, at least in part because states are reluctant to call the birth of a healthy child a harm.

(C) Carl would have been successful if he had sued for wrongful life rather than wrongful conception.

(D) Carl and Caroline will be unsuccessful in most jurisdictions if they discovered the pregnancy early enough that an abortion would not have endangered Caroline's life or health.

Ned and Nancy Newing are married and living in New Pennsey, a jurisdiction which recognizes wrongful life actions. Nancy is pregnant. She is feeling poorly and is afraid that she has caught German Measles. She is advised by her doctor that she need not worry because German Measles will not affect the fetus. When she delivers, she discovers that her child is suffering from numerous serious birth defects because of the exposure to German Measles during the first trimester. A wrongful life action is brought against the doctor. The doctor argues that he should not be forced to pay any damages.

192. What result?

(A) The doctor will likely be successful because the child's life was not wrongful, since the child was born into an existing marriage.

(B) The doctor will likely be unsuccessful only if it is established that he could have prevented the birth defects by, e.g., performing surgery in utero.

(C) The doctor will likely be successful if he can establish that he did not cause Nancy to contract German Measles.

(D) The doctor will likely be unsuccessful if there will be extraordinary medical costs incurred in raising the child and the Newings can establish that they would have secured an abortion had they been advised of the possible effects on the child from exposure to German Measles during the pregnancy.

Mary and John Smith have a beautiful three-year-old child, Kelly. One day, John received a telephone call while he was watching Kelly. John became engrossed in the conversation and did not notice that Kelly had wandered outside near the swimming pool in the backyard. Kelly fell into the pool.

When John finished his conversation he started looking for Kelly. By the time that John had figured out what had happened, Kelly had been in the pool for several minutes. While John was able to save Kelly, Kelly suffered permanent brain damage and requires very expensive medical care just to remain alive. Kelly sues John, claiming that John is liable for his negligent supervision of her.

193. What result?

(A) The success of the suit will depend in part on whether the state recognizes parent-child tort immunity. Some states have abolished that immunity entirely while other states would bar the kind of suit that would be brought here.

(B) Permitting a child to sue his or her parent is absurd and clearly violates public policy. Because permitting such suits would open the proverbial floodgates and permit children to sue their parents for all sorts of alleged mistakes, no state will recognize such a cause of action.

(C) The court will permit this suit to proceed. Because of the availability of insurance, permitting such suits is the only way to protect the family from what might otherwise be a financially disastrous situation. This type of action would be permitted in all of the states.

(D) This suit will be permitted if and only if a child is permitted to sue his or her parent for intentional torts.

Henrietta and Herman Hickerson live in North Virgiland, which recognizes the doctrine of parent-child immunity. Henrietta and Herman have a son, Icarus, whom Henrietta and Herman have been abusing for years. Before the statute of limitations has run, Icarus sues his parents for their intentional abuse of him. Henrietta and Herman argue that the doctrine of parent-child immunity bars this kind of suit.

194. What result?

(A) Henrietta and Herman may be subject to criminal penalty but they cannot be sued for their abuse of Icarus if the state recognizes this doctrine of immunity.

(B) Not only will the doctrine bar Icarus' civil suit, but Henrietta and Herman will be immune from criminal prosecution if the state recognizes this immunity doctrine.

(C) The suit may well go forward, because in many states this immunity doctrine does not preclude a child from suing a parent for an intentional tort.

(D) Because this is a criminal law doctrine, it would not prevent a child from suing his or her parents for either an intentional tort or a tort sounding in negligence.

Lyle and Lolita Langley live in Pensylginia, a comparative negligence state which has abrogated spousal immunity. One day as Lyle is driving the car, he is less careful than he should be and gets into an auto accident. He is unhurt but Lolita has serious injuries. Norman, the other driver, is 70% responsible for the crash while Lyle is held 30% responsible.

Lolita sues Norman for her injuries and Norman seeks contribution from Lyle.

195. What result?

   (A) Because Lolita is suing Norman and clearly does not want to sue her own husband, Norman will be totally responsible for the harm that she suffers.

   (B) Because spousal immunity has been abrogated and Lolita would be able to sue her husband for the costs of her injuries, Norman may well be held liable for only 70% of the costs of her injuries.

   (C) Because permitting suit against Lyle would undermine the marriage and deplete the family purse, Norman will be responsible for all of the harm incurred by Lolita.

   (D) Because Lyle was substantially at fault, Lolita will be barred from recovery.

Richard and Rhonda Waverly have a son, Norman, who has been known to hit other children. Norman has gotten into fights with schoolmates several times and in fact has been expelled from two different schools for fighting.

The Waverly family has just moved into a new house in a new school district. All seems to be going well for Norman until one day after school when Norman goes to the house of a classmate, Tom Thomas. That night, Richard and Rhonda receive a call from Tom's mother, Sarah, informing them that Norman had broken Tom's arm without any warning or provocation. Sarah threatens to sue Norman's parents for the harm that Norman has done. Richard and Rhonda consult an attorney to find out whether they are potentially liable.

196. What should the attorney say?

   (A) She should suggest that Richard and Rhonda are not liable unless they somehow encouraged or directed their son to break Tom's arm.

   (B) She should suggest that as Norman's parents, Richard and Rhonda are strictly liable for any harms caused by their son.

   (C) She should suggest that while jurisdictions vary, and thus she might have to do research to find out the law of the particular jurisdiction, Richard and Rhonda may well be liable if Norman's actions were reasonably foreseeable.

   (D) She should suggest that because Norman, rather than Richard or Rhonda, broke Tom's arm, Norman might be liable but Richard and Rhonda are not.

Kim and Sidney Smith wish to adopt a healthy child of at least average intelligence who has no known emotional or psychological disorders. They make this clear to a local adoption agency, Your Heart's Content, who assures them that Robert, the quiet child who will be placed with them, has no known problems. After the adoption is finalized, the Smiths discover that

Robert is not only severely psychologically and emotionally disturbed but that the adoption agency knew about these problems before placing Robert with them. The Smiths sue Your Heart's Content.

197. What result?

(A) The agency cannot be held liable because it cannot guarantee that adoptive parents will be completely satisfied and there would be no way to distinguish this case from those that might be filed by any dissatisfied adoptive parent.

(B) The agency will be held liable for all of the costs of raising the child because there would be no way to justify only compensating the family for some of the costs.

(C) The agency will not be held liable because they had no way of knowing that the child had severe psychological problems.

(D) While jurisdictions differ, the agency may well be held liable for the extraordinary costs associated with raising Robert including possible counseling or institutionalization costs.

Assume the same facts as in Question 197. However, the Smiths not only seek monetary damages but they also seek to abrogate or undo the adoption.

198. What result?

(A) While jurisdictions vary, some are willing to abrogate adoptions where an agency has misrepresented important facts about the child rather than has, e.g., merely failed to disclose salient information.

(B) The Smiths will be unsuccessful. Once the adoption is finalized, Robert is a member of their family for better or worse.

(C) The Smiths can of course return the child and get their money back. If consumer protections are in place when products are involved, they certainly should be in place when children are involved.

(D) While no state will allow the Smiths to undo the adoption, they can get the court to order the agency to put them first on the list for the next possible adoption.

Brenda and Brian Black are divorced, Brenda having custody of their two-year-old girl, Samantha. One Monday, Brian did not return Samantha from her weekend visit with him. When Brenda called Brian's apartment to find out what had happened, she discovered that his phone was no longer in service. She told herself not to worry, that he had probably again forgotten to pay the phone bill and that he was probably stuck in traffic.

When Brenda had not heard from Brian for a few days, she contacted a private detective agency to find her ex-husband and their daughter. Eventually, Brian and Samantha were found, living in another state using assumed names. Samantha was returned to Brenda.

Brenda sues Brian and those of his family members who helped him for intentional interference with the parent's custodial relationship.

199. What result?

(A) While Brian may be subject to criminal penalties for kidnaping his daughter, there is no civil remedy in this context.

(B) While a party with no relation to the child might be sued for interfering with the parental relationship, an individual with a legal relationship to the child cannot be held liable in this kind of suit.

(C) Brian may well be liable for this interference unless he has some legally valid justification or excuse.

(D) While Brian's family members might be liable because they have no legally recognized relationship with Samantha, Brian is immune from liability in the context because he is Samantha's legal and biological father.

Jim and Judy Germain are divorced, Judy having custody of their three-year-old, Tabetha. On the past several occasions when Jim came to pick up Tabetha for his weekend visitation, he found nobody at home. While the first few times he had believed Judy's claims about inadvertent mistakes, he now believed that Judy was intentionally depriving him of visitation with his daughter, whom he had not seen in several months. Jim does not want custody of his daughter but does want to see her regularly. He decides to sue Judy for intentional interference with his parental relationship with his daughter.

200. What result?

(A) Jim will be awarded custody and damages, assuming that he would not interfere with Judy's visitation with the child.

(B) Jim will be awarded damages but not custody, since he does not want the latter. However, were he to want custody, he might well have been awarded that as well.

(C) If the jurisdiction recognizes a cause of action for intentional interference with the custodial parent's relationship with his or her child, then the jurisdiction will also recognize such an action for the non-custodial parent. As to whether damages would be awarded in this particular case, this is unclear because more of the facts would have to be known.

(D) While this is dependent upon the law of the individual jurisdiction, it is unlikely that Jim will be awarded damages. Even if the jurisdiction recognizes a cause of action for intentional interference with the custodial parent's relationship with his or her child, that may not help Jim, since many states recognize such a cause of action for the custodial parent but not for the non-custodial parent.

Horace and Gertrude Salamander have been having marital difficulties and are legally separated. Gertrude meets Matthew through a friend and starts dating him. They have sexual relations on different occasions. When Horace discovers this, he sues Matthew for criminal conversation and alienation of affections.

201. What result?

ANSWER:

Zelda and Xerxes have a beautiful two-year-old daughter, Agatha. One day, while Zelda was cutting the lawn and Xerxes was doing the laundry, Agatha walked into the backyard toward the pool. Each parent had thought that the other was watching Agatha, and it was not until Zelda was cutting the grass near the pool that she saw her daughter floating in it. While Zelda was able to save Agatha's life, Agatha has suffered permanent brain damage due to the deprivation of oxygen. An action is brought on behalf of Zelda against her parents for negligent supervision.

202. What result?

ANSWER:

John Jones has just been informed by his wife of 15 years, Joanna, that their 14-year-old son, Carl, was fathered by someone else. John not only divorces Joanna but sues her for intentional infliction of emotional distress.

203. What result?

ANSWER:

Assume the same facts as in Question 203. However, assume that the jurisdiction has abrogated spousal immunity.

204. What effect, if any, would this have on whether the intentional infliction action would be permitted?

ANSWER:

Xerxes and Yolanda have been living together for years without benefit of marriage and have had two children together. One day as they were crossing the street, a car ran into Xerxes who was several steps ahead of Yolanda. Yolanda was not in danger herself but watched as Xerxes was struck and killed by the motorist who had run the red light. She has suffered greatly as a result of the accident—she has had recurrent chest pain, migraines and nausea, and is now being treated for depression and post-traumatic stress disorder. She sues the driver for negligent infliction of emotional distress.

205. What result?

ANSWER:

TOPIC 19: PROFESSIONAL RESPONSIBILITY

QUESTIONS

Bob and Betty Bevins go to Arthur Attorney to consult him about getting a divorce. Arthur listens to their complaints about each other, believes that the problems are not insurmountable, and urges them to attempt to reconcile. Arthur charges them a small consultation fee. Eventually Betty files for divorce. After Betty has filed, Bob comes to Arthur, shows him a statement of Bob's finances and the report of the private investigator that Bob has hired, admits having committed adultery during his marriage, and then asks Arthur to represent him. Arthur declines, accepting a small fee. Arthur immediately calls Betty, suggesting that she hire him as her attorney in the case against her husband. Betty fires her own attorney, hires Arthur, and does extremely well in the division of the marital assets.

206. Arthur would not have been subject to discipline if only he

(A) had not called Betty to solicit her services.

(B) had not accepted payment after hearing Bob's confession to adultery and being shown the private investigator's report and a statement of Bob's finances.

(C) had agreed to represent Bob rather than Betty.

(D) had not agreed to represent either of them after they both had come to see him to discuss whether they should get a divorce.

Paula and Robert Samuelson have decided to divorce. To save money, they hire Andrea Attorney to represent them both. Andrea is familiar with both Paula and Robert, having done work for them in the past. Andrea advises them in writing that she will be representing both of them and that she will not be looking out for the interests of one of them to the detriment of the interests of the other. The Samuelsons agree and both seemed pleased with the result. However, someone reports Andrea to the Office of Disciplinary Council and she now faces the possibility of a sanction.

207. How should this be decided?

(A) Because the Samuelsons are satisfied, Andrea should not be sanctioned.

(B) Because of the possibility that one of the parties would not be satisfied, Andrea should be sanctioned. She is fortunate that she is not being sued for malpractice.

(C) Given that Andrea advised them both about what her role would be and given that Andrea did exactly what she said that she would do, she cannot be sanctioned.

(D) As to whether dual representation is permissible in a divorce even with full disclosure, this is a matter of state law. Some jurisdictions permit such representation if the parties give their informed consent. Others have a blanket prophylactic rule against such representation, and whether sanctions will be imposed should be resolved in light of the local rules regarding dual representation.

Donna is seeking an attorney because she wants a divorce from her husband, Fred. She does not have much money and is afraid that she will not be able to get very good representation. She finds an attorney, Arthur Attorney, who will represent her on a contingency fee basis. Donna gets a divorce and does very well in the property distribution and in the award of spousal support, but is reluctant to pay the agreed-upon one-third to her attorney. Arthur sues Donna.

208. What result?

(A) Contingency fees arrangements have been around for a long time and charging one third of the award is not unusual. Donna will be forced to pay Arthur his agreed-upon share.

(B) Contingency fee contracts in domestic relations matters are against public policy because the attorney has an incentive to promote the couple's divorcing rather than reconciling. No jurisdiction will enforce such a contract.

(C) While many states prohibit contingency fee arrangements in the domestic relations context, some permit them. As to whether this agreement will be enforceable, this depends upon the law of the particular jurisdiction.

(D) While contingency fee contracts violate public policy, no state would permit Donna to contest the agreement because she did very well and because Arthur was not instrumental in causing her to divorce but only in permitting her to receive generous spousal support and a very advantageous property distribution.

Lucy Counselor, attorney at law, is approached by two of her oldest friends, Fred and Ethel, who have decided to get a divorce. They want her to represent them. Carrie says that she is willing to help them but that she will merely act as a scribe—she will neither advise them about what they should do nor will she look out for the interests of one over the other. This is all explained in writing and they agree in writing.

When Lucy is putting the agreement that Fred and Ethel have reached in writing, she discovers that Fred is trying to defraud Ethel.

209. What, if anything, should Lucy do?

ANSWER:

TOPIC 20: FEDERAL-STATE POWER DISTRIBUTION

QUESTIONS

The Supreme Court has recognized a "domestic relations exception."

210. This exception

(A) divests the federal courts of power to issue divorce, alimony, and child custody decrees.

(B) precludes federal courts from addressing the right to marry.

(C) permits married couples wishing to invoke the exception and end their marriages without going through the bother and expense of getting a formal divorce or annulment.

(D) permits married adults to propose or agree to have an open marriage without fear that this will somehow be used against either of them in future.

211. Under what conditions, if any, can federal law displace state family law?

(A) Because federal law is supreme, state family law can be displaced whenever Congress is inclined to do so.

(B) Because family law is paradigmatically state law, Congress can never override state family law.

(C) Federal law can displace state family law when the latter does major damage to clear and substantial federal interests.

(D) Because there is no federal family law, the issue never arises.

PRACTICE FINAL EXAM: QUESTIONS

PRACTICE FINAL EXAM
(90 Minutes)

Questions

Alfred and Betty are both 17 and hence minors, who live in Marrylania, a jurisdiction which treats minor marriages as voidable. Alfred and Betty know that the law does not permit them to marry, but marry anyway after lying about their ages. They tell no one. They continue to live at their respective parents' homes until they can figure out how to tell their parents that they have married.

On his 18th birthday, Alfred suggests that he wants to date other people. Betty is upset but says that it is fine with her. One week later, Alfred and his date are killed in a tragic accident. Betty learns that Alfred received a substantial sum of money on his 18th birthday and she wishes to receive her share as his surviving widow.

212. What result?

(A) Because Alfred and Betty never lived together after either had reached majority, their marriage is void and of no legal effect. Betty is not entitled to inherit anything.

(B) Betty will be considered Alfred's widow if and only if Alfred's parents decide not to challenge the marriage.

(C) Betty will not be considered Alfred's widow unless they had sexual relations after they had been declared husband and wife.

(D) Betty will be entitled to her share as surviving widow.

Terry and Walter live in Arkanado, which treats minor marriages as voidable. They are both 17. They lie about their ages and are married by a Justice of the Peace. They live together for about a year and a half but then find that it is simply too difficult to stay together. Terry wishes to have the marriage annulled based on their incompetency to contract it in the first place.

213. What result?

ANSWER:

Laurence and Karen have been in love since the first day that they had met at Laurence's mother's house on his 21st birthday. Karen had been 14 years old when she had been adopted by Laurence's mother and Laurence had met Karen the following year. That had been four years ago and they now wish to marry.

214. If all family members approve, are there any obstacles to their marriage?

(A) Yes. Because they are not each over 21 years of age, they will be precluded from marrying unless they can get judicial approval of their marriage.

(B) No, because the fact that their families approve should obviate any difficulties posed by their marriage.

(C) Yes, if the state precludes siblings by adoption from marrying.

(D) No, because they are of age and because they are not related by blood.

Rodney has known his uncle's daughter, Sarah, for his entire life and has always known that, someday, he and Sarah would get married. However, their home state, Restrictsylvania, prohibits first-cousin marriages. They go to the neighboring state, Lesstrictsylvania, marry in accord with local law, and return home to Restrictsylvania. One year later, Rodney dies in an industrial accident at work and Sarah's receipt of benefits depends upon whether her marriage to Rodney is valid.

215. What result?

ANSWER:

Norman and Olga are celebrating. They will be attending a wedding of some dear friends, which will be performed by a Justice of the Peace. By the time the wedding is about to take place, they are so taken by the moment that they decide they should get married too. The Justice of the Peace is willing to accommodate their request and everyone attending is doubly pleased.

After the wedding, all attending decide that even more celebration is in order. They agree to meet at a local bar to carry on the festivities. On the way to the bar, Norman and Olga are in a traffic accident in which Norman is killed. Norman has died intestate and his children claim that Olga should not receive anything from the estate.

216. What result?

(A) Olga will be entitled to inherit if she and Norman were not so drunk as not to know what they were doing when they married. Even if they were that drunk, Olga will still be entitled to a widow's share if the jurisdiction treats marriages involving incompetents as voidable rather than void.

(B) Because Olga and Norman were overcome by emotion and had not considered the implications of getting married, the marriage will be considered void and Olga will not be entitled to any of Norman's estate.

(C) Olga will be entitled to inherit. Otherwise, the marriage of their friends would also be subject to annulment, since the same individual performed the ceremony for all of them.

(D) Olga will not be entitled to inherit. Because they were unable to consummate the marriage, it will not be recognized as valid and she will not receive her widow's share.

Ken and Miriam have been married for several years. Recently, Ken has grown more and more critical of Miriam. One day, he came home from work and announced that if she did not sign a postnuptial agreement he would divorce her. Miriam was surprised and said that she wanted to talk to an attorney. Ken said that would be fine. He handed her the agreement and a list of the marital assets with their values.

Miriam talked to an attorney who suggested that the agreement seemed fair if the assets had been accurately represented. Miriam went home and signed the agreement, hoping that this would save their marriage. However, within a year, they divorced. Miriam challenges the validity of the postnuptial agreement, claiming fraud and duress.

217. What result?

(A) Because Miriam signed the agreement to save her marriage, she cannot now claim duress merely because the marriage would have ended had she not signed. The agreement is enforceable.

(B) Because Miriam only signed the agreement because Ken would otherwise have filed for divorce immediately, her signing was not voluntary but instead under duress, and thus the agreement is unenforceable.

(C) If, indeed, Miriam can establish that Ken materially misrepresented the nature and value of the marital assets, then the agreement can be invalidated.

(D) Because Miriam consulted an attorney and then voluntarily signed the agreement, she cannot contest it now. The agreement is enforceable.

Terry and Samuel Ulander are divorcing after five years of marriage. Terry challenges the prenuptial agreement which she signed the day before their wedding as unenforceable because it was unconscionable and signed under duress. She points out that although Samuel had mentioned a year earlier that they would have to have a prenuptial agreement before they could marry, nothing more had been said about it until he had presented it to her two days before the wedding. His great wealth notwithstanding, Samuel argues that because Terry knew that there would be a prenuptial agreement and because she had knowingly and voluntarily signed the agreement specifying that she would receive no spousal support, that is the end of the matter, even if she does not have any job skills and even if she has custody of the three young children born of the marriage.

218. What result?

(A) Terry is correct that the prenuptial agreement is unenforceable. It is unconscionable to give one's betrothed a prenuptial agreement one day before the wedding, and hence the agreement is unenforceable. Even if such little notice is not unconscionable, such an agreement would have been signed under duress and would be unenforceable for that reason.

(B) Samuel is correct. It is not unconscionable to present a prenuptial agreement about which notice had been given over a year earlier. Further, being asked to sign such an agreement under these circumstances does not constitute duress. The agreement is enforceable.

(C) Terry may well be correct that the agreement is unenforceable, not because of when it was presented but because of its content. To enforce the agreement against an individual who has no skills and who has three young children in his or her care may well be held by a court to be manifestly unjust.

(D) Samuel may well be correct. Terry's having signed the agreement voluntarily establishes that the agreement is not unreasonable. Otherwise, she never would have signed it.

Beatrice and Carl are divorcing after eight years of marriage. At the time of their marriage, each had been a highly paid attorney and so it had seemed eminently reasonable to sign a prenuptial agreement stating that neither would have to support the other in the event of divorce. However, things are rather different now. Carl is no longer practicing law. In the interim, his firm had been dissolved and he has discovered that he has to have extensive cancer treatment.

Carl claims that the prenuptial agreement is unenforceable because conditions have changed so drastically. Beatrice claims that because there had been full disclosure, the agreement had been voluntarily signed by both parties, and the agreement had not been unconscionable when it was signed, the prenuptial agreement is enforceable, Carl's great misfortune notwithstanding.

219. What result?

(A) Because all of the conditions for a valid prenuptial agreement had been met, Beatrice is correct that the agreement is enforceable. No state would hold the agreement unenforceable.

(B) Because not all of the conditions for a valid prenuptial agreement have been met, no state would hold this agreement enforceable. It would be unconscionable not to require Beatrice to pay Carl some support, given her enviable financial position and his unenviable one, and no state will enforce an unconscionable premarital agreement.

(C) The states will split on whether such an agreement is enforceable. In some states, the agreement must be examined both when it is made and when its enforcement is sought to make sure that it is neither unconscionable nor manifestly unjust. In these states, the agreement might well be held unenforceable. However, other states only look to see whether the agreement was unconscionable when it was made. In those states, a party's illness after the agreement was signed will not be a basis for its invalidation.

(D) The states will split on whether such an agreement is enforceable in that states differ with respect to whether they still recognize the common law doctrine of necessaries. The agreement would be unenforceable in those states in which the doctrine is still recognized but enforceable in those states in which it is no longer recognized.

James and Katherine are considering marriage. They have discussed whether to have children. Katherine is willing to have children but does not feel that strongly about the matter one way or the other. James desperately wants to have children and, in fact, will only marry Katherine if she signs a prenuptial agreement specifying that he will have custody of the children should they divorce. In exchange, James agrees to very favorable property and support provisions for Katherine. They sign the agreement and marry.

James and Katherine have two children, Joanne and Conrad. Both parents adore their children. Regrettably, however, they start to have marital difficulties and eventually decide to divorce, each seeking custody of the children.

James and Katherine each seek to void part of the prenuptial agreement. Katherine seeks to have the custody division declared unenforceable and James seeks to have the support and property provisions declared unenforceable.

220. What result?

ANSWER:

Fred and Gertrude are discussing whether to execute a prenuptial agreement before their marriage. Fred wants to do so because his parents, who are quite wealthy, are quite insistent. Gertrude does not want to make one because she believes that making such an agreement implies an expectation that the marriage will not be successful. Fred is insistent. Gertrude reluctantly signs the agreement for fear that otherwise the marriage will not take place. A few years after the marriage is celebrated, Gertrude and Fred divorce. Gertrude, who has always been resentful that a prenuptial agreement had been signed in the first place, challenges the validity of the agreement, claiming that she was coerced into signing it because of the implicit threat that the marriage would not otherwise take place.

221. Will the validity of the agreement be upheld?

(A) Assuming that Gertrude knew what she was signing, the validity of the prenuptial agreement will be upheld because coercion, even if established, is not a ground upon which to invalidate a prenuptial agreement.

(B) Assuming that Gertrude can establish the reasonableness of her subjective belief that the marriage would not take place unless she signed the agreement, the prenuptial agreement will be held void because she then will be found to have been coerced into signing it.

(C) While coercion is a ground upon which to invalidate a prenuptial agreement, the mere fear that the marriage would not otherwise be celebrated does not rise to the requisite level to establish coercion. Unless there is some other ground upon which to contest the agreement, the agreement will be held enforceable.

(D) Whether or not reasonable, Gertrude's subjective belief that the marriage would not otherwise take place, if proven, will suffice to establish coercion and hence be a basis upon which to invalidate the prenuptial agreement.

Alice Barton and Clarence Daniels have been married for three years. Alice has just discovered that Clarence lied about never having been married before and, further, that Clarence's former wife is still alive. Because Alice has sincere religious beliefs about the impermissibility of being married to someone who was previously married and whose ex-spouse is still alive, she seeks an annulment.

222. What result?

(A) Because Alice and Clarence have consummated the marriage, it cannot be annulled.

(B) Because Clarence knew that it was important to Alice that she marry someone who did not have a former spouse living and because Clarence nonetheless lied about this, Alice will be able to have the marriage annulled.

(C) Because three years have elapsed, Alice will be unable to have the marriage annulled even if she could have had it annulled on this basis earlier.

(D) If the court views this fraud as going to the essentials of marriage, then it will grant the annulment, notwithstanding that the couple has been married for three years.

John and Carol have been living together for the past several years in the state of New Caliyamo, whose constitutional protections for parental rights are no more robust than those afforded by the United States Constitution. Carol, who is three months pregnant, has again suggested that she wants to get married, but John has again replied that he does not believe in the institution of marriage.

When John returns from work the next day, he discovers that Carol has moved out. Confident that she will return soon, he does nothing.

After several months have gone by, John hires a private detective to find her. A few weeks later, the detective reports that Carol is living with her infant son and new husband in a different part of the city.

John seeks to establish his parental rights.

223. What result?

(A) Because John is the child's biological father, he will have no difficulty in establishing his parental rights.

(B) Because John did not marry Carol when he knew that she was pregnant, he would have been barred from establishing his parental rights even had Carol not married someone else.

(C) If Carol and her husband married before the birth of the child and the state affords a presumption of paternity to the husband when a child is born into the marriage, John may well be precluded from establishing parental rights if neither Carol nor her husband is willing to cooperate in John's having those rights legally recognized.

(D) John's rights will be respected because he did all that he reasonably could have done with respect to his child.

224. What is an equitable parent?

(A) This is a parent who tries to be fair at all times.

(B) This is the adult who is recognized as having legal ties to a child as a result of an equitable adoption.

(C) This is someone viewed by the law as a parent of a child when that adult has a parent-child relationship with the child and is willing to take on the rights and responsibilities of parenthood. The paradigmatic case involves a husband unaware that he is not biologically related to the child who had been born into or conceived during that adult's marriage.

(D) This is another term for the adult who has been designated as the guardian in a parental rights termination because the guardian has the parent-like responsibility of looking out for the best interests of the child.

Beverly has been divorced for several months. While she is pleased to be free of her ex-husband, Fred, she regrets that no children were born of the marriage. She decides that she will have and raise a child by herself. She talks to a longtime friend of hers, Carl, and asks whether he would be willing to donate some of his sperm so that she can artificially inseminate herself. Carl agrees.

Eventually, Beverly has a little girl, Juanita. Carl is ecstatic. He had always wanted to be a father and he would now be able to fulfill that dream. Carl starts dropping by Beverly's home more frequently. Sometimes, he stays with Juanita while Beverly does errands. When Carl asks when he can start having Juanita stay at his house, Beverly tells him that she does not want him to come to her house anymore. Carl goes to court to establish his parental rights.

225. What result?

(A) Because Carl is biologically related to Juanita, and legal paternity springs from biological paternity, Carl will be recognized as Juanita's father.

(B) Because Beverly only recently divorced and because a child needs a father, Fred rather than Carl will be recognized as Juanita's father.

(C) Because Beverly wants to raise Juanita alone, neither Carl nor Fred will be recognized as having parental rights with respect to Juanita.

(D) Whether Carl will be recognized as having paternal rights will likely depend, at least in part, on the agreement that he and Beverly had when he provided sperm for Juanita's conception.

Donna Davidson and Edward Erickson have been dating for several months. Donna announces that she is pregnant and Donna and Edward decide to get married. Not long after they marry, Donna gives birth to twin boys.

When the twins are two, Donna tells Edward that she has been seeing someone else and wants a divorce. Edward replies that Donna is free to do as she thinks best, but that he is going to seek custody of the twins. Donna tells Edward that he should not waste his time because as soon as she and Edward divorce, Donna is going to marry Herbert, the father of the twins.

All of this has occurred in Wissachusetts, which has a rebuttable presumption that children born into a marriage are the children of the husband and wife. The statute provides that courts are permitted to hear a challenge to that presumption by either the husband or the wife if that challenge is made within five years of the birth of the child whose paternity is at issue.

When Donna and Edward divorce, each seeks custody.

226. If the best interests of the children would be promoted by awarding custody to Edward but Edward is not the biological father of the twins, can he nonetheless be awarded custody of them given Donna's challenge to his paternity of the twins?

ANSWER:

Jack and Jill Johanson have decided to divorce, although they cannot agree about how the marital assets should be divided and, in fact, yell at each other every time that they discuss the issue. As far as Jack is concerned, Jill is being selfish and unreasonable.

Jack decides to teach Jill a lesson. He empties the joint bank account and brings about 25 of his closest friends to Exclusio, the most expensive restaurant in town. There, the group has the most sumptuous meal served in recent memory, complete with some of the most expensive wines from Exclusio's fabulous wine cellar. Jack pays the $30,000 bill in cash. When Jill hears what Jack has done, she suggests that they should get attorneys to work out the property distribution.

Neither Jack nor Jill seeks support and there are no children of the marriage. The sole contested issue involves how the assets should be divided. Jill insists that she should get a credit because of the money which Jack spent at the restaurant, whereas Jack insists that the statutory presumption that the assets be split equally should be followed and thus each should get roughly half of the remaining marital assets.

227. What result?

(A) Because Jack spent the money while they were still married, this expenditure will be treated as would any other expenditure during the marriage. The remaining assets will be divided roughly equally between Jack and Jill.

(B) Because Jack's expenditure is a paradigmatic example of dissipation of marital funds, Jill will be awarded the credit that she seeks.

(C) Whether or not Jack's expenditure involved dissipation, it would be unfair at this point to give Jill a credit for that use of funds.

(D) While Jill will be entitled to a credit for Jack's restaurant bill, Jack will be entitled to a credit for the $30,000 of marital funds which Jill had spent a year prior to talk of divorce for that new car. The credits will cancel each other out and the assets will be divided roughly equally.

Ethel and William Wainright are divorcing. They can agree about everything except how to characterize two items: (1) a diamond necklace given by William to Ethel on their third anniversary (he bought it by cashing the previous month's salary check), and (2) a car bought with funds earned by William before the marriage which was to replace Ethel's car, was driven primarily by her, and was used as a family car. Title of the latter is in both of their names.

228. How should these items be characterized?

(A) The diamond necklace was bought with marital funds and hence is a marital asset. The car was bought with separate funds and hence is the separate property of William.

(B) Because the diamond necklace was bought with funds earned by William, it is separate property owned by William. While Ethel may be allowed to keep it if she wants to do so, William will be entitled to a credit so that the value of this separate property will be accounted for with other assets. The car is also William's separate property.

(C) The car will likely be treated as marital property because it is used primarily by Ethel and both of their names are on the title. The necklace is also marital property because it was bought with marital funds.

(D) The car is likely to be treated as marital property because it replaced Ethel's car, was used primarily by her, and was used as a family car. The necklace may well be treated as Ethel's separate property. Notwithstanding that it was bought with marital funds, William may well be thought to have made a gift of it to his wife.

Lisa and Matthew Norris have been married for almost 20 years. They live in the home that Matthew owned before they were married. Over the years, Lisa and Matthew have contributed money from their paychecks to help retire the mortgage and to make improvements to the home. The property is still in Matthew's name, however. About a year after they completely paid off the mortgage, they decided to get a divorce. While both are pleased by the amount the house has increased in value over the years, they disagree strongly about how much Lisa should benefit from that increased value. She claims that the home is marital property subject to distribution and Matthew claims that it is separate property and that all of Lisa's contributions should either be treated as gifts or as compensated because she received the benefit of living in the house for all of these years.

229. How should the house be treated for distribution purposes?

ANSWER:

John and Katherine Molinsky are divorcing after 10 years of marriage. Each seeks custody of their daughter, Natasha. John has been a stay-at-home father while Katherine has been the primary wage-earner. Each has been found by the court to be a fit and loving parent. The jurisdiction employs a primary caretaker presumption.

230. Who is more likely to be awarded custody?

(A) Katherine, because as the primary wage-earner, she is the primary caretaker for the family.

(B) John, because as the adult who attends to Natasha's needs most of the time, he is the primary caretaker.

(C) It is impossible to say because primary caretaker is just a shorthand way of referring to the parent whose having custody would promote the best interests of the child.

(D) It is impossible to say because the primary caretaker is the parent who is most emotionally invested in the child.

Alexandria and Bernard Sutherland are expecting their first child. Alexandria is 38 years old and she is afraid that their child might have Downs Syndrome. She and Bernard insist on having an amniocentesis performed specifically to find out whether the child will have that disease. They are very relieved when they are told that their child will be fine.

When their child, Carolyn, is born, they are very upset when they discover that she is a Downs Syndrome child. Apparently, as a result of negligence, some test results had been confused and they had been told that their child would not have Downs Syndrome when the test results indicated that she would, and another couple had been told that their child would have the syndrome when the test had indicated that their child would not. The Sutherlands sue their doctor for their pain and suffering and for any extraordinary child-rearing expenses that they will incur as a result of the child having the illness.

231. Assuming that the jurisdiction recognizes the cause of action, what is the likely result?

(A) The Sutherlands will be successful in their wrongful life suit, but only if they can establish that but for the doctor's negligence their child never would have had the syndrome.

(B) The Sutherlands will be successful in their wrongful birth suit but only if they can establish that the symptoms are so severe that Carolyn would have been better off never having lived at all.

(C) The Sutherlands will be successful in their wrongful pregnancy suit but only because they specifically insisted on the amniocentesis to find out if the child would have the disease.

(D) The Sutherlands will be successful in their wrongful birth suit only if they can establish that they would have aborted Carolyn had they been apprised in a timely way of her condition.

Sarah and Avrum Williams, who are married and living in North Delawinia, have not been getting along for years. Finally, Sarah decides that she has had enough. She packs some things, including some objects of great sentimental value, and moves to the neighboring state of Libertyland, where she has relatives. She finds a job without much difficulty.

After she satisfies Libertyland's six-week residency requirement for divorce, she files for divorce, asking not only to be granted a dissolution of the marriage but also to have the property distributed. She asks for the car, all of the property that she has brought with her, and some of the property that she left in North Delawinia. Avrum makes a special appearance, contesting the court's jurisdiction to divide the property.

232. What result?

ANSWER:

Mary and Norman Oppenheimer have divorced, Norman having been awarded custody of their child, Peter. Mary has been ordered to pay $2,000 per month in child support. She decides that there is no reason for her to work so hard just to have to pay that much in child support so she voluntarily takes a decrease in hours and a cut in pay. She then files to have her child support payments reduced because of a material change in circumstances, namely, a significant decrease in her salary.

233. What result?

ANSWER:

Miguel and Juanita Marquez are married and living in the state of Texahoma. They have been having marital difficulties and have decided to divorce. Juanita is granted custody of the children and Miguel is ordered to pay child support. Miguel is offered a very attractive job in New Arizania with a company called Nurone. He accepts it and moves there. One year later, the company is forced to declare bankruptcy and Miguel loses his job. Miguel files in a New Arizania court to have his support obligations modified. Juanita opposes the modification, offering all of the appropriate arguments.

234. What result?

(A) Because Miguel has suffered an involuntary and substantial diminution in income, his support obligation will be modified.

(B) Because Miguel is very capable and doubtless will find another job before too long, his support obligation will remain unchanged.

(C) Because the Texahoma rather than the New Arizania court has jurisdiction under both states' Uniform Interstate Family Support Act statutes, the New Arizania court should decline to hear the case for lack of jurisdiction.

(D) The New Arizania court should refuse to modify the support obligation because Miguel knew when he took the job that there was a possibility that he would lose it and thus assumed the risk.

After Robert Patterson and Yeung Li have been dating for two months, they decide to marry. They go to a Justice of the Peace who marries them. Four months later, Yeung Patterson gives birth to a beautiful baby girl, Serenity, whom the doctor describes as having been born two weeks short of being full term. Robert accepts the child as his own.

Three years later, Robert and Yeung decide to divorce after Robert is discovered to be having an affair with someone else. Robert contests having to pay child support for a child that he claims is not his own.

235. What result?

(A) If indeed Robert is not the biological father of Serenity, he cannot be ordered to pay child support against his will.

(B) Because Serenity was born into the marriage, Robert will be forced to pay child support.

(C) Because Robert was on notice that he was not the father of Serenity and nonetheless accepted her as his daughter, he may well be estopped from denying his paternity now.

(D) Robert will be forced to pay child support unless he promises never to see Serenity again, in which case he cannot be forced to pay support.

Sven and Martha Johansson are married. They live with their three-year-old son, Eric, in the state of Monoming. Monoming has abrogated interspousal immunity.

One day, while Sven was supposed to be watching his son, Sven received an important call from a client. Sven could not have been on the phone for more than a few minutes, but by the time that he had finished, Eric had already found his way to the pool in the backyard and fallen into it. Sven was able to save him but only after Eric had suffered severe brain damage.

Martha sues Sven on behalf of her son for negligent supervision, hoping thereby to get money from their insurance company to cover some of the medical costs involved in Eric's care.

236. What result?

(A) Recovery is possible because the state has abrogated interspousal immunity. A separate issue is whether the insurance policy excludes these kinds of suits and whether the enforcement of such an exclusion would itself violate public policy.

(B) Even if the state permits suits by children against their parents, this kind of case is not actionable because it at most involves negligent supervision.

(C) Precisely because this may be the only way that the Johanssons will be able to pay for the needed medical care for their child, this suit will be permitted.

(D) Jurisdictions vary greatly with respect to whether these kinds of suits will be permitted. Among those permitting suits by children against their parents, some but not all will permit an action for negligent supervision and thus more information is needed before it will be clear whether Monoming permits this kind of suit.

Jamal and Tawanda Smith have been married for several years. Tawanda helped put Jamal through law school and the day after Jamal finished taking the bar exam he announced that he wanted a divorce. The Smiths have no children and can agree about how to divide what little property they have except Tawanda believes that she should receive credit in some way for having put Jamal though law school, while Jamal argues that she should not get a credit both because it is impossible to put a value on a law degree and because he does not even know if he passed the bar exam.

237. What result?

(A) Because a law degree is not transferable, it cannot be treated as property and, in any event, its value is too speculative for Tawanda to be given any credit for it in the marital asset distribution. No jurisdiction will permit Tawanda to receive credit for the law degree.

(B) Whether or not it is treated as property, the law degree will be treated as a marital asset. Each jurisdiction will permit Tawanda to receive a credit for half the cost of the degree plus one half of the expenses incurred which is more than her fair share.

(C) While the law degree may not be transferable, it has significantly increased Jamal's earning potential. Each jurisdiction will permit Tawanda to be credited with Jamal's increased earning potential, either reduced to present value or to be paid out over the years.

(D) While refusing to treat the degree as property or, possibly, even as a marital asset, many jurisdictions as a matter of equity will nonetheless consider the future value of the degree as something to be considered in the distribution of property or in the awarding of spousal support.

Akeem and Cynthia Walker have been married for several years. They have always lived in the house which Akeem inherited from his parents a few years before they married.

When they first discussed having children, they decided to make several improvements to the house. Those improvements were funded with monies that Cynthia had inherited from her grandmother one year after they had married. Maintenance costs and other improvements were funded from Akeem's and Cynthia's paychecks.

The Walkers eventually discovered that they were unable to have children. They tried adopting but that never worked out. In large part because of the pressures and disappointments associated with their difficulties in having children, they started to argue heatedly and eventually decided to divorce. Neither seeks spousal support. The sole issues involve whether to characterize the house as separate or marital property and whether Cynthia should receive some sort of credit if indeed the house is characterized as Akeem's separate property.

238. What result?

(A) Because the house was inherited before the marriage, it is Akeem's separate property. Monies contributed by Cynthia will not be credited but instead will be treated as her contribution to the household expenses.

(B) Because all of the monies contributed were marital, Akeem and Cynthia will be viewed as having shared the expenses equally. The house will remain Akeem's separate property and Cynthia will not be entitled to an offset.

(C) Because marital assets were used to pay for maintenance of and improvements to the house, the house might be viewed as having become marital property, or the increase in value of the house since the marriage may well be treated as a marital asset. Cynthia's contribution of separate funds to improve the house provides an additional reason to treat the house as part of the marital estate or to make her entitled to a credit, depending upon her intent when those separate funded were expended.

(D) Because marital funds were used to maintain the house, it will be treated as marital property. Cynthia is entitled to half of the value of the house.

John Jones and Sue Smith, both 17 and hence minors, wish to marry. However, their parents refuse to consent to the union as required by statute. The law requiring parental consent for minors is challenged in court.

239. What result?

(A) The challenge will likely be sustained because there is a fundamental right to marry.

(B) The challenge will likely not be sustained because minors do not have constitutional rights.

(C) The challenge will likely be sustained unless the parents have a good reason to prevent the marriage.

(D) The challenge will likely not be sustained because the marriage of John and Sue is only being delayed rather than precluded by the statute.

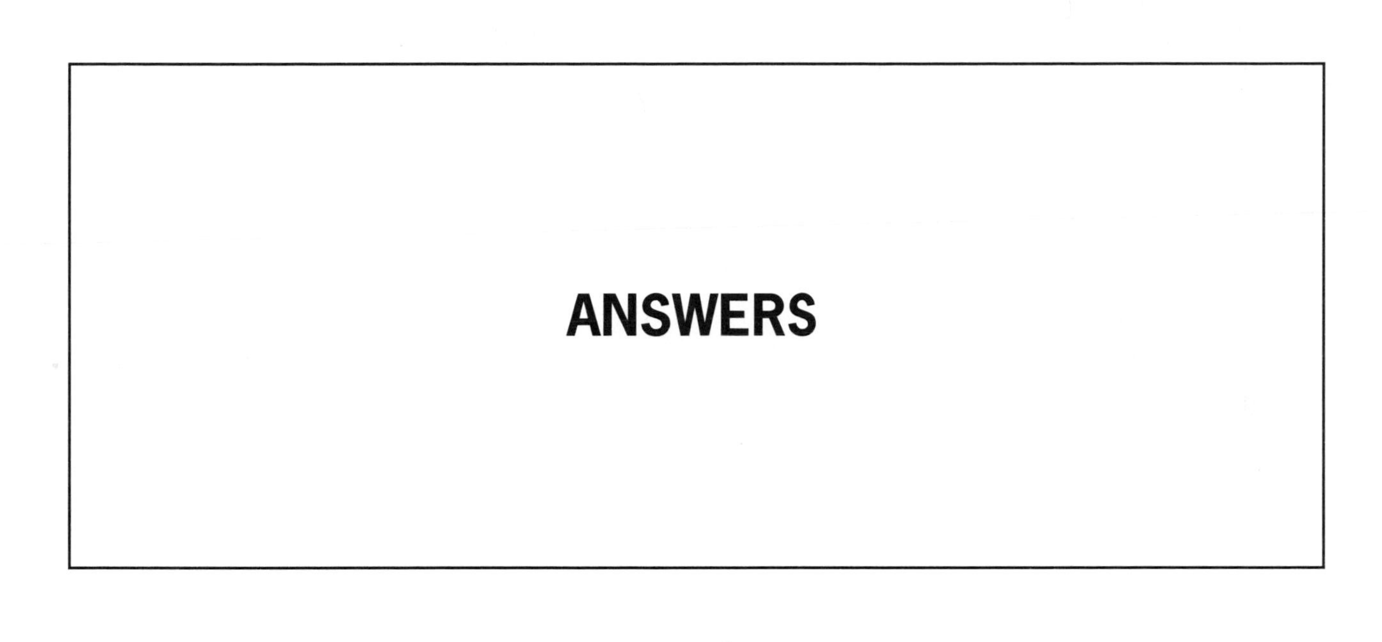

ANSWERS

TOPIC 1: MINOR MARRIAGES — ANSWERS

1. **Answer (B) is the best answer.** *See Greene v. Williams*, 9 Cal. App. 3d 559 (Ct. App. 1970) (voidable minor marriage in effect until declared void by a court).

   Answer (A) is incorrect. The marriage would not need to be annulled were it treated as void *ab initio* by the state. However, many states treat minor marriages as voidable rather than void and such marriages are valid until declared void by a court. *See Greene v. Williams*, 9 Cal. App. 3d 559 (Ct. App. 1970) (voidable minor marriage legally recognized until invalidated by a court).

   Answer (C) is incorrect. Were the marriage void rather than merely voidable, there would be no need to have it declared void by a court. *See Whitney v. Whitney*, 134 P.2d 357 (Okla. 1942) (marriage void *ab initio* does not require court decree to make marriage void).

   Answer (D) is incorrect. Even if Bonnie's parents never consented to the marriage, it would still need to be declared void by a court if the jurisdiction treated such marriages as voidable. *See Medlin v. Medlin*, 981 P.2d 1087 (Ariz. App. 1999) (minor marriage celebrated without parental consent voidable rather than void).

2. **Answer (B) is the best answer.** *See Medlin v. Medlin*, 981 P.2d 1087 (Ariz. App. 1999) (minor marriage ratified when couple lives together after minor reaches majority).

   Answer (A) is incorrect. Assuming that such marriages are merely voidable, they will be recognized as valid until declared void by a court. *See Medlin v. Medlin*, 981 P.2d 1087 (Ariz. App. 1999) (minor marriage celebrated without parental consent voidable rather than void).

   Answer (C) is incorrect. The marriage will be considered valid whether or not the jurisdiction recognizes common law marriage. However, if the jurisdiction had treated minor marriages as void but also had recognized common law marriages, then a separate way for the couple to have been recognized as legally married would be for them to have met the requirements of a common law marriage once each had reached the age of consent. *See Stilley v. Stilley*, 244 S.W.3d 958 (Ark. 1952) (common law marriage recognized even though marriage involving minor was void and hence could not later be ratified).

   Answer (D) is incorrect. Even where both parties agree that they no longer love each other and that the marriage is no longer viable, they must have a court declare that the marriage does not or, perhaps, never did exist. *See In re Leonard's Estate*, 207 N.W.2d 166, 168 (Mich. App. 1973) (discussing the presumption that "once entered, the marriage continues until ended by death or divorce").

3. **Answer (D) is the best answer.** Some states have an absolute bar precluding someone this young from marrying. *See* N. H. Stat. 457:4 (all marriage contracted

by children under a certain age are void). Others may not have an absolute bar but would only permit a marriage involving someone very young in extraordinary circumstances. *See* Nev. Stat. 122.025 (2) (person under 16 can marry in extraordinary circumstances if doing so would serve the best interests of the minor and parental consent has been given); *Kirkpatrick v. Eight Judicial District ex rel. County of Clark*, 43 P.3d 998, 1011 (Nev. 2002) ("Since the statute does not limit the youngest age at which a minor may seek judicial permission to marry, greater judicial protection is required for younger minors.").

Answer (A) is incorrect. Even with parental permission, individuals who are very young will simply be precluded from marrying. *See, e.g.*, N.H. Stat. 457:4 ("No male below the age of 14 years and no female below the age of 13 years shall be capable of contracting a valid marriage, and all marriages contracted by such persons shall be null and void.").

Answer (B) is incorrect. While it may well be that in this case Joanna is too young to marry even with parental permission, some minors are considered old enough to marry if their parents consent. *See* Alaska Stat. sec. 25.05.171(b) ("A superior court judge may grant permission for a person who has reached the age of 14 but is under the age of 18 to marry and may order the licensing officer to issue the license if the judge finds, following a hearing at which the parents and minor are given the opportunity to appear and be heard, that the marriage is in the best interest of the minor and that . . . (1) the parents have given their consent.").

Answer (C) is incorrect. While exposing a minor to pornographic materials might be one way to violate the prohibition against corrupting minors, that is not the only way. *See Com. v. Stafford*, 749 A.2d 489, 500 (Pa. Super. 2000) (defendant convicted for corrupting his minor wife by having sexual relations with her); *People v. Benu*, 385 N.Y.S.2d 222 (1976) (father convicted of endangering minor for taking active role in having his 13-year-old daughter marry a 17-year-old).

4. **Answer (C) is the best answer**. *See Greene v. Williams*, 88 Cal. Rptr. 261 (Ct. App. 1970) (parent cannot annul minor child's marriage after death of child merely because child married without parental consent).

Answer (A) is incorrect. A parent cannot have his or her child's voidable marriage annulled after the child has died. *See Greene v. Williams*, 88 Cal. Rptr. 261 (Ct. App. 1970) (parent cannot annul minor child's marriage after death of child merely because child married without parental consent).

Answer (B) is incorrect. This is a red herring. While reputation is one of the criteria for having a common law marriage, *see Metropolitan Life Ins. Co. v. Johnson*, 645 P.2d 356, 361 (Idaho 1982), it is not a condition of having a ceremonial marriage and thus does not provide an exception to the rule about when such marriages can be annulled.

Answer (D) is incorrect. This is a bad answer, since it does not describe a condition for challenging the marriage. Even had Penelope given Roberta a chance to establish her love for Paul, Penelope would still have been precluded from challenging the marriage at this point. *See Greene v. Williams*, 88 Cal. Rptr. 261

(Ct. App. 1970) (parent cannot annul minor child's marriage after death of child merely because child married without parental consent).

5. Yes, because New Vermshire treats minor marriages as voidable, Cindy and Don are married in the eyes of the law until a court declares their marriage void. Because Don has attempted to marry someone else while he is legally married, he faces a bigamy charge. *See Greene v. Williams*, 88 Cal. Rptr. 261, 262 (Ct. App. 1970) ("A marriage by an under-age child without parental consent is voidable only and remains in full force until dissolved."); *Kleinfield v. Veruki*, 372 S.E.2d 407, 409 (Va. App. 1988) ("a party to a voidable marriage must obtain an annulment, or any subsequent marriage is bigamous"). While a separate question is whether he in fact will be prosecuted, he is nonetheless at risk.

6. There are at least two issues here: (1) the age at which individuals can marry without getting someone else's consent, and (2) whether states make exceptions for those who either are pregnant or have already given birth. Each is a matter of state law. Most states require that individuals younger than 18 years of age have parental permission if they are to marry. However, some states permit a judicial bypass if the woman is pregnant or has a child. *See, e.g.*, Colo. Stat. sec. 14-2-108 (2); Flor. Stat. sec. 741.0405; Ill. Stat. Ch 750 sec. 5/208. Assuming that the jurisdiction in which they live does not permit individuals under 18 to marry without some sort of permission, Carol and David will be permitted to marry only if, e.g., local law permits a judicial bypass in these circumstances.

TOPIC 2: BIGAMOUS/POLYGAMOUS MARRIAGES — ANSWERS

7. **Answer (C) is the best answer**. A void marriage may be challenged even after the death of one of the parties. Because New Orrington does not recognize common law marriage and the ceremonial marriage was void, Tim's children will likely be successful in preventing Sara from getting any share of the estate. *See In re Estate of Crockett*, 728 N.E.2d 765, 769 (Ill. App. 2000).

   Answer (A) is incorrect. Assuming that no statute exists validating such marriages, *see Estate of Whyte v. Whyte*, 614 N.E.2d 372, 373 (Ill. App. 1993) (discussing such a statute), the marriage will be held void and thus not in effect even once the impediment has been removed. *See Dacunzo v. Edgye*, 111 A.2d 88, 95 (N. J. App. 1955).

   Answer (B) is incorrect. A void marriage can be challenged even after the death of a party. *See In re Estate of Crockett*, 728 N.E.2d 765, 769 (Ill. App. 2000) ("if a marriage is void *ab initio*, its validity is subject to attack in any proceeding in which the question of its validity arises, including actions in probate after death of the. . . party").

   Answer (D) is incorrect. Sara might well be protected were the marriage recognized. *See, e.g., In re Ruff's Estate*, 458 N.Y.S.2d 38 (1982) (widow allowed to elect against will notwithstanding deceased husband's intentions as reflected by his having left her out of his will).

8. There are two possible bases to Frankie's claim that she is Herbert's lawful widow. First, she might claim that the divorce was invalid, e.g., because Frankie was not given notice, *see Kalix v. Kalix*, 36 Pa. D. & C.3d 30 (Pa. Com. Pl. 1985) (divorce invalid because wife did not have notice of proceeding), or the court lacked jurisdiction to grant the divorce, *see Heckathorn v. Heckathorn*, 423 P.2d 410 (N.M. 1967) (divorce invalid because court lacked jurisdiction to grant it), although a separate issue is whether Frankie might be estopped from challenging the validity of the decree. *See Watson v. Watson*, 270 S.E.2d 542 (N.C. App. 1980) (ex-wife estopped from challenging validity of foreign divorce decree). Second, she might claim to have established a common law marriage after the divorce, assuming that the jurisdiction where they were living recognized such unions. If they agreed that they were husband and wife again after their divorce, lived as husband and wife, and held themselves out as husband and wife, then they would have contracted a valid common law marriage. *See Osteen v. Osteen*, 999 S.W.2d 28 (Tex. App. 1999) (discussing common law marriage allegedly established after ceremonial marriage dissolved); *Ballesteros v. Jones*, 985 S.W.2d 485, 489 (Tex. App. 1998) (listing conditions for valid common law marriage).

   Frankie's claims can only be evaluated after it is clear whether she is challenging the validity of the divorce or claiming instead that a common law marriage had been contracted after the divorce.

TOPIC 3: INCESTUOUS MARRIAGES	ANSWERS

9. **Answer (B) is the best answer**. If the marriage is treated as void, then Sarah will not receive the benefits to which she would have been entitled had she been John's legally recognized wife. *See Catalno v. Catalno*, 170 A.2d 726 (Conn. 1961) (death benefits denied because marriage between uncle and niece not recognized). If such marriages are permitted in the jurisdiction, then Sarah will receive the benefits.

   Answer (A) is incorrect. A marriage that is void because incestuous can be challenged after the death of one of the parties. *See In re Stiles*, 391 N.E.2d 1026 (Ohio 1979) (marriage between uncle and niece void and so can be challenged after death of one of parties).

   Answer (C) is incorrect. If the marriage is void *ab initio* for all purposes, the parent's permission will not make the marriage valid. In any event, Sarah at age 20 is old enough to marry without her parents' permission. *See, e.g.*, Okla. Stat. Ti. 43 sec. 3 ("Any unmarried person of the age of eighteen (18) years or upwards and not otherwise disqualified is capable of contracting and consenting to marriage with a person of the opposite sex"); Mich. Stat. 551.103(3)(1) ("Every person who becomes 18 years of age shall be capable by law of contracting marriage.") Iowa Stat. sec. 595.2(2) ("a marriage between a male and a female is valid only if each is eighteen years of age or older").

   Answer (D) is incorrect. Even if there is a record of the marriage, the marriage will not be considered valid if it is within the prohibited degrees of consanguinity.

10. The marriage may well not be recognized. While this is a matter of state law, many states will not only, e.g., prohibit a man from marrying his daughter but will also prohibit him from marrying his stepdaughter. *See* Conn. Stat. sec. 46b-21: Okla. Stat. Ti. 43, sec. 2; S. D. Stat. 25-1-7; *Rhodes v. McAfee*, 457 S.W.2d 522 (Tenn. 1970) (man's marriage to stepdaughter void). However, some courts may narrowly construe the statute and recognize the marriage on the theory that after the divorce the daughter was no longer the man's wife's daughter. *See Back v. Back*, 125 N.W. 1009 (Iowa 1910).

11. Wally would be prohibited by law from marrying his biological or adoptive daughter and many states preclude stepparents from marrying their stepchildren. *See, e.g.*, Conn. Stat. sec. 46b-21 (no man may marry his stepdaughter). Here, however, Wally is neither the biological or adoptive father of Soni nor is he her stepparent. He would thus not be precluded from marrying her based on those prohibitions and, indeed, there would seem to be no bar to the marriage absent a statute barring marriages between individuals if one has a parent-like relationship with the other. A separate issue would have been raised if, e.g., he had been having sexual relations with her before she reached the age of consent, *see Parrish v. State*, 494 So.2d 705 (Ala.

Cr. App. 1985) (mother's boyfriend convicted of first-degree sexual abuse of daughter), but that is not at issue here.

TOPIC 4: SEXUAL RELATIONS AND MARRIAGE — ANSWERS

12. **Answer (A) is the best answer**. Ethel has a misunderstanding of the condition that must be established. For purposes of annulments, impotency involves the inability to have sexual relations rather than the ability to have children. *See Dolan v. Dolan*, 259 A.2d 32, 37 (Me. 1969) ("As a ground for divorce or annulment of marriage it means an inability to engage in, or a lack of capacity for, normal and complete sexual intercourse."); *T. v. M.*, 242 A.2d 670, 673 (N. J. Super. Ch. 1968) ("Impotency is the inability to have sexual intercourse; impotence is not sterility.").

    Answer (B) is incorrect. While it is important to establish the permanence of the condition, *see S. v. S.*, 86 S.E.2d 103, 104 (Ga. 1955) (noting that the condition must be permanent if it is to be the basis of an annulment), mere inability to have children does not constitute impotence for these purposes. *See Dolan v. Dolan*, 259 A.2d 32, 37 (Me. 1969).

    Answer (C) is incorrect. The issue at hand is whether the couple can have sexual relations, not whether they can have children. *See T. v. M.*, 242 A.2d 670, 673 (N.J. Super. Ch. 1968).

    Answer (D) is incorrect. While it is true that once they have sexual relations during the marriage they will be unable to make use of this ground, *see Dolan v. Dolan*, 259 A.2d 32 (Me. 1969), the state may permit divorces for reasons other than adultery, so this part of the answer is false.

13. **Answer (C) is the best answer**. In Illinois, Marjorie would be barred on both grounds. *See* Ill. Stat. Ch. 750 sec 5/301(2) ("a party lacks the physical capacity to consummate the marriage by sexual intercourse and at the time the marriage was solemnized the other party did not know of the incapacity"); Ill. Stat. Ch. 750 sec 5/302(2) (action may be brought "by either party, no later than one year after the petitioner obtained knowledge of the described condition").

    Answer (A) is incorrect. Some states require that the party seeking the annulment was unaware at the time of the marriage that the marriage could not be consummated. *See* N. J. Stat. 2A:34-1(c) ("The parties, or either of them, were at the time of marriage physically and incurably impotent, provided the party making the application shall have been ignorant of such impotency or incapability at the time of the marriage, and has not subsequently ratified the marriage."); Del. Stat. Ti. 13 sec. 1506 (2) ("A party lacked the physical capacity to consummate the marriage by sexual intercourse and the other party did not, at the time the marriage was solemnized, know of the incapacity"); Wis. Stat. 767.03(2) ("A party lacks the physical capacity to consummate the marriage by sexual intercourse, and at the time the marriage was solemnized the other party did not know of the incapacity. Suit may be brought by either party no later than one year after the petitioner obtained knowledge of the incapacity."). *Cf. Marks v. Marks*, 77 N.Y.S.2d 269, 271

(N.Y. Sup. 1948) (noting that "it is entirely possible that two persons may wish to marry each other even though they knew in advance that there could never be issue of the marriage").

Answer (B) is incorrect. Even if the action could be brought in the state and she would not be estopped because of her prior knowledge, there may well be a deadline after which this ground will no longer be available. *See, e.g.*, Haw. Stat. 580-28 (action for annulment based on physical incapacity must be brought within two years of celebration of marriage).

Answer (D) is incorrect. While they might not be able to get the marriage annulled for lack of consummation, they may be able to have it dissolved on other grounds.

14. To have a marriage annulled on the ground of impotency, the party seeking to have the marriage annulled must establish both that the condition is incurable, *see Dolan v. Dolan*, 259 A.2d 32, 38 (Me. 1969), and that the condition existed when the marriage was contracted. *See Dolan v. Dolan*, 259 A.2d 32, 37 (Me. 1969) ("The incapacity must have existed at the time of the marriage."). Once the marriage was consummated, the plaintiff will be unable to have it annulled on this ground. A separate issue is whether instead the plaintiff will be able to get a divorce on the grounds of abandonment or cruelty, *see Chinnis v. Chinnis*, 501 N.Y.S.2d 227 (App. Div. 1986) (refusal to have marital relations held to help establish cruelty, thereby providing ground for divorce), or perhaps on a no-fault ground, but this is not a case of impotency.

TOPIC 5: MARRIAGE AND COMPETENCY — ANSWERS

15. **Answer (D) is the best answer**. If Yevgeny understood what he was doing at the time of the marriage, then he will be unable to have it annulled based on his own incompetency. *See Christoph v. Sims*, 234 S.W.2d 901, 904 (Tex. Civ. App. 1950). If Olga can establish that Yevgeny left the marital home without legal cause, e.g., a threat to physical safety, and has consistently refused to return, then she will have established abandonment. *See Mayes v. Mayes*, 743 So.2d 1257, 1260 (La. App. 1999) ("Abandonment by a spouse occurs when that spouse withdraws from the common dwelling without lawful cause and constantly refuses to return.").

    Answer (A) is incorrect. This is not true as a general matter, since Yevgeny will have to have been so inebriated that he did not understand what he was doing. *See Christoph v. Sims*, 234 S.W.2d 901, 904 (Tex. Civ. App. 1950) ("A party claiming he was intoxicated at the time of marriage cannot escape liability unless he was incapable at the time of understanding his acts; he must be so drunk that he did not understand what he was doing and the nature of the transaction.").

    Answer (B) is incorrect. While it is true that the marriage will likely be treated as valid if Yevgeny understood what he was doing, even if his cost-benefit calculation might have been different had he been sober, *see Christoph v. Sims*, 234 S.W.2d 901, 904 (Tex. Civ. App. 1950), a separate question is whether Olga will be successful in securing a divorce based on abandonment. *See Heilbut v. Heilbut*, 746 N.Y.S.2d 294, 296 (App. Div. 2002) ("Abandonment requires an unjustified, voluntary departure with an intention on the part of the departing spouse not to return against the will and without the consent of the complaining spouse."). It may well be that Yevgeny will not be able to have the marriage annulled, and Olga will be unable to establish abandonment.

    Answer (C) is incorrect. If Yevgeny knew what he was doing, it will not matter whether the jurisdiction treats marriages involving very, very drunk individuals as void or voidable, since in either event Yevgeny will have contracted a valid marriage. *See Mahan v. Mahan*, 88 So.2d 545, 547 (Fla. 1956) (noting that if an individual marries while drunk the marriage will be valid if he knew what he was doing).

16. **Answer (B) is the best answer**. *See Christoph v. Sims*, 234 S.W.2d 901, 904 (Tex. Civ. App. 1950) ("Living together in the same house after marriage, contributing financial support to the wife when sober, raise the inescapable presumption of cohabitation and must be held to show condonation; thus preventing annulment of a marriage superinduced by a state of intoxication."). *See also Mahan v. Mahan*, 88 So.2d 545, 548 (Fla. 1956) (discussing ratification or confirmation of the marriage which had taken place, when one of the parties was *non compos mentis* at the time that the marriage was celebrated).

    Answer (A) is incorrect. This is not the best answer because many states treat the marriage contracted under the circumstances described here as voidable rather than void. *See Dean v. Dean*, 146 A.2d 861, 863 (Md. 1958) ("annulment is confined to cases where a marriage has been performed, but by reason of fraud, duress, intoxication or the like, it is voidable").

Answer (C) is incorrect. This is false. If he was so drunk that he did not know what he was doing, then the marriage will at least be voidable, *see Dean v. Dean*, 146 A.2d 861 (Md. 1958).

Answer (D) is incorrect. This is false because if the marriage is merely voidable, then it can be ratified when the individual is sober. *See Christoph v. Sims*, 234 S.W.2d 901 (Tex. Civ. App. 1950).

17. **Answer (B) is the best answer**. Some states treat marriages involving the insane as void, *see Harris v. Harris*, 506 N.W.2d 3, 4 (Mich. App. 1993) (discussing statute specifying that such marriages are void), and some treat them as voidable. *See Woods v. Woods*, 638 S.W.2d 403, 405 (Tenn. App. 1982) ("A marriage is voidable from the beginning (1) when either party was insane."). Where the marriage is merely voidable rather than void, many states refuse to permit it to be challenged after one of the parties has died. *See Patey v. Peaslee*, 111 A.2d 194 (N.H. 1955); *Vance v. Hinch*, 261 S.W.2d 412 (Ark. 1953).

    Answer (A) is incorrect. This is false, since a void marriage can be challenged even after the death of the parties. *See Kleinfield v. Veruki*, 372 S.E.2d 407, 409 (Va. App. 1988).

    Answer (C) is incorrect. This is false, since she will be precluded from challenging the marriage after the death of one of the parties if the marriage is merely voidable. *See Patey v. Peaslee*, 111 A.2d 194 (N.H. 1955).

    Answer (D) is incorrect. Were the marriage merely voidable, it could not be challenged after the death of one of the parties, but if it were void it still could be challenged after one of the parties had died. *See Patey v. Peaslee*, 111 A.2d 194 (N.H. 1955); *Kleinfield v. Veruki*, 372 S.E.2d 407, 409 (Va. App. 1988).

18. To have the marriage annulled, Thomas will have to establish that at least one of them was so drunk that he or she did not know what he or she was doing when agreeing to marry. *See Christoph v. Sims*, 234 S.W.2d 901, 904 (Tex. Civ. App. 1950). Even if that could be established, a separate question would be whether the marriage had subsequently been ratified when the two had tried to make the marriage work. *See id.* If the state treats such marriages as voidable rather than void, then the marriage would have been ratified by the couple's later actions and they will need to get a divorce to end the marriage. They will have to make use of some other ground recognized by the state, e.g., incompatibility, living separate and apart, etc.

TOPIC 6: COHABITATION, PRENUPTIAL, AND POSTNUPTIAL AGREEMENTS — ANSWERS

19. **Answer (B) is the best answer**. Such agreements are enforceable, absent fraud, coercion, etc. *See Casto v. Casto*, 508 So.2d 330, 333 (Fla. 1987) (while enforceable, postnuptial agreement may be set aside "by establishing that it was reached under fraud, deceit, duress, coercion, misrepresentation, or overreaching").

    Answer (A) is incorrect. This is false. Postnuptial agreements are recognized and enforceable. *See In re Marriage of Friedman*, 122 Cal. Rptr. 2d 412 (Ct. App. 2002) (postnuptial agreement valid and enforceable).

    Answer (C) is incorrect. It is unlikely that this threat would be held coercive. *See Davis v. Miller*, 7 P.3d 1223, 1231 (Kan. 2000) (individual making agreement under stress of attempting to save the marriage nonetheless entered the agreement voluntarily).

    Answer (D) is incorrect. While the postnuptial agreement can be set aside if coercion or duress can be established, these are not the only conditions that will invalidate the agreement. Substantial misrepresentation and overreaching can also serve to invalidate the agreement. *See Casto v. Casto*, 508 So.2d 330, 333 (Fla. 1987).

20. **Answer (C) is the best answer**. There is clear fraud here that would invalidate the agreement. *See Fogg v. Fogg*, 567 N.E.2d 921, 923 (Mass. 1991) (Postnuptial agreements "at least have to meet the same threshold requirements of antenuptial and separation agreements. The agreement before us was signed as a result of the wife's implied fraudulent promise that she would attempt to preserve the marriage. Thus, it is invalid.").

    Answer (A) is incorrect. This is false because it misstates the rule. Merely because a postnuptial agreement is voluntary does not establish that it will be enforceable. *See Boudreaux v. Boudreaux*, 745 So.2d 61, 63 (La. App. 1999) ("spouses are free to contract with one another before or during marriage as to all matters that are not prohibited by public policy").

    Answer (B) is incorrect. This is false. The individuals proposing that a postnuptial agreement be made is not precluded from benefiting from that agreement. *See, e.g., Davis v. Miller*, 7 P.3d 1223 (Kan. 2000) (postnuptial agreement enforceable notwithstanding that husband proposed it and that husband filed for divorce).

    Answer (D) is incorrect. The issue here is not whether there was consideration, but whether there was fraud. *See Fogg v. Fogg*, 567 N.E.2d 921 (Mass. 1991).

21. **Answer (D) is the best answer**. Both provisions will likely be struck down as unenforceable, *see Combs v. Sherry-Combs*, 865 P.2d 50, 54 (Wyo. 1993), and

the custody and support will be decided as they would have been had the agreement never been made.

Answer (A) is incorrect. This is a misstatement of the relevant rule. Postnuptial agreements will be enforced only if they are not prohibited by public policy. This agreement will likely not be enforceable because deciding which parent would have custody before the children had even been born involves a failure to give adequate consideration to the children's best interests, which is contrary to public policy. *See Combs v. Sherry-Combs*, 865 P.2d 50, 54 (Wyo. 1993) ("the provision of the marriage document calling for custody to be granted to the same sex parent is void as against public policy").

Answer (B) is incorrect. This answer is only partially accurate. The answer is correct that the provision specifying custody without a consideration of the best interests of the child will likely be struck as violating public policy. *See Combs v. Sherry-Combs*, 865 P.2d 50, 54 (Wyo. 1993). However, the provision specifying no child support will also likely be struck down as violating public policy, *see Combs v. Sherry-Combs*, 865 P.2d 50, 54 (Wyo. 1993) ("The provision of the marriage document limiting potential support payments is void as against public policy."), and hence will likely not be enforced.

Answer (C) is incorrect. This answer is also only partially accurate. While the child support provision will likely be struck down, *see Combs v. Sherry-Combs*, 865 P.2d 50, 54 (Wyo. 1993), the provision specifying custody without even knowing which parent would best promote the interests of the child will also likely be struck down. *See id.*

22. **Answer (B) is the best answer**. It would be contrary to public policy to permit marriages formally celebrated to be dissolved on this basis. *See Lester v. Lester*, 87 N.Y.S.2d 517, 520 (Dom. Rel. 1949) (holding that an agreement between the parties that they were not really married despite having gone through a ceremonial marriage was unenforceable as a matter of public policy).

    Answer (A) is incorrect. *See, e.g., Crosson v. Crosson*, 668 So.2d 868 (Ala. Civ. App. 1995) (marriage upheld despite husband's subjective intent not to contract marriage). To permit a marriage not to be recognized if one of the parties subjectively intended that it not be recognized would create the potential for great injustice and would in addition be utterly unworkable. It would permit individuals to appear to marry but then to avoid the responsibilities of marriage by establishing that they had subjectively never intended to marry, outward manifestations to the contrary notwithstanding, if they subsequently wanted to get out of the marriage. Further, there would then always be a cloud associated with the rights and responsibilities arising from marriage, since they would always seem subject to invalidation based on a later showing of a subjective intent not to marry at the time of the marriage's celebration.

    Answer (C) is incorrect. This does not qualify as a prenuptial agreement in that such an agreement is entered into in contemplation and consideration of a future marriage. *See Matter of Estate of Crawford*, 730 P.2d 675, 77 (Wash. 1986) ("A prenuptial agreement is one entered into by prospective spouses *prior to marriage* but in contemplation and in consideration thereof.").

Answer (D) is incorrect. Individuals may be precluded from sitting on their rights for a very long time. However, a year would presumably not be too long a time. *See, e.g., Loiacono v. Loiacono*, 116 A.2d 881 (Pa. Super. 1955) (laches not a bar even though plaintiff waited six years before commencing suit to challenge divorce). Further, this statement implies that marriages cannot be dissolved once the parties are together for a year, which is simply untrue.

23. **Answer (D) is the best answer**. While agreements about property are enforceable, agreements about child custody which are made without a consideration of which parent's having custody would promote the best interests of the child would likely be held unenforceable as a matter of public policy. *See Osborne v. Osborne*, 428 N.E.2d 810 (Mass. 1981).

    Answer (A) is incorrect. While prenuptial agreements were once thought unenforceable because promoting divorce, *cf. Fricke v. Fricke*, 42 N.W.2d 500, 502 (Wis. 1950) ("At least a majority, if not all of the courts which have considered the matter have held that any antenuptial contract which provides for, facilitates, or tends to induce a separation or divorce of the parties after marriage, is contrary to public policy and is therefore void."), they now tend to be enforced provided that certain conditions obtain. *See, e.g., Cary v. Cary*, 937 S.W.2d 777, 782 (Tenn. 1996) ("So long as the antenuptial agreement was entered into freely and knowledgeably, with adequate disclosure, and without undue influence or overreaching, the provision limiting or waiving alimony will be enforced, with one exception . . . [namely,] if enforcement deprives one spouse of support that he or she cannot otherwise obtain and results in that spouse becoming a public charge.").

    Answer (B) is incorrect. Prenuptial agreements can specify property division, *see Osborne v. Osborne*, 428 N.E.2d 810, 816 (Mass. 1981) ("an antenuptial contract settling the alimony or property rights of the parties upon divorce is not per se against public policy and may be specifically enforced"), although the custody provision would not be enforceable if not promoting the best interests of the child. *See id.*

    Answer (C) is incorrect. This is false, precisely because the best interests of the child would also have to be considered insofar as custody was at issue.

24. **Answer (D) is the best answer**. A prenuptial agreement is enforceable where the agreement was informed and voluntary. *See Dematteo v. Dematteo*, 762 N.E.2d 792 (Mass. 2002).

    Answer (A) is incorrect. Merely because Zelda refused to marry Yogi unless he signed the agreement does not establish that Yogi was under duress when signing it. *See In re Marriage of Spiegel*, 553 N.W.2d 309 (Iowa 1996) (duress not established merely because husband threatened not to go through with marriage unless wife signed prenuptial agreement).

    Answer (B) is incorrect. Even if it represents the intentions of the parties, it can be struck down under certain conditions. *See Huck v. Huck*, 734 P.2d 417, 419

(Utah 1986) ("in general, prenuptial agreements concerning the disposition of property owned by the parties at the time of their marriage are valid so long as there is no fraud, coercion, or material nondisclosure").

Answer (C) is incorrect. Even an inequitable agreement may be upheld absent other difficulties. *See Lemaster v. Dutton*, 694 So.2d 1360, 1364 (Ala. Civ. App. 1996) ("a court should not concern itself with the disparity in income between parties to an antenuptial agreement in the absence of fraud, duress, or other culpable conduct on the part of one of the parties"). *See also Tubbs v. Tubbs*, 648 So.2d 817, 818-19 (Fla. App. 1995) (unreasonable agreement will not be set aside if both parties were informed and voluntarily agreed to the provisions).

25. Courts would be divided on whether an adultery clause like this should be given effect. Courts may be unwilling to give effect to a provision that they view as creating an economic incentive to cause the breakdown of a marriage. *See Davis v. Davis*, 1996 Conn. Super. Lexis 1922. On the other hand, giving effect to the adultery provision would simply nullify the prenuptial agreement. Without the prenuptial agreement, the state's public policy as manifested through its laws will be implemented and, arguably, it promotes public policy to permit the state's general approach to spousal support to be given effect. *See MacFarlane v. Rich*, 567 A.2d 585 (N.H. 1989). If the Legislature consciously decided that the commission of adultery should not be a bar to support, then it is not clear why it should be a bar here (express wishes of the parties to the contrary) but not in other cases.

26. **Answer (D) is the best answer**. *See Osborne v. Osborne*, 428 N.E.2d 810, 816 (Mass. 1981) (custody provision unenforceable if contrary to children's best interests)), and *In re Marriage of Bonds*, 5 P.3d 815 (Cal. 2000) (premarital agreement specifying that children would be raised in a particular religion is unenforceable).

    Answer (A) is incorrect. This is false. One part of the agreement may be upheld even if another is struck down as unenforceable. *See, e.g., Warren v. Warren*, 523 N.E.2d 680 (Ill. App. 1988) (upholding prenuptial provision regarding property but striking provision regarding maintenance).

    Answer (B) is incorrect. A court would not enforce a provision specifying that the children would be brought up in a particular faith. *See In re Marriage of Bonds*, 5 P.3d 815, 830 (Cal. 2000) ("a premarital agreement to raise children in a particular religion is not enforceable").

    Answer (C) is incorrect. The custody provision is also unenforceable if contrary to the best interests of the children. *See Osborne v. Osborne*, 428 N.E.2d 810, 816 (Mass. 1981).

27. **Answer (C) is the best answer**. *See Walther v. Walther*, 657 N.E.2d 332, 335 (Ohio App. 1995) ("when the parties enter into an in-court settlement agreement, so long as the court is satisfied that it was not procured by fraud, duress, overreaching or undue influence, the court has the discretion to accept it without finding it to be fair and equitable").

Answer (A) is incorrect. This is false. *See Lancaster v. Lancaster*, 530 S.E.2d 83, 86 (N.C. App. 2000) ("A separation agreement is not invalid merely because one party later decides that what she bargained for is not as good as she would have liked.").

Answer (B) is incorrect. This is false. *See Lancaster v. Lancaster*, 530 S.E.2d 83, 84 (N.C. App. 2000) (A court "may hold a separation agreement invalid if it is manifestly unfair to one because of the other's overreaching.").

Answer (D) is incorrect. This is false. *See, e.g., Lounsbury v. Lounsbury*, 752 N.Y.S.2d 103, 108 (App. Div. 2002) ("It is well established that a separation agreement is not invalid simply because one spouse was not represented by counsel.").

28. **Answer (D) is the best answer**. *See Posik v. Layton*, 695 So.2d 759, 762 (Fla. App. 1997) ("an agreement for support between unmarried adults is valid unless the agreement is inseparably based upon illicit consideration of sexual services").

    Answer (A) is incorrect. This is false because Paul might be making a contract claim. *See Doe v. Burkland*, 808 A.2d 1090, 1094 (R.I. 2002) (permitting domestic partner to bring contract claim).

    Answer (B) is incorrect. Informed consent and voluntariness notwithstanding, such agreements will not be upheld if they are based upon meretricious considerations which are inseparable from the agreement. *See Jones v. Daly*, 122 Cal. App. 3d 500, 508 (Ct. App. 1981).

    Answer (C) is incorrect. Paul might have expected that the agreement between them would be kept. *Cf. Doe v. Burkland*, 808 A.2d 1090 (R.I. 2002) (suggesting that cohabitation agreements, like other agreements, are enforceable where not based upon meretricious considerations).

29. Postnuptial agreements are enforceable if the parties made an informed and voluntary agreement, even if a different agreement might have been more equitable. *See, e.g., D'Aston v. D'Aston*, 808 P.2d 111, 113 (Utah App. 1990) (postnuptial agreement enforceable absent fraud, coercion, or material nondisclosure). Thus, for Ethel to be successful she will have to establish that Frederick somehow hid assets from her or somehow coerced her into signing the agreement. However, Frederick's threat to end the marriage unless Ethel signed the postnuptial agreement would not constitute duress or coercion.

30. Prenuptial agreements are presumptively enforceable if the parties are informed and the agreement is voluntary. Thus, this agreement might well be enforced assuming that there was no fraud or misrepresentation. However, given that he had legal representation and she did not and that this was presented shortly before the wedding, a court might hold it unenforceable. *See Miles v. Werle*, 977 S.W.2d 297, 301 (Mo. App. 1998) (factors which undermine enforceability of prenuptial agreement include lack of access to independent counsel and amount of time available to revise agreement). *See also Randolph v. Randolph*, 937 S.W.2d 815, 822 (Tenn. 1996) (while no state requires consultation with independent counsel to make a

prenuptial agreement enforceable, many consider it at the very least to be one factor among many which will help determine whether the agreement was made knowledgeably and can be enforced).

TOPIC 7: MARRIAGE AND FRAUD — ANSWERS

31. **Answer (C) is the best answer**. *See Husband v. Wife*, 257 A.2d 765, 768 (Del. Super. 1969) (discussing the "orthodox rule that only such fraud as goes to the very essentials of the marriage relation will suffice as ground for annulment").

    Answer (A) is incorrect. This is false. As a general matter, a marriage based on fraud is at most voidable and is not void. *See, e.g., Anonymous v. Anonymous*, 85 A.2d 706, 715 (Del. Super. 1951) ("A marriage procured by fraud is, at most, a voidable marriage, as distinguished from a void marriage.").

    Answer (B) is incorrect. This is false because most states require that the fraudulent misrepresentation not only be material but essential to the marriage. *See Houlahan v. Horzepa*, 135 A.2d 232, 234 (N.J. Super. Ch. 1957) ("The fraud required to annul consummated marriage must be of an extreme character and in an essential of the marriage relation.").

    Answer (D) is incorrect. This rule of law is inaccurate. A marriage can be declared void even if children have been born of the union. *Cf. Home of Holy Infancy v. Kaska*, 397 S.W.2d 208 (Tex. 1966) (voidable marriage declared void while mother pregnant, thereby making child born out of wedlock).

32. **Answer (A) is the best answer**. *See Anonymous v. Anonymous*, 85 A.2d 706, 717-18 (Del. Super. 1951) (pointing out that "antenuptial chastity is not an essential element of the marriage relation, and that, in the absence of statute, concealment of premarital unchastity does not amount to fraud affording ground for annulment of the marriage").

    Answer (B) is incorrect. This is not a good answer. In many states, the fraud must go to one of the essentials of marriage and will not simply be judged in light of the subjective importance of the matter to the deceived party. *See Houlahan v. Horzepa*, 135 A.2d 232, 234 (N.J. Super. Ch. 1957) ("The fraud required to annul consummated marriage must be of an extreme character and in an essential of the marriage relation.").

    Answer (C) is incorrect. This is false, since antenuptial chastity may well not be viewed as an essential of marriage. *See, e.g., Anonymous v. Anonymous*, 85 A.2d 706, 717-18 (Del. Super. 1951). In addition, there is no evidence here of a fraudulent misrepresentation on Mathilda's part.

    Answer (D) is incorrect. This is false, since the annulment is unlikely to be granted, *see Anonymous v. Anonymous*, 85 A.2d 706, 717-18 (Del. Super. 1951), and in any event there is no evidence here of a fraudulent misrepresentation on Mathilda's part.

33. **Answer (C) is the best answer**. *See V.J.S. v. M.J.B.*, 592 A.2d 328 (N.J. Super. 1991) (husband perpetrated fraud going to essentials of marriage when, expressed

statements prior to the marriage notwithstanding, he had a strong desire to have children).

Answer (A) is incorrect. In many states, an annulment will not be granted merely because one of the parties lied to the other about something subjectively important to the latter. The lie must go to one of the essentials of the marriage and the issue will be whether lying about one's desire to have children would be held to go to an essential of the marriage. While claiming that one wants to have children when one has a settled desire not to do so has traditionally sufficed for an annulment, *see Williams v. Witt*, 235 A.2d 902, 902 (N.J. Super. App. Div. 1967) (an annulment may be granted where one of the parties prior to the marriage forms a fixed determination never to have children and does not communicate that intention to his intended spouse), claiming that one does not want to have children when in fact one wants them has not traditionally been treated in the same way. *Cf. Frost v. Frost*, 181 N.Y.S.2d 562 (Sup. Ct. 1958) (husband's false claim that he believed in planned parenthood was not a ground upon which an annulment could be granted).

Answer (B) is incorrect. Even if the state has no-fault divorce, the annulment may be granted if the fraud is held to involve sufficiently important matter. *See, e.g., Murray v. Murray*, 706 N.Y.S.2d (Ct. App. 2000) (marriage annulled because of fraud material to the marriage).

Answer (D) is incorrect. This is false. A marriage can be annulled if one party fraudulently induced the other to marry and the fraud went to an essential of marriage. *See Houlahan v. Horzepa*, 135 A.2d 232, 234 (N.J. Super. Ch. 1957).

34. **Answer (C) is the best answer**. *See Estate of Leslie*, 689 P.2d 133, 136 n.4 (Cal. 1984) ("A putative marriage is one in which at least one of the parties to an invalid marriage has a good faith belief that the marriage is valid.").

    Answer (A) is incorrect. This is inaccurate. The doctrine does not help establish which marriage is valid but instead will offer some protection of one who has the false but good faith belief that he or she is a particular individual's spouse. *See* Neb. Stat. sec. 42-378 ("When the court finds that a party entered into the contract of marriage in good faith supposing the other to be capable of contracting, and the marriage is declared a nullity, such fact shall be entered in the decree and the court may order such innocent party compensated as in the case of dissolution of marriage, including an award for costs and attorney fees.").

    Answer (B) is incorrect. This is false. Although the putative spouse is offered protection, the marriage itself is not valid. *See* Neb. Stat. sec. 42-378.

    Answer (D) is incorrect. This is not a doctrine that protects the putative spouse while the validity of the marriage is being determined but instead protects that spouse even once the invalidity of that marriage has been established. *See* Neb. Stat. sec. 42-378.

35. **Answer (C) is the best answer**. *See In re Estate of Loveless*, 64 S.W.3d 564, 574 (Tex. App. 2001) ("The presumption that the most recent marriage is a valid one continues until a party proves the impediment of a previous marriage and its continuing validity.").

Answer (A) is incorrect. This is a red herring. While arriving late for one's wedding may cause one's marriage to start inauspiciously, *see Crockett v. Cardon*, 713 So.2d 802 (La. App. 1998) (plaintiff sues driver for mental anguish caused by driver making plaintiff late for his own wedding), this has nothing to do with the last-in-time presumption.

Answer (B) is incorrect. This is false. *See, e.g.*, Tex. Fam. Code sec. 6.202(a) ("A marriage is void if entered into when either party has an existing marriage to another person that has not been dissolved by legal action or terminated by the death of the other spouse.").

Answer (D) is incorrect. This is inaccurate. *See In re Estate of Loveless*, 64 S.W.3d 564, 574 (Tex. App. 2001) ("The presumption's strength increases with the lapse of time, acknowledgments by the parties to the marriage, and the birth of children.").

36. Even where one of the parties to a marriage has made a material misrepresentation going to the essentials of the marriage (*see Zutavern v. Zutavern*, 52 N.W.2d 254, 257 (Neb. 1952) ("The law differentiates between fraud in the essentials of the marriage relation and deceptive arts to which some persons resort with a view to an advantageous marriage by placing their accomplishments, character, and circumstances in a too optimistic view."), the marriage is voidable rather than void. If the innocent party learns of the fraud and then decides to continue with the marriage anyway, the marriage will be valid in the eyes of the law. Further, it is only the defrauded party that can challenge a marriage based on the fraudulent acts of his or her partner, *see Zutavern v. Zutavern*, 52 N.W.2d 254, 257 (Neb. 1952) ("A marriage contract induced by fraud may, under some circumstances, be voidable and annulled at the instance of the victim of the imposition."), and thus Bill would not have been able to challenge the marriage on this basis even had Abby not condoned his fraud. *Cf. Roger v. Roger*, 203 N.Y.S.2d 576 (Sup. Ct. 1960) (wife's acquiescence to use of contraception amounted to condonation of husband's fraud in inducing her to marry when he did not want to have children).

TOPIC 8: COMMON LAW MARRIAGES — ANSWERS

37. **Answer (D) is the best answer**. Wayne and Yolanda never met the relevant requirements while domiciled in a state recognizing such unions, which is the only exception to Pennio's general rule of non-recognition.

    Answer (A) is incorrect. Even if Texahoma would recognize that a common law marriage had been established by individuals merely visiting the state, Pennio has made clear that it will recognize a common law marriage only if it is established while the parties are domiciled in a state recognizing such marriages. *See Lynch v. Brown*, 681 F. Supp. 506 (N.D. Ill. 1988) (state will not recognize a common law marriage of its own domiciliaries allegedly contracted while visiting another state); *Laikola v. Engineered Concrete*, 277 N.W.2d 653 (Minn. 1979) (same); *Enlow v. Fire Protection Systems Inc.*, 803 S.W.2d 148, 150 (Mo. App. 1991) ("Missouri will not recognize a common law marriage between Missouri residents even if the marriage occurs in a state which recognizes common law marriage.").

    Answer (B) is incorrect. While the state has made clear that such marriages violate public policy, that does not settle the issue. Many states do not permit common law marriages to be contracted locally but will recognize them if contracted where the parties were domiciled or, sometimes, if contracted in another state which does recognize them. For an example of the latter, see *Carpenter v. Carpenter*, 617 N.Y.S.2d 903 (App. Div. 1994) (state will recognize its own domiciliaries' common law marriage even if that marriage was established while the couple was merely visiting a state recognizing such unions).

    Answer (C) is incorrect. While some states would recognize the marriage under these circumstances, Pennio has made clear that it will not because its own domiciliaries cannot establish such a marriage by merely visiting elsewhere even for extended periods.

38. **Answer (B) is the best answer**. There was no common law marriage in Texahoma and thus no relation that could be recognized in Pennio.

    Answer (A) is incorrect. This is inaccurate. The conditions of a common law marriage include (1) the capacity to marry, (2) an agreement between the parties to marry in the present (as opposed to some time in the future), and (3) holding out to the public of the relationship. *See Fleming v. Fleming*, 559 P.2d 329, 330-31 (Kan. 1977). Here, there was no capacity to marry at the time that they agreed (because Sally was still married to Robert when she lived with Thomas in Texahoma), and when Sally was free to marry she did not meet the other conditions in a state recognizing common law marriages. Her alleged common law marriage will not be recognized.

    Answer (C) is incorrect. Their common law marriage might have been recognized had they remained in Texahoma. *See In re Marriage of Hallgarth*, 2001 WL 574833,

*4 (Tex. App.) ("if the circumstances creating the common law marriage occur while one party is married to another person, the common law marriage comes to fruition upon dissolution of that marriage"). *But see Hill v. Vrooman*, 152 N.E. 421 (N.Y. 1926) (court refuses to recognize common law marriage because no affirmative act after woman could not become common law wife). However, because they moved out of the state before Sally was free to marry, the removal of the impediment could not cause the common law marriage to come into existence because their new domicile did not recognize such marriages in any event.

Answer (D) is incorrect. This is not a good answer because Pennio is willing to recognize common law marriages under certain conditions. Here, however, the conditions were not met.

39. **Answer (D) is the best answer.** If indeed they met Minnegan requirements to establish a common law marriage and if indeed Illiana will recognize a common law marriage validly established in another jurisdiction, then Illiana should recognize this marriage and Mary should be treated as Lyle's widow. Otherwise, she will not be recognized as his widow.

    Answer (A) is incorrect. This is inaccurate. While the state has decided not to recognize such unions if contracted within the state, it has also decided to recognize them if contracted elsewhere. The issue here will be whether in fact a common law marriage was celebrated in another state and thus should be recognized in Illiana.

    Answer (B) is incorrect. Merely because they traveled together in a state that recognizes common law marriage may not be enough for them to be recognized as having that status. This will depend upon the law of the forum state as well as upon what the couple did while in the state recognizing common law marriages. *Compare Goldin v. Goldin*, 426 A.2d 410, 415 (Md. App. 1981) ("We are unwilling to hold that a man and woman who travel from this State into a State that recognizes common-law marriages and cohabit for a few days are thereby deemed, in the eyes of the law, to be man and wife, unless there is shown a clear intent to enter into that status."), *with Lieblein v. Charles Chips Inc.*, 301 N.Y.S.2d 743, 745 (App. Div. 1969) ("Respondent's attack on the validity of appellant's alleged common-law marriage is based on the duration of the couple's stay in Georgia, which was approximately one week. Georgia law appears to prescribe no particular period of cohabitation within its borders as a predicate for a common-law marriage.").

    Answer (C) is incorrect. Some states recognizing common law marriages do not require that the individuals be domiciled there in order to establish the union. *See Lieblein v. Charles Chips Inc.*, 301 N.Y.S.2d 743 (App. Div. 1969) (discussing Georgia law).

40. **Answer (C) is the best answer.** State laws differ with respect to this issue and Audra must find out what local law provides in this kind of case. *Compare In re Marriage of Hallgarth*, 2001 WL 574833, *4 (Tex. App.), *with Hill v. Vrooman*, 152 N.E. 421 (N. Y. 1926).

    Answer (A) is incorrect. While some states will recognize a common law marriage if all of the conditions have been met and any existing impediment to the marriage has been removed, *see In re Marriage of Hallgarth*, 2001 WL 574833, *4 (Tex. App.) ("if the circumstances creating the common law marriage occur while one party is married to another person, the common law marriage comes to fruition upon dissolution of that marriage"), others require that some additional affirmative act be performed once the two are capable of marrying each other. *See Hill v. Vrooman*, 152 N.E. 421 (N.Y. 1926) (court refuses to recognize common law marriage because there was no affirmative act after the impediment was removed and the woman could become a common law wife).

Answer (B) is incorrect. They would be able to establish a common law marriage once the impediment had been removed by performing some affirmative act recognizing that they were now able to do so. The issue presented here is whether such an affirmative act is required once there is no impediment to their marriage in order for them to contract a common law marriage.

Answer (D) is incorrect. If Zena is still living, Walter cannot marry again until he and Zena have officially dissolved their marriage. This would be true even if Walter and Zena had contracted a common law rather than a ceremonial marriage. *See Skipworth v. Skipworth*, 360 So.2d 975, 977 (Ala. 1978) ("the only ways to terminate a common-law marriage are by death or divorce").

41. To establish a common law marriage in a state recognizing such unions, the couple must: (1) treat each other as husband and wife, (2) hold themselves out as married, and (3) be capable of marrying each other. *See Metropolitan Life Ins. Co. v. Johnson*, 645 P.2d 356, 361 (Idaho 1982). While Abigail and Bernard seem to have met the criteria for having a common law marriage, and are domiciled in a state which recognizes such marriage, there is still one additional difficulty—their behavior did not change when they acquired the capacity to marry, *i.e.*, when Abigail's husband died. Among those jurisdictions recognizing common law marriage, some require an additional act when the impediment to the common law marriage has been removed, *see In re Garges Estate*, 378 A.2d 307, 309 (Pa. 1977), while others do not. *See Hess v. Hess*, 176 P.2d 804 (Okla. 1947). Here, it is simply unclear whether the common law marriage will be recognized because it is unclear whether the jurisdiction requires an affirmative act once the impediment has been removed. If Marylania has such a requirement and if indeed no such act took place, then the common law marriage will not be recognized.

42. Morris and Nancy treat each other as husband and wife, and hold themselves out as married, and thus meet two of the three criteria for establishing a common law marriage. *See Metropolitan Life Ins. Co. v. Johnson*, 645 P.2d 356, 361 (Idaho 1982). However, they also must be capable of marrying. Once Oscar was dead, there was no longer an impediment to their marriage. When Oscar died, Nancy and Morris recognized the importance of that event, as is evidenced by Nancy placing a ring on Morris's finger. At this point, their common law marriage should be recognized by the state, whether or not the state requires an affirmative act once the impediment to the marriage no longer exists. *See In re Garges Estate*, 378 A.2d 307, 309 (Pa. 1977). Because they have met the requirements of having a common law marriage and because West Marriagelandia recognizes such unions,

their marriage will be recognized and There When You Need Us will have to give Nancy the benefits due her.

TOPIC 9: CIVIL UNIONS

ANSWERS

43. **Answer (A) is the best answer**. *See* Vt. Stat. Ti. 15 sec. 1201(2) (" 'Civil union' means that two eligible persons have established a relationship pursuant to this chapter, and may receive the benefits and protections and be subject to the responsibilities of spouses.") & Vt. Stat. Ti. 15 sec. 1201(2) ("For a civil union to be established in Vermont, it shall be necessary that the parties to a civil union . . . [b]e of the same sex and therefore excluded from the marriage laws of this state.").

    Answer (B) is incorrect. This is false. The state does not have a separate category for marriages performed by a justice of the peace rather than a member of the clergy.

    Answer (C) is incorrect. While one might describe such a marriage as rather civil, this is not the meaning of the legal term.

    Answer (D) is incorrect. This is false. A common law marriage is a type of marriage whereas a civil union imposes the rights and benefits of marriage but is not itself a kind of marriage.

44. **Answer (B) is the best answer**. *See* Vt. Stat. Ti. 15 sec. 1206 (specifying the required procedure for the dissolution of civil unions).

    Answer (A) is incorrect. This is false. Just as would be true had they married, they need to go through a formal procedure to have their civil union dissolved. *See* Vt. Stat. Ti. 15 sec. 1206.

    Answer (C) is incorrect. This is false. *See* Vt. Stat. T. 15 sec. 1206. While reputation in the community is an element of common law marriage, *see Metropolitan Life Ins. Co. v. Johnson*, 645 P.2d 356, 361 (Idaho 1982), it has no bearing on the issue here.

    Answer (D) is incorrect. This is false both because they must go through a formal procedure and because they would continue to have the rights and obligations accompanying that status until the union was formally dissolved, just as would be true had they married. *See* Vt. Stat. Ti. 15 sec. 1206.

TOPIC 10: DIVORCE — ANSWERS

45. **Answer (B) is the best answer**. *See Grant v. Grant*, 765 So.2d 1263, 1267 (Miss. 2000) ("If either party, by reason of such conduct on the part of the other as would reasonably render the continuance of the marital relationship unendurable, or dangerous to life, health or safety, is compelled to leave the home and seek safety, peace and protection elsewhere, then the innocent one will ordinarily be justified in severing the marital relation and leaving the domicile of the other, so long as such conditions shall continue, and in such case the one so leaving will be not guilty of desertion. The one whose conduct caused the separation will be guilty of constructive desertion and if the condition is persisted in for a period of one year, the other party will be entitled to a divorce.").

    Answer (A) is incorrect. A divorce can be granted even though both parties are at fault, *see Heard v. Heard*, 424 So.2d 1177, 1179 (La. App. 1982), although it is not clear here that both parties are at fault.

    Answer (C) is incorrect. Alice could have been found at fault if she abandoned the marital home without adequate reason. Here, however, she had adequate reason, since it was dangerous for her to stay. *See Grant v. Grant*, 765 So.2d 1263, 1267 (Miss. 2000).

    Answer (D) is incorrect. Here, absent additional evidence, there would be no reason to find Alice unfit and hence no reason to remove her children from her care.

46. **Answer (C) is the best answer**. *See Sibley v. Sibley*, 693 So.2d 1270, 1271 (La. App. 1997) ("Even in this era of declining mores, adultery is usually not committed in the presence of witnesses. Thus in most cases where adultery is alleged, as in this case, only circumstantial evidence is offered to prove the allegations.").

    Answer (A) is incorrect. Some states preclude such testimony in an action for adultery, *see Lee v. Lee*, 378 N.Y.S.2d 459 (App. Div. 1976) (discussing provision precluding husband or wife testifying against the other in a divorce action based on adultery). In any event, such a requirement would be too strong in that it would preclude an action where adultery was witnessed by various people other than the spouse of the accused.

    Answer (B) is incorrect. There is no requirement that the spouse admit to an affair in order for a divorce to be granted on the ground of adultery. *See Harmon v. Harmon*, 757 So.2d 305 (Miss. App. 1999) (divorce granted on ground of adultery, husband's denial notwithstanding).

    Answer (D) is incorrect. *See Laccetti v. Laccetti*, 225 A.2d 266, 270 (Md. 1967) ("to support a finding of adultery there must be evidence of disposition as well as of opportunity"); *Reynolds v. Reynolds*, 755 So.2d 467, 469 (Miss. App. 1999) ("A charge of adultery may be established by showing an adulterous inclination coupled with an opportunity to consummate the inclination."), because otherwise it would be much too difficult a requirement to meet. *Cf. Sibley v. Sibley*, 693 So.2d 1270, 1271 (La. App. 1997). However, it should not be thought that this is an easy standard to meet. *See Bodne v. King*, 835 So.2d 52, 58 (Miss. 2003) ("Adultery, for example, requires clear and convincing proof."); *Seemann v. Seemann*, 355 S.E.2d 884, 886 (Va. 1987) ("One who alleges adultery has the burden of proving it by clear and convincing evidence.").

47. **Answer (A) is the best answer**. *Compare Scott v. Scott*, 586 A.2d 1140 (Vt. 1990) (married couple may meet standard even if living under same roof), *with Jackson v. Jackson*, 284 A.2d 654 (Md. App. 1971) (married couple cannot meet standard if living under same roof).

    Answer (B) is incorrect. Some jurisdictions will permit a divorce under these circumstances. *See Flynn v. Flynn*, 491 A.2d 156, 159 (Pa. Super. 1985) (Pennsylvania law does not require individuals to be living in separate residences to be living separate and apart.).

    Answer (C) is incorrect. Some jurisdictions require the separation. *See In re Marriage of Norviel*, 102 Cal. App. 4th 1152, 1162 (Ct. App. 2002) ("living apart physically is an indispensable threshold requirement to separation, whether or not it is sufficient, by itself, to establish separation").

    Answer (D) is incorrect. While this view has been suggested in some opinions, *see Schmidt v. Krug*, 624 A.2d 183, 185 (Pa. Super. 1993) ("the gravamen of the phrase 'separate and apart' becomes the existence of separate lives not separate roofs"), it is by no means universally held.

48. **Answer (B) is the best answer**. While they are maintaining separate residences, a court may well hold that having frequent relations indicates that there is hope that the marriage might continue and thus refuse to find that the couple is living separate and apart for purposes of getting a divorce. *See McClure v. McClure*, 172 S.W.2d 243 (Ark. 1943) (couple continuing to have sexual relations is not living separate and apart for purposes of divorce ground notwithstanding their maintaining separate residences).

    Answer (A) is incorrect. Living separate and apart implies more than maintaining separate residences; it also implies that the couple has ceased having marital relations. While occasional or isolated incidents may not toll the statutory period for living separate and apart, *see Smith v. Smith*, 564 S.E.2d 591, 592 (N.C. 2002) ("Isolated incidents of sexual intercourse between the parties shall not toll the statutory period required for divorce predicated on separation of one year."); *Thomas v. Thomas*, 483 A.2d 945, 948 (Pa. Super. 1984) ("instances of sexual relations during a separation period do not, without more, defeat a claim that the parties have lived separate and apart"), whether the couple is continuing to have sexual relations is also relevant here.

    Answer (C) is incorrect. The question the court will examine is whether their having relations precludes their having a divorce, *compare Smith v. Smith*, 564 S.E.2d

591 (N.C. 2002) *with McClure v. McClure*, 172 S.W.2d 243 (Ark. 1943). The court will not examine their post-divorce plans.

Answer (D) is incorrect. Many states will not toll the statutory period for an isolated occurrence for fear that couples would be induced not even to try to get back together. *See Smith v. Smith*, 564 S.E.2d 591 (N.C. 2002); *Thomas v. Thomas*, 483 A.2d 945 (Pa. Super. 1984).

49. **Answer (C) is the best answer**. This is a paradigmatic example of a ground that does not impute fault to either party.

    Answer (A) is incorrect. This is false. Even if the couple has agreed that their marriage is over, they still must meet one of the grounds established by the state, *e.g.*, living separate and apart for the relevant period. *See, e.g., Jackson v. Jackson*, 284 A.2d 654 (Md. App. 1971) (couple denied divorce because they failed to meet the statutory requirements for living separate and apart).

    Answer (B) is incorrect. This is false. A couple might be able to get a divorce on no-fault grounds even if both have committed marital faults. *See, e.g., Davis v. Davis*, 377 S.E.2d 640 (Va. App. 1989).

    Answer (D) is incorrect. This is false. Each party may blame the other for the breakdown of the marriage but they nonetheless might make use of a no-fault ground like irreconcilable differences. *See, e.g., Neidviecky v. Niedviecky*, 657 N.W.2d 255 (N.D. 2003) (divorce granted on basis of irreconcilable differences, although husband treated wife badly and wife was unfaithful to husband).

50. **Answer (A) is the best answer**. *See McLendon v. McLendon*, 169 So.2d 767, 769 (Ala. 1964) ("A decree of divorce from bed and board . . . is only a legal separation, the marriage continuing in regard to everything not necessarily withdrawn from its operation by the decree.").

    Answer (B) is incorrect. While husbands or wives may feel this way about their respective spouses, this is not what the term means.

    Answer (C) is incorrect. While decrees sometimes precluded an adulterous individual from remarrying during the life of the innocent spouse, *see, e.g., D'Arcangelo v. D'Arcangelo*, 102 N.Y.S.2d 100 (App. Div. 1951), that is not what is at issue here.

    Answer (D) is incorrect. Absolute divorce or divorce *a vinculo matrimonii* permits remarriage. *See Watkins v. Watkins*, 231 So.2d 904, 907 (Ala. Civ. App. 1970) (describing divorce *a vinculo matrimonii* as a total divorce of husband and wife, wholly releasing them from their marital duties).

51. **Answer (B) is the best answer**. *See Estin v. Estin*, 334 U.S. 541, 549 (1948) ("The result in this situation is to make the divorce divisible—to give effect to the Nevada decree insofar as it affects marital status and to make it ineffective on the issue of alimony.").

    Answer (A) is incorrect. A divisible divorce is a term of art which does not speak to whether individuals may get a legal separation but instead to the possibility that a court may be able to grant a divorce even if it does not have jurisdiction to award support or distribute the marital property. *See Rice v. Rice*, 336 U.S. 674, 679 (1949) (Jackson, J., dissenting) (describing divisible divorce as "a divorce good to end a marriage but invalid to affect dependent property rights").

Answer (C) is incorrect. While some states would impose such a disability on an adulterous spouse, *see, e.g., D'Arcangelo v. D'Arcangelo*, 102 N.Y.S.2d 100 (App. Div. 1951), that is not what the term involves.

Answer (D) is incorrect. This is false. A court may be able to issue a divorce decree but nonetheless not be able to make a finding concerning spousal support. *See Vanderbilt v. Vanderbilt*, 354 U.S. 416, 418-19 (1957) (suggesting that although a Nevada ex parte divorce was valid, "the Nevada divorce court was as powerless to cut off the wife's support right as it would have been to order the husband to pay alimony if the wife had brought the divorce action and he had not been subject to the divorce court's jurisdiction").

52. **Answer (C) is the best answer**. *See Holofcener v. Holofcener*, 219 A.2d 869 (Md. 1966); *Davis v. Davis*, 832 So.2d 492 (Miss. 2002).

    Answer (A) is incorrect. This is false. Various states permit adultery to be the ground for divorce even if the parties have already separated and even if the parties would not have reconciled even without the adulterous incident. *See Holofcener v. Holofcener*, 219 A.2d 869 (Md. 1966) (divorce granted on ground of adultery even though adultery committed during period of separation); *Davis v. Davis*, 832 So.2d 492, 496 (Miss. 2002) ("It has never been required that the adultery be causally related to the final separation of the parties to be a valid basis for granting a divorce.").

    Answer (B) is incorrect. This is false. Whether or not Olga would have done this if she had met the right person, the fact remains that she did not commit adultery and Oscar did.

    Answer (D) is incorrect. This is false. In many states, Olga would be able to use this ground as a basis for divorce.

53. **Answer (C) is the best answer**. *See Gee v. Gee*, 39 So.2d 406 (Ala. 1949). *See Gee v. Gee*, 39 So.2d 406, 408 (Ala. 1949) ("It is our view that if the court has jurisdiction over the res because the respondent is a resident of Alabama, it would be immaterial by virtue of the proviso whether complainant was such a resident when the bill was filed, or that he had been for twelve months.").

    Answer (A) is incorrect. Because Sonny is a Pennio domiciliary, the action can be filed, even though Sarah is not a Pennio domiciliary. *See Gee v. Gee*, 39 So.2d 406, 408 (Ala. 1949) (if respondent is a domiciliary, it is not necessary for the complainant also to be a domiciliary in order for the court to have jurisdiction to grant a divorce).

    Answer (B) is incorrect. This is false. Pennio courts will be deciding whether a divorce will be granted and they can decide in light of local law. *See Gee v. Gee*,

39 So.2d 406 (Ala. 1949) (applying local law to determine whether the divorce should be granted).

Answer (D) is incorrect. The court's personal jurisdiction over both parties will not suffice if neither of the parties is domiciled in the state. Unless at least one of the parties is domiciled in the state, the state will not have jurisdiction to grant the divorce. *See Gee v. Gee*, 39 So.2d 406 (Ala 1949).

54. **Answer (D) is the best answer**. *See, e.g., In re Roedell's Estate*, 112 N.W.2d 842 (Iowa 1962) (wife entitled to be treated as surviving widow when she had no notice of divorce and her address had been known by husband).

    Answer (A) is incorrect. The question here is whether the divorce was valid, not whether the marital assets were divided equitably.

    Answer (B) is incorrect. This is false. Andrew filed for divorce in Hawifornia and he is a Hawifornia domiciliary. The correct law to apply is that of Hawifornia rather than Washegon.

    Answer (C) is incorrect. While it is true that Alice would have learned of Andrew's intentions if she had bought a subscription to the local paper, Andrew knew where Alice was living. Publication in the local paper would not be adequate notice in this case. *See Corrigan v. Corrigan*, 184 So.2d 664 (Fla. App. 1966) (fundamental due process required that notice of suit be mailed to defendant at known address).

55. **Answer (C) is the best answer**. *See, e.g., Estate of Hafner*, 184 Cal. App. 3d 1371 (Ct. App. 1986) (dividing estate between putative spouse and surviving spouse and her children).

    Answer (A) is incorrect. Even if she had committed adultery, this might have established a ground for the divorce but would not have established the validity of the divorce.

    Answer (B) is incorrect. While Alice's due process rights were not respected, Betina might be able to collect some of the proceeds as a putative spouse if she had believed in good faith that she and Andrew were validly married. *Cf. Estate of Leslie*, 689 P.2d 133, 136 n.4 (Cal. 1984) ("A putative marriage is one in which at least one of the parties to an invalid marriage has a good faith belief that the marriage is valid.").

    Answer (D) is incorrect. There is no requirement that a putative spouse can collect only if children are born of the putative marriage. *See King v. Cancienne*, 316 So.2d 366 (La. 1975) (putative husband allowed to collect damages for wrongful death notwithstanding that no children were born of the marriage).

56. **Answer (B) is the best answer**. *See Self v. Self*, 893 S.W.2d 775 (Ark. 1995) (first wife barred by laches from asserting her rights after waiting for 24 years).

    Answer (A) is incorrect. While Betina never validly married Andrew, that does not settle the issue. She may nonetheless be entitled to some of the proceeds as a putative spouse or perhaps by pleading laches.

Answer (C) is incorrect. While Betina might collect as a putative spouse, that is not her only avenue of recovery. The court may preclude Alice from challenging the marriage because she sat on her rights for so long. *See Brown v. Brown*, 274 Cal. App. 2d 178 (Ct. App. 1969) (wife barred from challenging validity of subsequent marriage about which she had known for many years).

Answer (D) is incorrect. This is false. The determination will not simply be made in terms of which spouse lived with the individual for a longer period. *See, e.g., Caruso v. Lucius*, 448 S.W.2d 711 (Tex. Civ. App. 1970) (first wife entitled to some proceeds after husband's death notwithstanding that putative wife had lived with him for a much longer period than had his first wife).

57. **Answer (B) is the best answer**. *See Pacheo v. Pacheo*, 246 So.2d 778, 782 (Fla. 1970) (upholding constitutionality of denial of spousal support to adulterous spouse); *Collier v. Collier*, 183 S.E.2d 769 (Ga. 1971) (sustaining custodial award to husband because of wife's adultery); *see Schreier v. Schreier*, 625 S.W.2d 644, 650 (Mo. App. 1981) (fault can be taken into account in distribution of marital property).

    Answer (A) is incorrect. Marital fault might also affect spousal support or the property distribution. *See, e.g., Coggin v. Coggin*, 837 So.2d 772, 776 (Miss. App. 2003) (specifically noting that marital fault is a consideration in determining spousal support).

    Answer (C) is incorrect. *See Schreier v. Schreier*, 625 S.W.2d 644 (Mo. App. 1981).

    Answer (D) is incorrect. *See Collier v. Collier*, 183 S.E.2d 769 (Ga. 1971). Further, the adultery might be considered as a factor militating in favor of the finding that the children's best interests would be promoted by awarding custody to the non-adulterous parent. *See Gustaves v. Gustaves*, 57 P.2d 775, 780-81 (Idaho 2002).

58. **Answer (C) is the best answer**. *See M.T. v. J.T.*, 355 A.2d 204 (N.J. App. 1976) (recognizing marriage between man and postoperative male-to-female transsexual).

    Answer (A) is incorrect. State courts deciding whether to recognize marriages involving post-operative transsexuals have thought it important to decide in light of how the state defined the sex of the transsexual. *See, e.g., In re Estate of Gardiner*, 42 P.3d 120 (Kan. 2002), and *Littleton v. Prange*, 9 S.W.3d 223 (Tex. App. 1999).

    Answer (B) is incorrect. This is false. *See M.T. v. J.T.*, 355 A.2d 204 (N.J. App. 1976) (recognizing marriage between man and postoperative male-to-female transsexual).

    Answer (D) is incorrect. This is false. *See M.T. v. J.T.*, 355 A.2d 204 (N.J. App. 1976) (recognizing marriage between man and postoperative male-to-female transsexual).

59. Jurisdictions vary with respect to what is required for a couple to live separate and apart for purposes of establishing that state's divorce ground. Some will require no sexual contact for the relevant period while others will permit an occasional sexual interlude without requiring that the clock begin again. *Compare Fletcher v. Fletcher*,

474 S.E.2d 802, 804 (N.C. 1996) (isolated incidents of sexual relations does not constitute resumption of marital relations), *with Santostefano v. Santostefano*, 712 S.W.2d 324, 326 (Ark. App. 1986) (parties must live separate and apart for relevant period without sexual intercourse). If the jurisdiction requires that sexual relations have not taken place, then the divorce on this ground will be denied. If the jurisdiction permits isolated incidents, then the question will be whether their relations will be viewed as too frequent and thus a resumption of marital relations. If the parties are viewed as having resumed marital relations, then they will have to assert some other ground for the divorce or, perhaps, wait until they have met the requirements for living separate and apart.

60. In order for a divorce to be granted, both the residency and the domicile requirements must be met. These are separate requirements and one can meet one without meeting the other. While many cases involve someone who meets the residency requirement without also meeting the domicile requirement, *see Williams v. North Carolina*, 325 U.S. 226 (1945), it is possible for the domicile but not the residency requirement to be met in a particular case unless, e.g., local law defines the two as synonymous. *Compare Ross v. Ross*, 208 So.2d 194 (Miss. 1968) (residence and domicile are synonymous for purposes of divorce), *with Robinson v. Robinson*, 67 A.2d 273 (Pa. 1949) (suggesting that the two are distinguishable in that residence speaks to physical presence while domicile speaks to intent). Here, it is simply unclear whether local rules require that the individual have been residing there, e.g., for the last 60 days, *cf.* Ark. Stat. sec. 9-12-307 (specifying that the plaintiff or defendant must have resided in the state 60 days prior to the commencement of the action), and thus unclear whether the state's residency requirement has been met.

61. While Oscar may well be correct that Olga had not established domicile in Lasnevania, he should have contested the divorce there. Because he was served in the state and nonetheless elected not to appear, he has lost his opportunity to challenge the divorce and it should be given full faith and credit. *See Cook v. Cook*, 342 U.S. 126, 128 (1951) (defendant who is personally served in state would be barred from collaterally attacking divorce decree in another state). Oscar will be unsuccessful in his attempt to contest the divorce now and the marital assets will have to be divided.

TOPIC 11: DIVORCE DEFENSES

ANSWERS

62. **Answer (A) is the best answer.** *See Cain v. Cain*, 795 So.2d 614, 617 (Miss. App. 2001) (in divorce proceedings, collusion is an agreement between husband and wife that one of them shall commit or appear to have committed acts constituting a cause of divorce, for the purpose of enabling the other to obtain a divorce).

    Answer (B) is incorrect. *See Hollis v. Hollis*, 427 S.E.2d 233, 235 (Va. App. 1993) (condonation is one spouse's forgiveness of the other spouse's misconduct, usually evidenced by resumption and continuation of matrimonial relations).

    Answer (C) is incorrect. The contract might well be treated as void because it violates public policy. *See Schulz v. Fox*, 345 P.2d 1045, 1050 (Mont. 1959) (any agreement, the purpose of which is to facilitate the granting of a divorce without proper grounds existing, is void).

    Answer (D) is incorrect. This is inaccurate. *See Brandt v. Brandt*, 33 N.W.2d 620, 623 (N.D. 1948) (recrimination involves a showing by the defendant of any cause of divorce against the plaintiff).

63. **Answer (C) is the best answer.** This is an example of connivance. *See Hollis v. Hollis*, 427 S.E.2d 233, 235 (Va. App. 1993) ("Connivance is the consent, either expressed or implied, of one spouse to the proposed misconduct of the other spouse. One who consents to another's misconduct may not seek a divorce based on the misconduct.").

    Answer (A) is incorrect. Laches involves a delay in enforcing one's rights. *See Dorsett v. Moore*, 61 P.3d 1221, 1224 (Wyo. 2003) ("Laches is defined as such delay in enforcing one's rights that it works to the disadvantage of another.").

    Answer (B) is incorrect. Condonation involves forgiveness of a marital breach. *See Hollis v. Hollis*, 427 S.E.2d 233, 235 (Va. App. 1993).

    Answer (D) is incorrect. This conduct is not an example of recrimination. *See Davis v. Davis*, 377 S.E.2d 640, 643 (Va. App. 1989) ("If the plaintiff alleges misconduct that will constitute grounds for a divorce from the bonds of matrimony, his or her application may be barred, in recrimination, by proof that he or she was guilty of conduct that could be a basis for the defendant to obtain a divorce from the bonds of matrimony.").

64. **Answer (A) is the best answer.** Recrimination involves an assertion by defendant that plaintiff has committed a marital fault which could be the basis of divorce. *See Davis v. Davis*, 377 S.E.2d 640, 643 (Va. App. 1989).

    Answer (B) is incorrect. Recrimination involves a charge that the plaintiff was also at fault, see *Davis*, 377 S.E.2d at 643, but does not require that the individual committed the fault more than once. *See Surbey v. Surbey*, 360 S.E.2d 873 (Va. App. 1987) (single act of extreme cruelty sufficed for purposes of recrimination).

Answer (C) is incorrect. The marital fault need not rise to the level of being criminal. Adultery would be a ground for divorce even if the statute prohibiting adultery has been repealed. *See, e.g.*, 17 Me. Rev. Stat. Ann. sec. 101 (former adultery statute repealed) and 19 Me. Rev. Stat. Ann. sec. 902(1)(a) (adultery is ground for divorce).

Answer (D) is incorrect. There is no general requirement that a marital fault must occur more than once in order for it to be a ground for divorce. *See, e.g., Surbey v. Surbey*, 360 S.E.2d 873 (Va. App. 1987).

65. **Answer (B) is the best answer**. *See Davis v. Davis*, 377 S.E.2d 640, 643 (Va. App. 1989) ("[T]he husband's suit on the ground of willful desertion was proven, but that the defense of cruelty, in recrimination, bars the granting of a divorce to him. We further hold that the wife's suit on the ground of cruelty was proven, but that the defense of desertion, in recrimination, bars the granting of a divorce to her. Because both parties were at fault, the only ground for divorce is their separation. The trial court properly refused to grant either party a divorce based upon fault, but granted the divorce on the ground that the parties had lived separate and apart without any cohabitation or interruption for one year."). *But see R.G.M v. D.E.M.*, 410 S.E.2d 564, 567 (S.C. 1991) ("the defense of recrimination does not constitute an exception to the statute barring alimony").

    Answer (A) is incorrect. Were another marital fault subsequently committed, the parties could divorce. Further, they might be able to divorce on a no-fault ground such as living separate and apart for the requisite period. *See Davis v. Davis*, 377 S.E.2d 640 (Va. App. 1989).

    Answer (C) is incorrect. This is inaccurate. Recrimination is a defense in divorce, *see Davis*, 377 S.E.2d at 643, and thus does not speak to whether any crimes have been committed or could be prosecuted.

    Answer (D) is incorrect. This is false because it can affect whether support will be paid. In some jurisdictions, a defense of recrimination will remove the fault ground for divorce. If the divorce is granted without a showing of fault, then support might be ordered whereas had fault been established, e.g., because the defense of recrimination was not established, then there might be no support award. *See Surbey v. Surbey*, 360 S.E.2d 873, 875 (Va. App. 1987) ("We hold that because neither party is entitled to successfully assert adultery as a ground for divorce, and because there was a finding supported by the evidence that both parties were at fault in causing the separation, there did not exist a ground for divorce under any other section of the Code except [living separate and apart]. The right to spousal support is not affected by an award of a no-fault divorce since neither party's duty of support is affected absent a finding of fault on one party or the other.").

66. **Answer (D) is the best answer**. *See Tesch v. Tesch*, 399 N.W.2d 880, 883 (S.D. 1987) ("continuation of cohabitation, marital relations, and passive endurance,

absent an express agreement to condone, was insufficient to support a finding of condonation").

Answer (A) is incorrect. By forgiving Kathy, Ken did not forever give up his right to get a divorce. Were she to resume the past pattern of infidelity, he would have grounds for divorce. *See Padova v. Padova*, 183 A.2d 227, 229 (Vt. 1962) ("[C]ondonation is a doctrine of conditional forgiveness. Marital relations accomplishes the forgiveness, but with the continuance of the marriage the obligation is then on the forgiven partner to desist from the misconduct."). Here, he did have marital relations one more time but did not forgive her and it is simply unclear what courts would do, i.e., it is unclear whether this sole act of marital relations would be held to constitute condonation.

Answer (B) is incorrect. Once the spouse's fault has been forgiven, that fault will no longer be a ground for divorce. The question here is whether the resumption of marital relations that single time would constitute forgiveness. *See Prytherch v. Prytherch*, 247 N.Y.S.2d 579, 581 (App. Div. 1964) ("While a single act of sexual intercourse may not establish condonation as a matter of law, we are of the opinion that such an act is some evidence of forgiveness, and that it should not be held as a matter of law that under no circumstances may a finding of condonation be based upon a single act.").

Answer (C) is incorrect. This is inaccurate. Condonation of a past fault does not mean permission to do it again. *See Dorsey v. Dorsey*, 227 A.2d 617, 618 (Md. 1967) ("Condonation is forgiveness with the implied condition that the marital offenses shall not be repeated and the offended shall be treated with conjugal kindness, and, as in this case, where the husband breaches this condition by maintaining his illicit relationship, the right to the remedy for former marital offenses revives."). The question at hand is whether the resumption of marital relations on a single occasion will be viewed as forgiveness. This varies within the states. *Cf. Malloy v. Malloy*, 234 S.E.2d 199, 202 (N. C. App. 1977) ("Voluntary sexual intercourse by the innocent spouse, with knowledge or reason to know that the other has committed adultery, usually operates as a condonation of the offense."); *Tigert v. Tigert*, 595 P.2d 815, 818 (Okla. App. 1979) ("When the parties resume cohabitation and sexual intercourse after the condoning spouse learns of the offense, and there are no further offenses, condonation is implied.").

67. If Katrina can establish that John has committed adultery, she can offer the defense of recrimination, which basically means that the other partner has also committed a marital fault which provides a ground for ending the marriage. The defense of recrimination, where established, might prevent the couple from getting a divorce or, instead, might merely prevent one of the members of the couple from securing benefits based on the other partner's wrongdoing. *See Hartstern v. Hartstern*, 224 S.W.2d 447, 449 (Ky. 1949) ("Recrimination is a complete bar to the right of a party to obtain a divorce, although he may have established the grounds supporting his charge by conclusive evidence. It is strictly a plea in defense of an action, and may be established by showing that the plaintiff has been guilty of such conduct toward the defendant as, standing alone, would justify the Court in granting a divorce to the defendant."); *Burns v. Burns*, 400 P.2d 642, 645 (Mont. 1965) ("[W]hen the

trial court, as here, has found that both parties to a divorce action have established grounds for divorce and it further finds that the legitimate objects of marriage have been destroyed, it may, in its discretion, award a divorce to both parties."). It is thus unclear whether Katrina's successfully establishing the defense of recrimination will preclude their divorce or instead will merely prevent Katrina from bearing the burden imposed on the party at fault. This will depend upon Punitania's law.

68. Melissa has committed a marital fault by having an affair. However, Douglas has verbally forgiven her and, further, has had sexual relations with her since then. Her adultery has been condoned and can no longer be a basis for divorce. *See Tigert v. Tigert*, 595 P.2d 815, 819 (Okla. App. 1979) ("Condonation having been shown, its effect was to bar a divorce for adultery."). Where Melissa has done all that she can to make the marriage work and Douglas is at least as much at fault for the eventual breakdown of the marriage, her condoned marital fault cannot be used as the basis for the divorce. *See id.* at 820-21 (where "the fault for the troubles since the condonation lies as much with the complaining spouse as with the errant spouse, it should not grant a divorce on the ground of the condoned offense"). The court will presumably grant the divorce on the ground suggested by Melissa rather than by Douglas.

TOPIC 12: RECOGNITION OF FOREIGN MARRIAGES AND DIVORCES

ANSWERS

69. **Answer (D) is the best answer**. Because William did not establish domicile in Nevada, the Nevada court did not have jurisdiction to grant the divorce. *See Williams v. North Carolina*, 325 U.S. 226 (1945) (Nevada divorce decree not entitled to full faith and credit because neither party to the divorce had been domiciled in Nevada).

    Answer (A) is incorrect. This is not a particularly persuasive argument. Even if both had committed adultery, this might not preclude the divorce.

    Answer (B) is incorrect. This is not a particularly persuasive argument. Even if William had been at fault and Wanda had not been, this might not preclude a divorce on no-fault grounds.

    Answer (C) is incorrect. This is not a particularly persuasive argument, since the Nevada court does not need to have personal jurisdiction over her in order to grant a divorce. *See Estin v. Estin*, 334 U.S. 541 (1948).

70. **Answer (B) is the best answer**. Because Paul made an appearance in Nevada to litigate the jurisdictional question, the decree is subject to full faith and credit guarantees. *See Boudreau v. Welch*, 192 So.2d 356 (La. 1966) (where wife sues husband for divorce and husband makes an appearance, the divorce decree must be given full faith and credit).

    Answer (A) is incorrect. However, it would have been correct if Paul had not made an appearance in Nevada. *See Williams v. North Carolina*, 325 U.S. 226 (1945).

    Answer (C) is incorrect. For residency purposes, the relevant requirement is that of Nevada rather than that of Illinois, since a Nevada court was issuing the decree.

    Answer (D) is incorrect. The issue has already been litigated and the court should not be making a determination of her domicile for purposes of determining the validity of the Nevada judgment. *See Dusesoi v. Dusesoi*, 498 So.2d 1348 (Fla. App. 1986) (where wife made special appearance in Texas court to contest jurisdiction and the court rejected her claim that it had no jurisdiction, the divorce decree issued by the Texas court is entitled to full faith and credit).

71. **Answer (D) is the best answer**. The husband might be estopped from challenging the validity of the decree, *see In re Marriage of Gryka*, 413 N.E.2d 153 (Ill. App. 1980) (husband estopped from challenging the validity of his own divorce), although the court might refuse to estop him from challenging it. *See Wampler v. Wampler*, 170 P.2d 316 (Wash. 1946) (wife not estopped from challenging validity of her own divorce).

    Answer (A) is incorrect. Full faith and credit is not owed to judgments from other countries. *See Magner v. Hobby*, 215 F.2d 190, 193 (2d Cir. 1954) ("As this divorce was granted by a court in a foreign country there is no constitutional requirement that it be given the full faith and credit which should in one state be given to the judgment of a court of a sister state.").

Answer (B) is incorrect. *See, e.g., Christopher v. Christopher*, 31 S.E.2d 818 (Ga. 1944) (refusing to recognize foreign divorce decree out of comity where the latter court did not have jurisdiction to issue the judgment).

Answer (C) is incorrect. A marriage might be declared void even if a child had been born to the putative marriage. *See Henderson v. Henderson*, 46 S.E.2d 10 (Va. 1948) (declaring marriage void notwithstanding that a child had been born to the couple).

72. **Answer (D) is the best answer**. *See Estate of Anderson*, 60 Cal. App. 4th 436, 440 (Ct. App. 1997) (Estoppel "prevents a person from acting in a manner inconsistent with his former position or conduct to the injury of another.").

Answer (A) is incorrect. This is false. Because Betty Lou has established domicile in Texarkana, the Texarkana courts have jurisdiction to grant the divorce and can do so in light of local law. *Brady v. Brady*, 158 S.E.2d 359, 365 (W. Va. 1967) ("Unless a divorce decree from a foreign state is attacked on jurisdictional grounds a sister state must give it full faith and credit under the provisions of that clause of the Constitution of the United States."); *cf. Rosenstiel v. Rosenstiel*, 209 N.E.2d 709 (N.Y. 1965) (recognizing foreign divorce on grounds not recognized locally). The state will have jurisdiction over the divorce if one of the parties is domiciled there and has met the relevant residence requirement. *See Johnson v. Muelberger*, 340 U.S. 581, 585 (1951) ("domicile of one party to a divorce creates an adequate relationship with the state to justify its exercise of power over the marital relation").

Answer (B) is incorrect. This is false because the court could recognize another state's law out of comity. *See Hawsey v. Louisiana Dept. of Social Services*, 934 S.W.2d 723, 726 (Tex. App. 1996) ("Comity is a principle under which the courts of one state give effect to the laws of another state or extend immunity to a sister sovereign not as a rule of law, but rather out of deference or respect.")

Answer (C) is incorrect. While the court could look at Lorsiona law with respect to this issue, it would not be required to do so, since its own law would govern whether a divorce could be granted. *Cf. Williams v. North Carolina*, 317 U.S. 287 (1942) (Nevada divorce applying local law entitled to full faith and credit, notwithstanding its contravening another state's public policy, if the Nevada court had jurisdiction to issue the decree).

73. **Answer (A) is the best answer**. While Nevada only has a six-week residency requirement before the divorce action can be commenced, *see* Nev. Stat. 125.020, Donald would have to have been domiciled in Nevada for the divorce decree to be entitled to full faith and credit. When Donna challenges Donald's divorce and remarriage, the Caloregon court will likely treat both as invalid and hold that Donna is Donald's lawful widow. *See Still v. Sunderman*, 77 N.W.2d 629 (Iowa 1956) (where state does not have jurisdiction to grant divorce, divorce and subsequent remarriage will be treated as null and void and first wife will be treated as lawful widow).

Answer (B) is incorrect. This is false. Donna could wait and challenge the marriage later. Further, the fact that Donald had died would not bar a challenge to the invalidity of the marriage. *See Still v. Sunderman*, 77 N.W.2d 629 (Iowa 1956). While there is a certain period of time after which the plaintiff will be denied the opportunity to challenge the marriage because of laches, here she only waited a matter of months and thus would not be so barred. *See, e.g., Loiacono v. Loiacono*, 116 A.2d 881 (Pa. Super. 1955) (laches not a bar even though plaintiff waited six years before commencing suit to challenge divorce).

Answer (C) is incorrect. This is false. A void marriage cannot be ratified. *See Kleinfield v. Veruki*, 372 S.E.2d 407, 409 (Va. App. 1988) ("A void marriage may not be ratified and may be attacked, either collaterally or directly, either before or after the death of the parties."). This marriage would be subject to challenge whether or not Donald had lived with Carrie in Caloregon.

Answer (D) is incorrect. While Donna will be recognized as Donald's lawful widow, this is not because Donald and Carrie had failed to live together for six months in the state. Even had they done so, their marriage still would not have been valid. *See Kleinfield v. Veruki*, 372 S.E.2d 407 (Va. App. 1988); *Loiacono v. Loiacono*, 116 A.2d 881 (Pa. Super. 1955); and *Still v. Sunderman*, 77 N.W.2d 629 (Iowa 1956).

74. **Answer (C) is the best answer**. *See, e.g., Hesington v. Hesington's Estate*, 640 S.W.2d 824, 826 (Mo. App. 1982) (as a matter of comity, Missouri will recognize a marriage valid where contracted unless to do so would violate the public policy of this state).

    Answer (A) is incorrect. This is false. *See In re Estate of Toutant*, 633 N.W.2d 692 (Wis. App. 2001) (rejecting that Wisconsin is required to give full faith and credit to marriage of Wisconsin resident celebrated in Texas).

    Answer (B) is incorrect. This is false. Merely because a marriage is prohibited locally does not mean that it cannot be recognized if it has been validly celebrated elsewhere. *See Mazzolini v. Mazzolini*, 155 N.E.2d 206 (Ohio 1958) (recognizing marriage between first cousins celebrated in Massachusetts even though it could not have been celebrated in Ohio); *Mason v. Mason*, 775 N.E.2d 706 (Ind. App. 2002) (recognizing marriage between first cousins celebrated in Tennessee even thought the marriage could not have been celebrated in Indiana).

    Answer (D) is incorrect. *See Farah v. Farah*, 429 S.E.2d 626, 629 (Va. App. 1993) ("A marriage that is valid under the law of the state or country where it is celebrated is valid in Virginia, unless it is repugnant to public policy.")

75. For a state to have jurisdiction to grant a divorce, at least one of the parties must have met the residency requirement and at least one of the parties must be domiciled in the state. *See Johnson v. Muelberger*, 340 U.S. 581 (1951). Here, although Wendy has met the residency requirement, neither she nor Walter is domiciled in Tennio so the Tennio court did not have jurisdiction to grant the divorce and the divorce need not be given full faith and credit. Without a valid divorce, Wendy

and Walter are still legally married and Wendy will have committed adultery if she voluntarily had sexual relations with Thomas while she was still married to Walter.

76. States differ about whether adoptive siblings can marry without violating the incest ban. In *Israel v. Allen*, 577 P.2d 762 (Colo. 1978), the Colorado Supreme Court recognized the marriage of a brother and adoptive sister. However, other states specifically prohibit marriages between individuals within the prohibited degrees of consanguinity or affinity even if one of the individuals was adopted and is not related by blood. *See* Ill. St. Ch. 750 sec. 5/212; Minn. Stat. sec. 517.03. Even if the marriage cannot be celebrated locally, however, all may not be lost. A separate question is whether the marriage will be recognized locally, even if violating local law, if it was validly celebrated elsewhere. *Compare* N.M. Stat. 40-1-4 ("All marriages celebrated beyond the limits of this state, which are valid according to the laws of the country wherein they were celebrated or contracted, shall be likewise valid in this state, and shall have the same force as if they had been celebrated in accordance with the laws in force in this state."), *with* Ga. Stat. sec. 19-3-43 ("All marriages solemnized in another state by parties intending at the time to reside in this state shall have the same legal consequences and effect as if solemnized in this state. Parties residing in this state may not evade any of the laws of this state as to marriage by going into another state for the solemnization of the marriage ceremony."). To answer whether Coloming will recognize the marriage, one must know whether Coloming prohibits such marriages to be celebrated within the state and, if so, whether it is nonetheless willing to recognize the union if validly celebrated elsewhere.

TOPIC 13: PROPERTY — ANSWERS

77. **Answer (D) is the best answer**. This is an example of dissipation. *See In re Marriage of Shuster*, 586 N.E.2d 1345, 1360 (Ill. App. 1992) ("Dissipation of marital assets occurs when a spouse (1) uses marital property (2) for his or her own benefit for a purpose unrelated to the marriage (3) at the time when the marriage is in serious jeopardy or undergoing an irreconcilable breakdown.").

    Answer (A) is incorrect. While Samuel might not enjoy the painting, it may well be a good investment and thus would not constitute dissipation. Dissipation involves the frivolous spending of marital assets. *See Bojrab v. Bojrab*, 786 N.E.2d 713, 726 (Ind. App. 2003).

    Answer (B) is incorrect. While the result may not have been desired, this would not count as dissipation. Promoting good relations with one's in-laws would promote the marriage and would seem unlikely to be attempted when the marriage was coming to an end. *See Bratcher v. Bratcher*, 26 S.W.3d 797, 799 (Ky. App. 2000) (To establish dissipation, one must establish that the "dissipation occurred during a separation or when dissolution was pending and that there was a clear intent on the part of the dissipator to deprive the spouse of marital assets.").

    Answer (C) is incorrect. Here, there seems to be a good faith attempt to increase marital wealth which is unsuccessful because of unanticipated difficulties. It would have been different if the investment were made in highly speculative stocks. *See Gadomski v. Gadomski*, 664 N.Y.S.2d 886, 888 (App. Div. 1997) (husband dissipated assets when investing in highly speculative stocks).

78. **Answer (B) is the best answer**. Assuming that the jurisdiction permits separate property to be distributed, *see Carson v. Carson*, 436 P.2d 7 (Haw. 1967) (suggesting that separate property can be distributed to promote equity), the court might indirectly bring it about that Jill receives the proceeds from the property or the property itself, *see Miller v. Miller*, 441 N.Y.S.2d 339, 341 (Super. Ct. 1981) ("The court holds that while it may not affect title to real property situated outside the State of New York, it may make an equitable distribution thereof and order one of the parties to convey same"), even if the court could not simply award the property to Jill. *See Bondurant v. Bondurant*, 283 A.2d 26, 28 (D.C. 1971) ("A District of Columbia court has no power to enter a judgment dissolving title to real estate in another jurisdiction.").

    Answer (A) is incorrect. Even if the jurisdiction permits separate property to be distributed, awarding real property to Jill which is located in another state will likely be viewed as beyond the court's power. *See Bondurant v. Bondurant*, 283 A.2d 26, 28 (D.C. 1971) ("A District of Columbia court has no power to enter a judgment dissolving title to real estate in another jurisdiction.").

Answer (C) is incorrect. This is false, since some jurisdictions will permit a court to distribute separate property in the interest of promoting equity. Here, the court might order Jack to sell the property and split the proceeds. *See Miller v. Miller*, 441 N.Y.S.2d 339 (Sup. Ct. 1981).

Answer (D) is incorrect. If indeed children were born of the marriage, custody should be awarded in light of what would best promote the interests of the children. It should not be awarded to punish a parent. *See Durham v. Durham*, 2003 WL 21398903 (Ark. App.).

79. **Answer (A) is the best answer**. The court might well do this. *See Ware v. Ware*, 748 A.2d 1031 (Md. App. 2000) (treating lottery winnings during separation as marital).

    Answer (B) is incorrect. This is false, since many jurisdictions would treat the winnings as marital property. However, a separate issue is whether each party would be entitled to half of the winnings. *See Alston v. Alston*, 629 A.2d 70 (Md. 1990) (holding in case involving similar circumstances that the wife should not receive half of the winnings).

    Answer (C) is incorrect. This is false. *See Ware v. Ware*, 748 A.2d 1031 (Md. App. 2000) (dividing some of the lottery winnings that would be distributed after the divorce was final).

    Answer (D) is incorrect. While fault may play a role in how the assets are distributed, *see In re Letende*, 815 A.2d 938, 942 (N. H. 2002) (noting with approval that fault had played a role in the trial court's division of property pursuant to a divorce), it does not play a role in determining whether the asset is marital or separate.

80. **Answer (D) is the best answer**. Property acquired by gift or descent during the marriage is non-marital but property acquired during the marriage using marital funds is marital property. *See* Ill. Stat. Ch. 750 sec. 5/503(a) (defining marital property).

    Answer (A) is incorrect. While both were acquired during the marriage, that does not make the painting marital property, since it was acquired by bequest. For a definition of marital property, *see* Ill. Stat. Ch. 750 sec. 5/503(a).

    Answer (B) is incorrect. For purposes of distinguishing between marital and separate property, the question is how and when they were acquired rather than who uses them. *See* Ill. Stat. Ch. 750 sec 5/503(a) (defining marital and non-marital property).

    Answer (C) is incorrect. This is false. The car was acquired with marital funds and thus is marital property, absent evidence that it was given to John as a gift. *See, e.g., Jablonski v. Jalonski*, 25 S.W.3d 433 (Ark. App. 2000) (cars bought with marital funds were marital property).

81. **Answer (A) is the best answer**. Items that are bought with marital funds are marital property unless they have been made gifts. *See Batson v. Batson*, 769 S.W.2d 849, 856 (Tenn. App. 1988) ("gifts by one spouse to another of property that would

otherwise be classified as marital property are the separate property of the recipient spouse").

Answer (B) is incorrect. The question here is not who ultimately will get the cars but whether their value should be accounted for in the marital distribution. Because they are marital property (absent evidence that they have been made gifts), their value should be taken into account in the distribution of marital assets. *Cf. Ott v. Ott*, 2001 WL 32675 (Va. App.) (treating antique car collection as marital and granting wife 50% of its value).

Answer (C) is incorrect. This is false. The salaries earned during the marriage are marital, absent agreement to the contrary. *See* Ill. Stat. Ch. 750 sec. 5/503(a).

Answer (D) is incorrect. The question here is not whether she should get the car but whether its value should be accounted for in the distribution of other assets. Even if she does not want to drive it, her share of the marital estate should reflect that he received (all of) the Ferrari. *See, e.g., Roe v. Roe*, 429 S.E.2d 830, 832-33 (S. C. App. 1993) (awarding husband and wife their respective cars but including the value of those cars in the calculation regarding the distribution of the other marital property).

82. **Answer (D) is the best answer**. This is the least likely scenario. Much more would have to be shown to establish that this was Abigail's intent. *Cf. Browning v. Browning*, 551 S.W.2d 823, 825 (Ky. App. 1975) ("The burden is on the Appellant to prove by clear and convincing proof that he acquired his interest by gift.").

    Answer (A) is incorrect. This is a possible outcome if Abigail can show that Arnold's contributions were intended as gifts. *See Batson v. Batson*, 769 S.W.2d 849, 856 (Tenn. App. 1988) ("gifts by one spouse to another of property that would otherwise be classified as marital property are the separate property of the recipient spouse").

    Answer (B) is incorrect. This is a possible outcome if funds have been commingled and it is too difficult to do tracing. *See Moran v. Moran*, 512 S.E.2d 834, 836 (Va. App. 1999) ("When marital property and separate property are commingled by contributing one category of property to another, resulting in the loss of identity of the contributed property, the classification of the contributed property shall be transmuted to the category of property receiving the contribution. However, to the extent the contributed property is retraceable by a preponderance of the evidence and was not a gift, such contributed property shall retain its original classification.").

    Answer (C) is incorrect. This is a possible outcome if the funds can be traced. *See Moran v. Moran*, 512 S.E.2d 834, 836 (Va. App. 1999).

83. **Answer (C) is the best answer**. *See Bass v. Bass*, 448 S.E.2d 366, 367 (Ga. 1994) ("if the separate non-marital property of one spouse appreciates in value during the marriage solely as the result of market forces, that appreciation does not become a marital asset which is subject to equitable division; but, if the separate non-marital property of one spouse appreciates in value during the marriage as the result of efforts made by either or both spouses, that appreciation does become a marital asset which is subject to equitable division").

Answer (A) is incorrect. While both owned their properties before the marriage, that does not settle the issue. The court will have to examine whether marital funds were used for upkeep and improvements. *See Hall v. Hall*, 462 A.2d 1179, 1182 (Me. 1983) (discussing the "source of funds" rule, which might mean that property owned prior to the marriage but improved during it would be included in part marital and in part separate property).

Answer (B) is incorrect. This is false. Separate property that is kept separate will remain separate unless it is contributed to the marital estate. *See, e.g., Etterman, v. Etterman*, 2002 WL 31058072, *1 (Mich. App. 2002) ("generally, property received as an inheritance by a married party and kept separate from marital property is deemed separate property").

Answer (D) is incorrect. Regardless of the wealth of the parties, the court will have to decide which property is marital and which separate for distribution purposes.

84. **Answer (A) is the best answer**. This is the least likely to occur. It would be too speculative for the court to assume that she would be made partner. *See Mahoney v. Mahoney*, 453 A.2d, 527, 532 (N.J. 1982) ("Valuing a professional degree in the hands of any particular individual at the start of his or her career would involve a gamut of calculations that reduces to little more than guesswork.").

    Answer (B) is incorrect. This is not a good answer because it is a possible way of handling the distribution. *See In re Marriage of Olar*, 747 P.2d 676, 689 (Colo. 1987) ("The contribution of one spouse to the education of the other spouse may be taken into consideration when marital property is divided.").

    Answer (C) is incorrect. This is a possible way of handling the distribution. *See In re Marriage of Watt*, 214 Cal. App. 3d 340, 351 (Cal. App. 1989) ("in the case of a career-threshold marriage where the working spouse provided a far greater share of living expenses while the student spouse acquired a professional degree, . . . the trial court [should] consider the totality of the nonstudent's contributions and efforts toward attainment of that degree, including contributions for ordinary living expenses").

    Answer (D) is incorrect. This is a possible way of handling the distribution. *See Becker v. Perkins-Becker*, 669 A.2d 524, 531 (R.I. 1996) ("The value of a professional degree or a license may not be included in the distribution of marital assets upon the dissolution of a marriage.").

85. **Answer (A) is the best answer**. *See Marshall v. Marshall*, 688 S.W.2d 279 (Ark. 1985) (wife only entitled to proportion of pension benefits earned during marriage).

    Answer (B) is incorrect. The court might retain jurisdiction and decide the appropriate distribution once everything is clearer. *See Krafick v. Krafick*, 663 A.2d 365, 375 (Conn. 1965) ("Alternatively, under the 'reserved jurisdiction' method, the trial court reserves jurisdiction to distribute the pension until benefits have matured. Once matured, the trial court will determine the proper share to which each party is entitled and divide the benefits accordingly.").

Answer (C) is incorrect. This is false. *See Marshall v. Marshall*, 688 S.W.2d 279 (Ark. 1985).

Answer (D) is incorrect. As a general matter, the benefits will be distributed in light of the proportion between the benefits earned during the marriage years and the total number of years in which the benefits were earned. *See Marshall v. Marshall*, 688 S.W.2d 279 (Ark. 1985). Of course, the court might award spousal support were that appropriate.

86. **Answer (B) is the best answer**. *See Snider v. Snider*, 551 S.E.2d 693, 697 (W. Va. 2001).

    Answer (A) is incorrect. This is false. While the Texas court could grant an ex parte divorce, *see Snider v. Snider*, 551 S.E.2d 693, 697 (W. Va. 2001) ("It is a common occurrence for one party to a marriage to seek a divorce in a jurisdiction that is foreign to the other party. This practice, where one spouse obtains a divorce in a foreign jurisdiction without the participation of the other spouse, is known as an 'ex parte divorce,' "), it could not distribute the New York marital property. *See id.* ("Courts examining these occurrences have developed the 'divisible divorce' doctrine, thereby allowing courts to separate resolution of the ex parte divorce from the resolution of the parties' other marital interests—such as child custody and support, spousal support, and the distribution of marital property.").

    Answer (C) is incorrect. While the Texas court had jurisdiction to grant the divorce, it did not have jurisdiction to distribute the marital property. *See Snider v. Snider*, 551 S.E.2d 693 (W. Va. 2001).

    Answer (D) is incorrect. This is false. The Texas court had jurisdiction to grant the divorce. *See Snider v. Snider*, 551 S.E.2d 693, 697 (W. Va. 2001).

87. **Answer (B) is the best answer**. This, basically, is the definition of community property. *See* Ariz. Stat. sec. 25-211 (explaining community property and the exceptions).

    Answer (A) is incorrect. The property owned by the town would be public property rather than community property, notwithstanding that there is a sense in which the property might be said to be owned by the entire community.

    Answer (C) is incorrect. Community property refers to property acquired during a marriage in a community property state which does not meet certain exceptions, *see* Ariz. Stat. sec. 25-211. Further, mere use of property would not transmute separately owned property into property owned by both parties to the marriage. *See Ray v. Ray*, 372 S.E.2d 910, 911 (S.C. App. 1988) ("The mere use of separate property to support the marriage, without some additional evidence of intent to treat it as property of the marriage, is not sufficient to establish transmutation.").

    Answer (D) is incorrect. Community property refers to who owns rather than who uses the property. *Cf. Muckleroy v. Muckleroy*, 498 P.2d 1357, 1358 (N.M. 1972) (one of hallmarks of community property is that it can be jointly owned).

88. **Answer (C) is the best answer**. *See Zorilla v. Wahid*, 83 S.W.3d 247, 251 (Tex. App. 2002) (describing quasi-community property as "property acquired while

domiciled in another state that would have been community property if the acquiring spouse was domiciled in Texas at the time of acquisition").

Answer (A) is incorrect. While frozen embryos have been described as deserving special respect and as being neither persons nor property, *see Davis v. Davis*, 842 S.W.2d 588, 596 (Tenn. 1992), quasi-community property refers to property acquired in a common law jurisdiction which would have been community property if acquired in a community property jurisdiction. *See, e.g.*, Cal. Fam. sec. 125. (discussing quasi-community property).

Answer (B) is incorrect. However, upon dissolution of the marriage the spouse not owning such property would be given a credit for one half of the community funds used to improve the separate property. *See, e.g.*, La. Stat. Ann. Civ. Code art. 2366 (discussing the credit that will be given when community property is used for the benefit of separate property).

Answer (D) is incorrect. *See, e.g.*, Cal. Fam. sec. 125 (discussing definition of "quasi-community property"). A separate issue is now how the property of such couples should be treated. *Cf. In re Marriage of Carrillo*, 2003 WL 1735641, *3 (Wash. App.) ("Where parties live in a stable, quasi-marital relationship, upon the demise of such a relationship, the characterization of property as separate and community will apply by analogy even though no marriage and no community property exists.").

89. Notwithstanding that the property was owned separately by Thomas before the marriage, his putting the property in both of their names may well be interpreted as his making a gift of his separate property to the marital estate. *See Carter v. Carter*, 419 A.2d 1018 (Me. 1980). Further, the fact that marital funds (money from their paychecks) were used to pay the mortgage and to make improvements on the house would also support treating the house as marital property subject to distribution rather than as his separate property. *See Hebron v. Hebron*, 566 S.W.2d 829 (Mo. App. 1978) (spouse's contributions to house as well as house being jointly titled helped justify its being treated as marital). While different jurisdictions would treat this situation differently, the house might well be treated as marital property rather than his separate property.

90. The appropriate treatment of these items depends upon the intent of the individual making the gift. If the court finds that the jewelry was given by Ken to Julie as an irrevocable gift, then it will be treated as Julie's separate property. *See Michael v. Michael*, 469 S.E.2d 14, 19 (W. Va. 1996). If the painting was not clearly meant to be an irrevocable gift to Ken by Julie but was instead viewed as an investment for the benefit of the marriage, then the painting will be viewed as marital property subject to distribution. *See Michael v. Michael*, 469 S.E.2d 14, 19 (W. Va. 1996). The important issue will be to establish the understandings of the individuals making and receiving the gifts at the time the gifts were made. *See In re Balanson*, 25 P.3d 28, 37 (Colo. 2001) ("In order to qualify as a 'gift,' a transfer of property must involve a simultaneous intention to make a gift, delivery of the gift, and acceptance of the gift.").

TOPIC 14: CUSTODY/VISITATION

ANSWERS

91. **Answer (B) is the best answer**. *See Thomas v. Thomas*, 987 P.2d 603, 607 (Utah App. 1999) (standard determine which fit parent will be awarded custody).

    Answer (A) is incorrect. The standard does not determine whether a parent is unfit but, rather, which of two fit parents will be awarded custody. *See Thomas v. Thomas*, 987 P.2d 603, 607 (Utah App. 1999).

    Answer (C) is incorrect. Support will be determined in light of a variety of factors including the state's child support guidelines. *See In re T.H.*, 657 N.W.2d 273, 275 (N. D. 2003) ("Child support guidelines determine, as a rebuttable presumption, the amount of a parent's child support obligation.").

    Answer (D) is incorrect. The state cannot second-guess parental decisions merely because it disagrees about what would promote a child's best interests. *See Lassiter v. Dept. of Social Services*, 452 U.S. 18, 27 (1981) ("a parent's desire for and right to the companionship, care, custody and management of his or her children is an important interest that undeniably warrants deference and, absent a powerful countervailing interest, protection").

92. **Answer (C) is the best answer**. *See Sistrunk v. Sistrunk*, 245 So.2d 845, 847 (Miss. 1971) (tender years doctrine presumes that mothers are better suited to have custody of young children). Note, however, that the presumption is not irrebuttable.

    Answer (A) is incorrect. The tender years doctrine applies to the child of tender years, not to the parent of relatively young age. *See Sistrunk v. Sistrunk*, 245 So.2d 845, 847 (Miss. 1971) ("It is presumed that when children are of tender years that the mother is best fitted to have their custody.").

    Answer (B) is incorrect. A child's preferences are considered, but only when the child is older and of sufficient intelligence, understanding, and experience to express a preference. *See DesLauriers v. DesLauriers*, 642 N.W.2d 892, 895 (N.D. 2002).

    Answer (D) is incorrect. An unfit mother will not be given custody of even a very young child. *See Buntyn v. Smallwood*, 412 So.2d 236, 238 (Miss. 1982) (suggesting that the tender years doctrine only applies when mother is fit). Mississippi still includes this presumption as one factor among many to be considered in custody decisions. *See Pellegrin v. Pellegrin*, 478 So.2d 306, 307-08 (Miss. 1985).

93. **Answer (D) is the best answer**. *See Farmer v. Farmer*, 735 N.E.2d 285, 288 (Ind. App. 2000) ("a parent may not withhold child support payments even though the other parent interferes with visitation rights").

    Answer (A) is incorrect. This can be considered when deciding who will be awarded custody. *See In re McGivney*, 748 N.Y.S.2d 794, 795 (App. Div. 2002) (listing among considerations militating in favor of awarding custody to father that he would promote contact with other parent while the mother if awarded custody would be less likely to promote contact with the father).

Answer (B) is incorrect. This can be considered in a modification of custody. *See Chafin v. Rude*, 391 N.W.2d 882 (Minn. App. 1986) (custody modified from mother to father because the latter but not the former would promote the child's having contact with both parents).

Answer (C) is incorrect. If the parent's reluctance to promote contact with the other parent is due to a reasonable belief that the other parent is abusing their child, then the parent's reluctance will not be held against him or her. *Cf. Ford v. Ford*, 2000 WL 33200935 (Del. Fam. Ct) (mother continues to have primary custody and father continues to have only supervised visitation given court's belief that mother's charges of inappropriate behavior by father are not unfounded).

94. **Answer (B) is the best answer**. *See Myers v. Myers*, 601 N.W.2d 264, 267 (N.D. 1999) (preference of mature child significant but not dispositive with respect to what custodial arrangement would promote best interests).

Answer (A) is incorrect. *See Neidviecky v. Neidviecky*, 657 N.W.2d 255, 258 (N.D. 2003) (explicitly listing reasonable preference of the child as a factor).

Answer (C) is incorrect. This overstates the significance of the mature child's preference. *See Myers v. Myers*, 601 N.W.2d 264 (N.D. 1999) (child's preference not dispositive).

Answer (D) is incorrect. This is false. *See Barstad v. Barstad*, 499 N.W.2d 584, 588 (N.D. 1993) ("Although age is not the exclusive indicator of a child's maturity and capacity to make an intelligent choice, generally, a child's preference is entitled to more weight as he or she grows older.").

95. **Answer (A) is the best answer**. *See, e.g., Todd v. Casciano*, 569 S.E.2d 566, 568 (Ga. App. 2002) ("A trial court is authorized to modify an original custody award upon a showing of new and material changes in the conditions and circumstances substantially affecting the interest and welfare of the child.").

Answer (B) is incorrect. Modifying custody does not abridge a fundamental right of the former custodial parent because both parents have a fundamental interest in the care and custody of their children. *See Cookson v. Cookson*, 514 A.2d 323, 326 (Conn. 1986).

Answer (C) is incorrect. A higher salary alone would likely not constitute a material change in circumstances justifying a modification of custody. *See Spoor v. Spoor*, 641 N.E.2d 1282 (Ind. App. 1994). The children might well benefit from the higher salary in that higher child support might be ordered. *See Kerby v. Kerby*, 60 P.3d 1038, 1041 (Okla. 2002) ("this Court recognize[s] that a significant change of income, without a showing of change in need, warrant[s] modification of a child support award").

Answer (D) is incorrect. This is false. A custody award can be modified if there has been a material change in the circumstances, even if the custodial parent is not unfit. *See, e.g., Todd v. Casciano*, 569 S.E.2d 566 (Ga. App. 2002).

96. **Answer (C) is the best answer**. *See Kelly v. Kelly*, 640 N.W.2d 38, 41 (N.D. 2002) (the circumstances must be different from what they were at the time of the last decree).

    Answer (A) is incorrect. A material change in income alone will likely not suffice to meet this standard. *See Spoor v. Spoor*, 641 N.E.2d 1282 (Ind. App. 1994).

    Answer (B) is incorrect. The question is not whether there has been any change, however minor, in certain "material" circumstances but instead whether there has been a material or significant change. *See Milliken v. Milliken*, 339 N.W.2d 573, 575 (Wis. 1983) (must be substantial change in relevant factor rather than any change however slight).

    Answer (D) is incorrect. While a change in residence may involve a material change, it need not. *See In re Marriage of Eikermann*, 48 S.W.3d 605, 611 (Mo. App. 2001) ("a change of residence alone does not require a change of custody").

97. **Answer (C) is the best answer**. *See Ellis v. Ellis*, 840 So.2d 806, 813 (Miss. App. 2003) (suggesting that "the child suffered from parental alienation syndrome due to Nancy's continuous intrusion into the child's relationship with her father").

    Answer (A) is incorrect. While many individuals do not wish to be parents, this term is used to discuss a parent who is attempting to alienate his or her child from the other parent. *See Davis v. Hilton*, 780 So.2d 974, 975 (Fla. App. 2001) (describing parental alienation as an attempt to alienate a child from his or her parent).

    Answer (B) is incorrect. While parents may sometimes be upset with their children, that does not count as parental alienation in the relevant sense. *See Davis v. Hilton*, 780 So.2d 974, 975 (Fla. App. 2001).

    Answer (D) is incorrect. While individuals going through a divorce may well feel animosity toward their soon-to-be ex-spouses, this term is not used to refer to that alienation.

98. **Answer (C) is the best answer**. Because Divorca rather than Newstartania is the home state of the children, Divorca rather than Newstartania has jurisdiction to hear this case for custody modification. *See, e.g., Matthews v. Riley*, 649 A.2d 131 (Vt. 1994) (Vermont has jurisdiction to modify custody because it is the home state of the child.).

    Answer (A) is incorrect. Newstartania would have been permitted to modify Divorca's decree had the facts been different and Newstartania had become the children's home state. In that event, the Newstartania court would have had jurisdiction. Where a court has jurisdiction to hear the case, "the party seeking modification must demonstrate (1) that since the time of the previous decree, there have been changes in the circumstances upon which the previous award was based; and (2) that those changes are sufficiently substantial and material to justify reopening the question of custody." *See Hogge v. Hogge*, 649 P.2d 51, 54 (Utah 1982).

Answer (B) is incorrect. Even were there a material change in the circumstances, a prior question would be whether the Newstartania court would have jurisdiction to hear the case. *See, e.g., Phillips v. Beaber*, 995 S.W.2d 655 (Tex. 1999) (denying that Texas courts have jurisdiction to modify the custody decree in a particular case).

Answer (D) is incorrect. The Uniform Interstate Family Support Act is a Model Act concerning support rather than custody issues. *See In re Marriage of Doetzl*, 65 P.3d 539, 541 (Kan. App. 2003) ("UIFSA was promulgated and intended to be used as a procedural mechanism for the establishment, modification, and enforcement of child support and spousal support obligations.").

99. **Answer (B) is the best answer**. *See, e.g., Matthews v. Riley*, 649 A.2d 131 (Vt. 1994) (Vermont had jurisdiction to modify custody because it was the home state of the child).

Answer (A) is incorrect. Because the children have been living in South Florilina for the past 18 months, North Florilina no longer has jurisdiction to decide the custody modification. *See, e.g., Phillips v. Beaber*, 995 S.W.2d 655 (Tex. 1999) (declining jurisdiction under the Uniform Child Custody Jurisdiction Act and the Parental Kidnaping Prevention Act because the child had been living in Colorado for more than six months and thus Colorado was the child's home state).

Answer (C) is incorrect. While the children are appropriately in the state, that does not give the court jurisdiction, given that Georgiana is not the home state of the children. *See Phillips v. Beaber*, 995 S.W.2d 655 (Tex. 1999).

Answer (D) is incorrect. The issue here is not whether the court has personal jurisdiction over Liana but whether it has the equivalent of subject matter jurisdiction so that it can modify custody. *See Amin v. Bakhaty*, 798 So.2d 75, 81 (La. 2001) (describing "the limitations imposed by the UCCJA as equivalent to declarations of subject matter jurisdiction which mandate that the jurisdictional requirements of the UCCJA be met when the custody request is filed").

100. **Answer (D) is the best answer**. *See Ireland v. Ireland*, 717 A.2d 676 (Conn. 1998) (relocation permitted where for legitimate reason and in best interests of child).

Answer (A) is incorrect. *See Kaiser v. Kaiser*, 23 P.2d 278, 286 (Okla. 2001) (The cases uniformly hold that visitation rights alone are an insufficient basis on which to deny relocation.).

Answer (B) is incorrect. *See In re C.R.O.*, 96 S.W.3d 442 (Tex. App. 2002) (upholding relocation restriction).

Answer (C) is incorrect. While a relocation might be denied for these reasons, *see In re C.R.O.*, 96 S.W.3d 442 (Tex. App. 2002), it might also be permitted, notwithstanding the burdens that would thereby be placed on the non-custodial parent's relationship with his or her children.

101. **Answer (B) is the best answer**. *See Gorham v. Gorham*, 692 P.2d 1375, 1379 (Okla. 1984) (discussing "the requisite nexus between the behavior and detriment to the child").

Answer (A) is incorrect. The amount of time might be important insofar as the court was deciding whether to grant the divorce, but here the granting of the divorce is a given and the issue is who will have custody of the child. As a general matter, the best interests of the child are paramount in custody determinations. *See Habecker v. Giard*, 820 A.2d 215, 219 (Vt. 2003) ("The best interests of the child must be the court's paramount consideration in awarding custody.").

Answer (C) is incorrect. This is a red herring. Regrettably, parents sometimes blame their children for the parents' bad behavior. *See, e.g., State v. Peterson*, 557 N.W.2d 389, 395 (S.D. 1996) (discussing individual who seemed to believe that his sexual abuse of his daughter was somehow her fault).

Answer (D) is incorrect. This misconstrues the purpose of a custody proceeding. *See Leppert v. Leppert*, 519 N.W.2d 287, 291 (N.D. 1994) ("the goal in custody determinations is to foster the health and well-being of the child, not to punish either of the parents").

102. The touchstone of establishing which parent should have custody is the best interests of the child. *In re Custody of Smith*, 969 P.2d 21, 41-43 (Wash. 1998) ("the best interests of the child remain the touchstone by which all other rights are tested"). While jurisdictions differ, many recognize that it may be in a child's best interests for the adulterous spouse to be awarded custody of the child. *See, e.g., Hollon v. Hollon*, 784 So.2d 943, 949 (Miss. 2001) ("Our cases well recognize that it may be in the best interest of a child to remain with its mother even though she may have been guilty of adultery."). Here, it seems likely that, all else equal, Winona will be awarded custody.

103. For the party seeking to modify custody to be successful, he or she must show that there has been a material change in the circumstances and that the child's best interests would be served by modifying custody. *See Shioji v. Shioji*, 712 P.2d 197, 200 (Utah 1985). The mere fact that the mother is starting to date someone may well not suffice either to modify custody or to require that the boyfriend only visit when the child is away from the home. Rather, the father may be required to show that the new boyfriend is having some detrimental effect on the child. *See Moore v. Moore*, 544 So.2d 479, 483 (La. App. 1989) ("The fact that a mother has a steady boyfriend who frequents her home is not sufficient reason to justify change in custody in the absence of proof that the mother's relationship with the boyfriend is having a detrimental effect on the child."). However, if the court believes that the mother's relationship with the boyfriend will have a detrimental effect on the child, then the court might take some sort of action.

104. While some state courts have struck down the tender years doctrine, *see, e.g., Ex parte Devine*, 398 So.2d 686 (Ala. 1981), that doctrine involves an express preference for women in certain cases involving a custody dispute. Absent an express classification on the basis of sex, it is quite unlikely that a mere statistical difference, even if significant, would trigger equal protection guarantees. *Cf. Personnel Administrator of Massachusetts v. Feeney*, 442 U.S. 256 (1979) (neutral statute with disproportionately adverse effect upon women upheld because there

was no showing of an intent to discriminate on the basis of sex). Betty's argument is unlikely to be successful.

105. A modification of custody may be granted when there has been a material change in the circumstances and the child's best interest would be promoted by changing the custodial arrangement. *See In re Thompson*, 659 N.W.2d 864, 866 (N.D. 2003). Here, the relevant issues might include whether Xerxes is just having some initial adjustment problems with his step-siblings or instead is suffering some sort of harm. Further, depending upon his age and maturity, Xerxes' stated preference for living with his father will be given some weight. Ultimately, it is unclear whether Zeus' custody modification request will in fact be granted. The new living arrangement coupled with difficulty in getting along with step-siblings might constitute a material change in circumstances and it might be held to be in Xerxes' best interest to live with his father. *Compare Elder v. Elder*, 2001 WL 1077961 (Tenn. Ct. App.) (no modification notwithstanding difficulties with stepparent and step sibling), *with Mosbrucker v. Mosbrucker*, 562 N.W.2d 390 (N. D. 1997) (modification justified in light of difficulties with step-family).

106. Xerxes' home state is West Carolandia. Assuming that no exceptions apply, the West Carolandia court has jurisdiction under the Uniform Child Custody Jurisdiction Act and the Parental Kidnaping Prevention Act. Thus, while there may have been a material change in the circumstances, the proper forum to hear the request for a custody modification is West Carolandia and the East Carolanida court should decline to exercise jurisdiction. *See Bates v. Jackson*, 28 S.W.3d 476 (Mo. App. 2000) (Missouri court lacks jurisdiction to determine custody where Indiana court had already issued initial custody order and both states had adopted the Uniform Child Custody Jurisdiction Act.).

107. West Monaho permits second-parent adoptions and thus it could not be argued that it would somehow violate public policy to legally recognize that Gina has two parents of the same sex. Nonetheless, Samantha did not establish a legal tie with Gina by adopting her and thus may be precluded from being awarded custody or visitation rights. The jurisdictions differ with respect to how to treat this kind of case. *Compare Titchenal v. Dexter*, 693 A.2d 682 (Vt. 1997) (no visitation or custody rights), *with V.C. v. M.J.B.*, 748 A.2d 539 (N.J. 2000) (same-sex partner was psychological parent to child and thus could be awarded visitation rights).

108. Jurisdictions vary with respect to the enforceability of surrogacy contracts. Some require that various procedures be followed. *See, e.g.*, Va. Stat. sec. 20-158. Others make them enforceable, *see* Ark. Stat. sec. 9-10-201, and still others make such agreements either void or voidable at the instance of the surrogate. *See R.R. v. M.H.*, 689 N.E.2d 790 (Mass. 1998) (holding surrogacy agreement unenforceable). It will be important to find out what New Arisey law says with respect to this issue and whether the Wainwrights have followed the required procedures, if any. In many but not all jurisdictions, Eva would get to keep Adam, although a separate issue would involve whether any fees or expenses that had been paid would have to be returned.

109. This again would be a matter of state law. However, some states treat gestational and genetic surrogate agreements differently, treating the former as enforceable and the latter as voidable. *See Johnson v. Calvert*, 851 P.2d 776 (Cal. 1993) (gestational surrogacy agreement enforceable); *In re Marriage of Moschetta*, 25 Cal. App. 4th 1218 (Ct. App. 1994) (genetic surrogacy agreement voidable). Were this such a jurisdiction, then Eva as a gestational surrogate would likely not be able to keep the child, even if she would have been able to keep the child had she been a genetic surrogate.

110. Jurisdictions tend to require that the relocation will promote the best interests of the child. However, they differ in what they presume will achieve that end. *Compare Hollandsworth v. Knyzewski*, 109 S.W.3d 653 (Ark. 2003) (presumption in favor of relocation for custodial parent with primary custody), *with Dranko v. Dranko*, 824 A.2d 1215 (Pa. Super. 2003) (burden of proof to establish advantages of move on parent seeking to relocate). Here, some factors would militate in favor of permitting the relocation, *e.g.*, that she has family in East Michsylvania and their standard of living would improve, while other factors militate against permitting the relocation, *e.g.*, that it would be more difficult for the child to maintain a relationship with his father. *Compare In re Marriage of Collingbourne*, 791 N.E.2d 532 (Ill. 2003) (permitting relocation), with *Sullivan v. Knick*, 568 S.E.2d 430 (Va. App. 2002) (denying relocation request, at least in part, because it would interfere with visitation with the father). As to whether the benefits would outweigh the costs, this would depend upon various factors including whether suitable alternative visitation arrangements could be set up with the father as well as whether the state had a presumption in favor of relocation for the custodial parent.

111. John is unlikely to be successful in his attempt to have custody modified. Eileen is correct that the West Tennucky court does not seem to have jurisdiction to modify custody. The home state of the children continues to be Pennio, see Uniform Child Custody Jurisdiction Act sec. 3(1), and unless some kind of exception can be offered to justify West Tennucky's asserting jurisdiction, e.g., some emergency or the children having been abandoned in the state, see Uniform Child Custody Jurisdiction Act sec.3 (3), a Pennio rather than a West Tennucky court should be addressing the substantive merits of whether a custody modification would be appropriate.

TOPIC 15: SUPPORT

ANSWERS

112. **Answer (A) is the best answer**. *See Joye v. Yon*, 547 888, 890 (S.C. App. 2001) ("A majority of courts reinstate the alimony obligation upon annulment of the subsequent marriage where the attempted remarriage was void *ab initio* but deny reinstatement if the attempted remarriage was merely voidable.").

    Answer (B) is incorrect. As a general matter, states will not reinstate a support obligation if the second marriage was voidable rather than void. *See Joye v. Yon*, 547 888, 890 (S.C. App. 2001).

    Answer (C) is incorrect. While an individual's having taken on additional family responsibilities would make the resumption of spousal support seem even more unfair, courts have not suggested, e.g., that payments should resume unless the individual has started a new family. *See Glass v. Glass*, 546 S.W.2d 738, 743 (Mo. App. 1977).

    Answer (D) is incorrect. This is a red herring. Georgina, the innocent spouse, will not have to indemnify anyone.

113. **Answer (B) is the best answer**. *See Eagerton v. Eagerton*, 328 S.E.2d 912, 914 (S.C. App. 1985).

    Answer (A) is incorrect. While many individuals might believe that their ex-spouses are in need of such training, rehabilitative spousal support is not designed to make the ex-spouse more civil but, instead, to enable the person to improve his or her job skills. *See Eagerton v. Eagerton*, 328 S.E.2d 912, 914 (S.C. App. 1985) ("The purpose of rehabilitative alimony is to encourage a dependent spouse to become self-supporting by providing alimony for a limited period of time during which the dependent spouse might retrain and rehabilitate himself or herself thereby limiting the duration of the time in which the supporting spouse is burdened by spousal support.").

    Answer (C) is incorrect. While rehabilitative services may be those that will help an individual improve functioning, *see Ferrante v. Allstate Insur. Co.*, 40 Pa. D. & C.3d 594, 595 (1986), rehabilitative spousal support is a term of art and does not refer to such services.

    Answer (D) is incorrect. While seeking counseling to save a marriage may be viewed favorably by the courts, *see, e.g., Strickland v. Strickland*, 2002 WL 31440829, *1 (Conn. Super.) (mentioning husband's refusal to attend counseling as one of the factors supporting his being more at fault for the breakdown of the marriage), rehabilitative support does not involve such services.

114. **Answer (B) is the best answer**. *See Maynard v. Maynard*, 399 A.2d 900, 901 (Md. App. 1979) ("an award of alimony *pendente lite* is a monetary payment pending

the outcome of litigation which has been instituted but which has not been concluded").

Answer (A) is incorrect. What is described is rehabilitative support. *See Eagerton v. Eagerton*, 328 S.E.2d 912, 914 (S.C. App. 1985).

Answer (C) is incorrect. The amount of the award is a separate matter. *See Knott v. Knott*, 806 A.2d 768, 784 (Md. App. 2002) (pointing out that *pendente lite* orders "are designed to provide for purely temporary needs on a short term basis, whereas the provisions for support in a final judgment of divorce are perforce intended to be more permanent and cover equally essential but less frequent recurring living expenses").

Answer (D) is incorrect. The *pendente lite* award is supposed to provide income while matters are being decided.

115. **Answer (D) is the best answer**. The gender of the parties should not be considered in the determination of spousal support. *See In re Marriage of Bethke*, 484 N.W.2d 604, 608 (Iowa App. 1992) (suggesting that gender must be ignored in the determination of alimony).

    Answer (A) is incorrect. Duration of the marriage is a factor often considered in determining support. *See, e.g., Powell v. Powell*, 648 P.2d 218, 221 (Kan. 1982) (explicitly mentioning this factor).

    Answer (B) is incorrect. The employability of the spouse is a factor often considered in determining support. *See, e.g., McPhee v. McPhee*, 440 A.2d 274, 277 (Conn. 1982) (explicitly mentioning employability as one of the factors to consider in spousal support determinations).

    Answer (C) is incorrect. The standard of living during the marriage is often considered as a factor. *See Capps v. Capps*, 699 So.2d 183, 184 (Ala. Civ. App. 1997) (specifically mentioning this factor).

116. **Answer (C) is the best answer**. *See Hertz v. Hertz*, 48 Pa. D. & C.4th 424 (Pa. Com. Pl. 2000) (upholding waiver of spousal support but not upholding waiver of child support).

    Answer (A) is incorrect. *See, e.g., Hertz v. Hertz*, 48 Pa. D. & C.4th 424, 430 (Pa. Com. Pl. 2000) (enforcing waiver of spousal but not of child support).

    Answer (B) is incorrect. *See Pierce v. Pierce*, 397 So.2d 62, 64 (La. App. 1981) ("The legal duty of support owed to a child cannot be renounced.").

    Answer (D) is incorrect. Child support is not the parent's claim to waive. *See Wyatt v. Wyatt*, 408 S.E.2d 51, 54 (W. Va. 1991) ("The duty of a parent to support a child is a basic duty owed by the parent to the child, and a parent cannot waive or contract away the child's right to support.").

117. **Answer (C) is the best answer**. *See Ellis v. Taylor*, 449 S.E.2d 487 (S.C. 1994) (enforcing non-custodial parent's agreement to pay private college tuition).

Answer (A) is incorrect. The court is not likely to treat the agreement as merely aspirational. *See Gaddis v. Gaddis*, 314 N.E.2d 627, 632-33 (Ill. App. 1974) ("the defendant's agreement to provide for Beverly's college education was based upon adequate consideration and a promise to do more than the law required which is specifically enforceable").

Answer (B) is incorrect. This is false. A parent might be forced to pay for a child's college education if he or she had agreed to do so. *See Golay v. Golay*, 210 P.2d 1022, 1023 (Wash. 1949) ("A rich man, well able to pay, might very well be held for a college education of an extended and expensive sort.").

Answer (D) is incorrect. A court would be unlikely to order a parent to pay postgraduate expenses absent an agreement to do so. *See In re Marriage of Belsby*, 754 P.2d 1269 (Wash App. 1988) (trial court abused discretion when ordering support for child during graduate school).

118. **Answer (C) is the best answer**. *Compare Neudecker v. Neudecker*, 577 N.E.2d 960 (Ind. 1991) (upholding statute requiring divorcing parents to pay for their child's college education), *with Jennings v. Jennings*, 783 P.2d 178 (Wyo. 1989) (no duty of post majority support beyond what is included in divorce agreement).

Answer (A) is incorrect. *See Neudecker v. Neudecker*, 577 N.E.2d 960 (Ind. 1991) (upholding statute permitting courts to order divorcing parents to pay for their child's college education).

Answer (B) is incorrect. *See Propst v. Propst*, 776 P.2d 780 (Alaska 1989) (holding that there is no duty to pay for children's college education).

Answer (D) is incorrect. This is false. *See Neudecker v. Neudecker*, 577 N.E.2d 960 (Ind. 1991) (upholding such a requirement).

119. **Answer (A) is the best answer**. *See K.S. v. G.S.*, 440 A.2d 64 (N.J. Super. Ch. 1981) (husband required to support child born during marriage as a result of artificial insemination to which he had consented).

Answer (B) is incorrect. This is false. *See K.S. v. G.S.*, 440 A.2d 64 (N.J. Super. Ch. 1981) (requiring husband to pay notwithstanding lack of genetic link to child).

Answer (C) is incorrect. If the child had been the product of an extramarital affair, then the husband might not be forced to pay child support. *See Ferradaz v. Ortiz*, 754 So.2d 867 (Fla. App. 2000) (DNA tests ordered to determine whether husband or putative father was the biological father; biological father would be ordered to support child).

Answer (D) is incorrect. A parent will not be immune from suit by simply deciding neither to support nor to visit his or her children. Indeed, a court might well decide that such an agreement between the parents is unenforceable. *See Blisset v. Blisset*, 526 N.E.2d 125 (Ill. 1988).

120. **Answer (C) is the best answer**. *See Tregoning v. Wiltschek*, 782 A.2d 1001 (Pa. Super. 2001) (mother estopped from challenging paternity of child born during the marriage).

Answer (A) is incorrect. This result is unlikely, given that Douglas has acted as the father of these children for several years, wants to continue the relationship, and was led to believe by the wife that he was the father. *See Tregoning v. Wiltschek*, 782 A.2d 1001 (Pa. Super. 2001) (mother estopped from challenging paternity of child born during the marriage). Further, if there is a statute requiring that paternity be contested within, say, a few years, neither Danielle nor Edward will be allowed to contest paternity now. *Cf. David V.R. v. Wanda J.D.*, 907 P.2d 1025 (Okla. 1995) (putative father cannot now challenge husband's paternity after two years had elapsed and there had been no challenge by either the husband or the wife).

Answer (B) is incorrect. Here, Douglas is not requesting custody and there is no reason to believe the mother unfit. Given that awarding custody to the mother would promote the best interests of the child, it would not make sense to award custody to the father. *See Hollon v. Hollon*, 784 So.2d 943, 946 (Miss. 2001) ("The polestar consideration in child custody cases is the best interest and welfare of the child.").

Answer (D) is incorrect. This alternative makes the least sense, since it would mean that the children would be without a father notwithstanding the (possible) willingness of two different individuals to take on that responsibility.

121. **Answer (C) is the best answer**. *See William L. v. Cindy E.L.*, 495 S.E.2d 836 (W. Va. 1997) (husband precluded from contesting paternity when he had been on notice that he was not the father and he nonetheless continued to act as father to the child).

Answer (A) is incorrect. *See Richard B. v. Sandra B.B.*, 625 N.Y.S.2d 127 (App. Div. 1995) (husband estopped from denying paternity).

Answer (B) is incorrect. *See Knill v. Knill*, 510 A.2d 546 (Md. 1986) (husband not estopped from denying paternity of child born during marriage to avoid paying child support).

Answer (D) is incorrect. This is false. *See, e.g., Williams v. Williams*, 843 So.2d 720 (Miss. 2003) (ex-husband relieved of support obligation after discovering that he was not the father of his son even though the identity of the biological father was not established).

122. **Answer (B) is the best answer**. *See, e.g., Erwin L.D. v. Myla Jean L.*, 847 S.W.2d 45, 47 (Ark. App. 1993) ("a mother's agreement or assurances that she would not pursue a paternity action to request support cannot validly be interposed by a putative father as a defense").

Answer (A) is incorrect. The court is unlikely to take this approach. *See C.A.M. v. R.A.W.*, 568 A.2d 556, 561 (N.J. App. 1990) ("the birth of a normal, healthy child as a consequence of a sexual relationship between consenting adults precludes inquiry by the courts into representations that may have been made before or during that relationship by either of the partners concerning birth control").

Answer (C) is incorrect. Steven is unlikely to be successful pursuing this route. *See Stephen K. v. Roni L.*, 105 Cal. App. 3d 640 (Ct. App. 1980) (mother not liable in tort for misrepresentation with respect to her use of birth control when child born as a result of father's detrimental reliance).

Answer (D) is incorrect. This is unlikely to occur. *See Beard v. Skipper*, 451 N.W.2d 614 (Mich. App. 1990) (mother's alleged misrepresentation about birth control cannot be used as factor to reduce child support owed by father).

123. **Answer (C) is the best answer**. *See McHale v. McHale*, 612 So.2d 969, 973 (La. App. 1993) ("Proof of a change in circumstances does not justify the reduction of the child support award where an obligor's inability to pay arises from his own voluntary actions.").

Answer (A) is incorrect. This is false. Loss of a job can constitute a material change of circumstances. *See Tucker v. Tucker*, 908 S.W.2d 530, 534 (Tex. App. 1995).

Answer (B) is incorrect. This is not a good answer both because Robert presumably could get another job and because the court would not want to encourage the voluntary loss of a job to avoid paying support. *Cf. In re Marriage of Hester*, 565 N.W.2d 351, 354 (Iowa App. 1997) (although "mindful of the apparent futility of ordering Sherry to pay such support," the court thought that "[t]o do otherwise rewards Sherry for her misdeed").

Answer (D) is incorrect. A parent who has little or no contact with his son can nonetheless be required to pay child support. *See Michaels v. Weingartner*, 864 P.2d 1189 (Kan. 1993).

124. **Answer (B) is the best answer**. *See Wright v. Wright*, 623 P.2d 97, 99 (Haw. App 1981) ("Where the father has remarried and a child or children have been born of the second marriage, the family court can properly take into account the needs of those children or the needs of the new wife when determining whether to modify an order for the support of the children of the first marriage.").

Answer (A) is incorrect. While the decision to remarry and start a new family is certainly voluntary, courts have nonetheless permitted it to be considered for purposes of support modification. *See, e.g., Young v. Young*, 762 S.W.2d 535, 536 Mo. App. 1988) ("The birth of father's child of the second marriage is a factor to consider as to father's ability to pay.").

Answer (C) is incorrect. While one of the goals, where possible, is to assure that the child would have the same standard of living that he or she would have had if the parents had not divorced, *see Peterson v. Peterson*, 748 P.2d 593, 596 (Utah App. 1988) ("Child support awards should . . ., when possible, assure the children a standard of living comparable to that which they would have experienced if no divorce had occurred."), other goals are included as well, such as tying the support amount to the parent's ability to pay. *See Cochran v. Buffone*, 359 N.W.2d 557, 560 (Mich. App. 1984).

Answer (D) is incorrect. This is false. *See, e.g., Young v. Young*, 762 S.W.2d 535, 536 (Mo. App. 1988) ("Father's remarriage and voluntary assumption of support of his stepchildren is immaterial to the determination of his obligation to support his own child.").

125. **Answer (C) is the best answer**. *See Peterson v. Peterson*, 748 P.2d 593, 596 (Utah App. 1988) (where possible, the child's standard of living should be comparable to what it would have been had there been no divorce).

Answer (A) is incorrect. Courts may well change a support award where a non-custodial parent's income has increased substantially, even if the child's needs have not changed significantly. *See Kerby v. Kerby*, 60 P.3d 1038, 1041 (Okla. 2002) ("Because the parents' income is a fundamental factor in the initial award, a significant change in the income is material even where there is no change in the children's needs."). Further, the children should benefit from the non-custodial parent's increased income, *see id.* at 1042, although courts "are not required to provide opulence and excess." *Id.*

Answer (B) is incorrect. This is false. A court might even order an increase in support and a reduction in visitation. *See Gibson v. Barton*, 455 N.E.2d 282 (Ill. App. 1983) (upholding lower court doing both).

Answer (D) is incorrect. Because the child's standard of living should not be tied to the standard of living of his or her parents at the time of divorce, *see Peterson v. Peterson*, 748 P.2d 593 (Utah App. 1988), Greta will likely be ordered to pay increased support even if such a policy might induce some non-custodial parents to work less hard.

126. **Answer (C) is the best answer**. See Uniform Interstate Family Support Act sec. 205 (specifying the conditions under which the state establishing the support order will have continuing exclusive jurisdiction to modify that order).

Answer (A) is incorrect. Where the father and child continue to live in the issuing state, only that state has jurisdiction to modify the support order. *See In re Marriage of Zinke*, 967 P.2d 210, 213 (Colo. App. 1998) ("as long as one of the individual parties or the child continues to reside in the issuing state, the issuing tribunal retains continuing, exclusive jurisdiction over its order").

Answer (B) is incorrect. The Washington court did not have jurisdiction to nullify the order. *See In re Marriage of Zinke*, 967 P.2d 210 (Colo. App. 1998).

Answer (D) is incorrect. The question here involves jurisdiction rather than the substantive merits. An Alaska rather than a Washington court should be deciding this case.

127. **Answer (D) is the best answer**. *See* the Uniform Interstate Family Support Act sec. 211(a) (specifying the conditions under which the court establishing the spousal support order will have continuing exclusive jurisdiction to modify that order).

Answer (A) is incorrect. While the Washington court would have personal jurisdiction over Andrew, it would not have subject matter jurisdiction to modify the spousal support order. See the Uniform Interstate Family Support Act sec. 211.

Answer (B) is incorrect. The court would not have jurisdiction to modify the decree. See the Uniform Interstate Family Support Act sec. 211(a).

Answer (C) is incorrect. This is not a good answer because it suggests that the issue is substantive rather than jurisdictional. The modification of support should be decided by an Alaska rather than a Washington court. See the Uniform Interstate Family Support Act sec. 211(a). A separate issue is whether the support would be modified by an Alaska court.

128. **Answer (D) is the best answer.** *See* Hines v. Clendening, 465 P.2d 460 (Okla. 1970) (court has personal jurisdiction over defendant via the state's long-arm statute in case involving similar facts).

Answer (A) is incorrect. The Oklahoma court might well find that it has jurisdiction over Oscar through its long-arm jurisdiction statute, since Oscar had many contacts with the state including that he had married there, had lived there with his wife, and arguably had abandoned his wife there. *See Hines v. Clendening*, 465 P.2d 460 (Okla. 1970).

Answer (B) is incorrect. It could not have ordered support without having jurisdiction over him. *See Wray v. Wray*, 73 S.W.3d 646, 649 (Mo. App. 2002) ("The court must have jurisdiction over the person of Husband to adjudicate a personal liability against him, such as maintenance, support, attorney's fees, and suit money.").

Answer (C) is incorrect. If the court had personal jurisdiction over him, then it could order support. *See Hines v. Clendening*, 465 P.2d 460 (Okla. 1970).

129. **Answer (C) is the best answer.** This is not an indicator of emancipation. A separate question is whether someone having sexual relations with an emancipated minor would be subject to the same criminal penalties as might be imposed were the minor not emancipated. *See Campbell v. State*, 771 So.2d 1205 (Fla. App. 2000) (40-year-old man subjected to criminal penalties for having sexual relations with non-emancipated minor).

Answer (A) is incorrect. This would emancipate her. *See Vaupel v. Bellach*, 154 N.W.2d 149, 150 (Iowa 1967) ("all minors attain their majority by marriage").

Answer (B) is incorrect. This would support her being emancipated. *See Fevig v. Fevig*, 559 P.2d 839, 840 (N.M. 1977) ("An express emancipation of a minor takes place when the parent freely and voluntarily agrees with his child, who is able to care and provide for himself, that he may leave home, earn his own living, and do as he pleases with his earnings.").

Answer (D) is incorrect. Here, she would be emancipated. *See Lawson v. Lawson*, 695 N.E.2d 154, 156 (Ind. App. 1998) ("Emancipation may also occur when a minor child enters the military service.").

130. **Answer (B) is the best answer.** *See Fernandez v. Fernandez*, 717 S.W.2d 781, 783 (Tex. App. 1986) ("[T]hat part of the judgment finding the minor child emancipated and terminating Appellee's duty of child support is reversed and judgment

is rendered that Appellee's duty of support is hereby reinstated effective from the date of the granting of the annulment of the marriage of the minor daughter, Jo-Ann Fernandez.").

Answer (A) is incorrect. *See In re Marriage of Fetters*, 584 P.2d. 104, 106 (Colo. App. 1978) (father's support obligation for daughter did not exist during period that her voidable marriage was still recognized by law and hence he would not be responsible for those payments when daughter's marriage declared void by a court).

Answer (C) is incorrect. Many states will reinstitute the minor's non-emancipated status upon the voiding of the minor's marriage. *See In re Marriage of Fetters*, 584 P.2d 104, 106 (Colo. App. 1978) ("emancipation is not necessarily a continuing status; rather, it may be terminated at any time during the child's minority").

Answer (D) is incorrect. The support obligation might be revived even absent a specification in the divorce decree to that effect. *See Eyerman v. Thias*, 760 S.W.2d 187 (Mo. App. 1988) (father's support obligation of formerly emancipated minor revived, notwithstanding the absence of any agreement about the revival of that support obligation).

131. **Answer (D) is the best answer**. This is not a basis for personal jurisdiction. Rather, it is one way that one might give someone notice of the proceeding.

Answer (A) is incorrect. This is a basis for personal jurisdiction. See the Uniform Interstate Family Support Act sec. 201(a)(3) (specifying that there is a basis for jurisdiction if the parent once resided with the child in the state).

Answer (B) is incorrect. This is a basis for personal jurisdiction. See the Uniform Interstate Family Support Act sec. 201(a)(6) (specifying that there is a basis for jurisdiction if the parent had sexual relations within the state and the child might thereby have been conceived).

Answer (C) is incorrect. This is a basis for personal jurisdiction. See the Uniform Interstate Family Support Act sec. 201(a)(1) (specifying that there is a basis for jurisdiction if the parent was personally served within the state).

132. **Answer (A) is the best answer**. *See Cermak v. Cermak*, 569 N.W.2d 280, 285 (N.D. 1997) ("cohabitation cannot be the sole basis for termination of spousal support at least where cohabitation is not included as a condition for termination in the divorce decree") and Utah Stat. sec. 30-3-5(9) ("Any order of the court that a party pay alimony to a former spouse terminates upon establishment by the party paying alimony that the former spouse is cohabitating with another person.").

Answer (B) is incorrect. *See In re Marriage of Dwyer*, 825 P.2d 1018, 1019 (Colo. App. 1991) ("a former spouse's unmarried cohabitation is not, in and of itself, sufficient ground for suspending, reducing, or terminating maintenance"); *In re Marriage of Ales*, 592 N.W.2d 698, 703 (Iowa App. 1999) ("[T]he petitioner in a modification action will be required to show there is a cohabitation to meet the substantial change of circumstances requirement. . . . Then, the burden will shift to the recipient to show why spousal support should continue in spite of the cohabitation because of an ongoing need, or because the original purpose for the support award makes it unmodifiable.").

Answer (C) is incorrect. This is false. *See, e.g.*, Utah Stat. sec. 30-3-5(9).

Answer (D) is incorrect. This is false. *See, e.g.*, Utah Stat. sec. 30-3-5(9).

133. **Answer (A) is the best answer**. *Compare Van Dyck v. Van Dyck*, 425 S.E.2d 853 (Ga. 1993) (cohabitation with member of same sex does not meet the requirement to have spousal support terminated), *with Garcia v. Garcia*, 60 P.3d 1174 (Utah App. 2002) (cohabitation with member of same sex meets the requirement to have spousal support terminated).

Answer (B) is incorrect. This is false. *See Garcia v. Garcia*, 60 P.3d 1174 (Utah App. 2002).

Answer (C) is incorrect. This is false. *See Van Dyck v. Van Dyck*, 425 S.E.2d 853 (Ga. 1993).

Answer (D) is incorrect. The issue is not whether the payor is cohabitating but whether the payee is cohabitating, *see, e.g.*, Utah Stat. sec. 30-3-5(9), perhaps with the additional consideration that the payee spouse is receiving economic benefit. *Cf. In re Marriage of Ales*, 592 N.W.2d 698 (Iowa App. 1999).

134. A court will not permit an individual who has voluntarily taken a pay cut, so that his support obligations will be reduced to have those support obligations decreased. *See Fox v. Fox*, 942 P.2d 1084 (Wash. App. 1997). Rather, the amount that he could be making will be imputed to him and the support obligations will be determined in light of that imputed income. However, an individual who has involuntarily had his salary reduced materially may have his support obligation reduced in light of the decrease in income. *See Crockett v. Crockett*, 575 So.2d 942 (La. App. 1991) (involuntary termination from employment justified child support reduction). Here, Quentin will likely be unsuccessful in his attempt to have his payments reduced if his motivation for getting a new job is discovered or inferred.

135. Because the lottery ticket was bought after the marriage had ended, the ticket was not bought with marital property but with Mabel's separate property. Norman as a general matter would not be entitled to an increase in support unless his support had been artificially low for some reason. *See Foster v. Foster*, 1997 WL 583567 (Ohio App.); *Gerrits v. Gerrits*, 482 N.W.2d 134 (Wis. App. 1992). Had the ticket been bought during the marriage even if during a legal separation, however, then the winnings would have been subject to distribution. *See Ware v. Ware*, 748 A.2d 1031 (Md. App. 2000).

136. The goal of child support is not to freeze the child's standard of living at what it was during the marriage, *see Laird v. Laird*, 650 N.W.2d 296 (S.D. 2002), but to allow it to improve if possible. As a general matter, child support will be increased if the non-custodial parent has had a positive material change in income. *See Stofer v. Linville*, 662 S.W.2d 783 (Tex. App. 1983); *McKee v. McKee*, 820 P.2d 1362 (Okla. App. 1991). Thus, a lottery winner might well be ordered to increase his or

her child support payments. *See In re Marriage of Boyden*, 517 N.E.2d 1144 (Ill. App. 1987); *In re Marriage of McCord*, 910 P.2d 85 (Colo. App. 1995).

137. Frederick is correct. The Wydaho court does not have jurisdiction to modify either support order. Hermione still lives in Washegonia with her father. Given that both live there and that the Washegonia court retained jurisdiction, Ethel must file in Washegonia to have the support decrees modified. *See In re Marriage of Erickson*, 991 P.2d 123 (Wash. App. 2000) (holding that the Washington court does not have jurisdiction to modify custody support order because the obligor still lives in California, the initiating state).

138. David might be held to have agreed to support the child and then forced to live up to the agreement. Or, he might be equitably estopped from denying his obligation, especially because Cindy can argue detrimental reliance. *See In re Parentage of M.J.*, 787 N.E.2d 144 (Ill. 2003). It is likely that David will be ordered to pay child support, notwithstanding his never having married Cindy and his having no biological connection to the child.

139. While winning the lottery certainly increases income, courts have split on whether this justifies reducing support payments. Were Myron to take this in a lump sum payment, then he would not be receiving the increased monies annually and thus might be held not to have recurring increased income. *See Burnette v. Bender*, 908 P.2d 1086 (Ariz. App. 1995). However, some jurisdictions will require that lottery winnings be treated as income for child support purposes, even if the monies are not recurring. *See Clary v. Clary*, 54 S.W.3d 568 (Ky. App. 2001); *In re Marriage of Bohr*, 8 P.3d 539 (Colo. App. 2000).

140. If Terry's earnings have increased significantly and Thomas' have not, Thomas' support obligation may decrease. An increase in the custodial parent's income is proper to consider when deciding whether child support should be modified, *see Luker v. Luker*, 861 S.W.2d 195, 198-99 (Mo. App. 1993), and the issue will be what the relevant support tables say is the appropriate amount for Thomas to be paying given the two parents' incomes. The children will be receiving more than they were before even if a higher percentage is coming from the custodial parent.

141. While income may be imputed if an individual has a voluntary decrease in salary, *see Mittendorf v. Mittendorf*, 515 S.E.2d 464, 466 (N.C. App. 1999) ("A *voluntary* decrease in a parent's income, even if substantial, does not constitute a changed circumstance which alone can justify a modification of a child support award."), some states will modify a support obligation if a parent decides to stay home with a very young child, e.g., one under two years of age. *Compare Thomas v. Thomas*, 589 A.2d 1372 (N.J. Super. Ch. 1991) (parent who stays home with infant not ordered to pay support), *with Hershman v. Fountain*, 2003 WL 1827153 (Ark. App.) (income imputed to parent who stays home to take car of infant). The question at hand will be whether the jurisdiction treats the parent who quits a job to stay home to take care of his or her young infant as voluntarily (and unjustifiably) stopping employment, in which case the salary will presumably be imputed, or instead as justifiably stopping employment, in which case the salary may well not be imputed.

142. **Answer (C) is the best answer**. *See St. Luke's Presbyterian Hospital v. Underwood*, 957 S.W.2d 497, 499 (Mo. App. 1997) ("Although historically the doctrine required only a husband to pay the necessary expenses of his wife, the doctrine is now gender neutral and applies equally to each spouse."); *Geisinger Medical Center v. Salerno*, 40 Pa. D. & C., 668, 669 (Pa. Com. Pl. 1986) ("The 'doctrine of necessaries' provides that a husband may be held liable for the 'necessary' goods and services provided to his wife or family, despite the absence of any express written consent on his part.").

Answer (A) is incorrect. This is not a good answer because the doctrine may well apply in this case. *See* Haw. Stat. sec. 572-24 ("Both spouses of a marriage, whether married in this State or in some other jurisdiction, and residing in this, shall be bound to maintain, provide for, and support one another during marriage, and shall be liable for all debts contracted by one another for necessaries for themselves, one another, or their family during marriage.")

Answer (B) is incorrect. *See St. Luke's Presbyterian Hospital v. Underwood*, 957 S.W.2d 497, 499 (Mo. App. 1997) ("Under the doctrine of necessaries, if the medical services patient received were necessary and patient maintained no separate assets, wife would be liable for the reasonable value of the medical services patient received.").

Answer (D) is incorrect. She may well be held responsible, notwithstanding that she thinks it inadvisable. *See* Haw. Stat. sec. 572-24.

TOPIC 16: FAMILY PRIVACY AND THE CONSTITUTION

ANSWERS

143. **Answer (C) is the best answer**. *See Beltram v. Allan*, 926 P.2d 892, 895 (Utah App. 1996) (putative father can establish rights only if he acts in a timely way).

 Answer (A) is incorrect. While a husband does not have the legal right to veto his wife's getting an abortion, *see Planned Parenthood of Central Missouri v. Danforth*, 428 U.S. 52 (1976), a woman will not be able to put a child up for adoption if the father disagrees and he has established a relation with the child. *See, e.g., Petition of Doe*, 638 N.E.2d 181 (Ill. 1994) (unmarried father's consent to adoption required).

 Answer (B) is incorrect. While the interest of parents in the care, custody, and control of their children is fundamental, *see Troxel v. Granville*, 530 U.S. 57, 65 (2000), that interest is not absolute. *See id.* at 88 (Stevens, J., dissenting).

 Answer (D) is incorrect. The father's rights are not contingent on his reconciling with the mother. *See, e.g., In re Riggs*, 612 S.W.2d 461 (Tenn. App. 1981) (unwed father's right recognized notwithstanding no reconciliation with the child's mother).

144. **Answer (D) is the best answer**. *See, e.g., In re C.B.*, 2002 WL 1072245 (Iowa App. 2002) (father's rights terminated after taking no action to begin relationship with his son).

 Answer (A) is incorrect. This is false. While *Stanley v. Illinois*, 406 U.S. 645 (1972), stands for the proposition that unmarried fathers have an important interest in the care and custody of their children, the case does not establish that the interest can never be overridden by the state.

 Answer (B) is incorrect. While *Lehr v. Robertson*, 463 U.S. 248 (1983), establishes that in some cases it is unnecessary to get a consent to adoption from an unmarried father who fails to establish a connection with his child, the case does not suggest that consent is never necessary to obtain if the mother no longer wishes to have any contact with the father.

 Answer (C) is incorrect. This is inaccurate. The promise to be a better father now will not suffice to safeguard a father's interest in his child when the father has failed to establish any connection with his child. *See, e.g., Lehr v. Robertson*, 463 U.S. 248 (1983) (individual who had never established a relationship with his daughter could not block her being adopted by her mother's husband).

145. Carl is unlikely to be successful as a matter of federal constitutional right. In *Michael H. v. Gerald D.*, 491 U.S. 110 (1989), a plurality of the Supreme Court held that the Fourteenth Amendment did not protect the parental rights of a man who had in all probability fathered a child with a woman married to someone else. While Carl might be more successful if the state constitution protected his parental rights, *see*

In re J.W.T., 872 S.W.2d 189 (Tex. 1994) (state constitution afforded protection to parental rights of man who fathered a child with a woman in an intact marriage with someone else), he is unlikely to succeed by claiming that the Fourteenth Amendment affords him protection unless *Michael H.* is overruled.

146. **Answer (D) is the best answer**. *See Coleman v. Coleman*, 471 A.2d 1115 (Md. App. 1984) (husband constitutionally prohibited from enjoining wife's abortion).

 Answer (A) is incorrect. A husband does not have the right to veto his wife's decision to seek an abortion. *See Planned Parenthood of Central Missouri v. Danforth*, 428 U.S. 52 (1976).

 Answer (B) is incorrect. This is an overstatement. *See Planned Parenthood of Southeastern Pennsylvania v. Casey*, 505 U.S. 833, 875 (1992) ("it is an overstatement to describe it as a right to decide whether to have an abortion without interference from the State").

 Answer (C) is incorrect. The decision is for the wife rather than the husband to make and the court should not be engaging in this kind of balancing test. *See Conn v. Conn*, 525 N.E.2d 612 (Ind. App. 1988) (court erred in using balancing test to decide whether wife should be allowed to obtain abortion).

147. **Answer (A) is the best answer**. *See Bellotti v. Baird*, 443 U.S. 622, 643 (1979) ("if the State decides to require a pregnant minor to obtain one or both parents' consent to an abortion, it also must provide an alternative procedure whereby authorization for the abortion can be obtained").

 Answer (B) is incorrect. This does not accurately reflect the law. *See Planned Parenthood of Southeastern Pennsylvania v. Casey*, 505 U.S. 833, 846 (1992) ("Before viability, the State's interests are not strong enough to support a prohibition of abortion or the imposition of a substantial obstacle to the woman's effective right to elect the procedure.").

 Answer (C) is incorrect. This statement is too strong. A state can require that a minor either have parental permission to get an abortion or, instead, have permission from a court. *See Casey*, 505 U.S. at 899 ("a State may require a minor seeking an abortion to obtain the consent of a parent or guardian, provided that there is an adequate judicial bypass procedure").

 Answer (D) is incorrect. The law will be struck down. *See Casey*, 505 U.S. at 846.

148. **Answer (C) is the best answer**. *Cf. Davis v. Davis*, 842 S.W.2d 588, 604 (Tenn. 1992) ("The case would be closer if Mary Sue Davis were seeking to use the preembryos herself, but only if she could not achieve parenthood by any other reasonable means.").

 Answer (A) is incorrect. While they might well be awarded to Tara, this would not be because she would be able to abort had they been implanted. Rather, it is more likely that a balancing approach would be used where there was no prior agreement about what to do in this case. *See Davis v. Davis*, 842 S.W.2d 588 (Tenn. 1992).

Answer (B) is incorrect. While the state may favor life over non-life, that interest would likely be held not to suffice to require that Vince receive the embryos. *See Davis*, 842 S.W.2d at 602 ("the state's interest in potential human life is insufficient to justify an infringement on the gamete-providers' procreational autonomy").

Answer (D) is incorrect. This does not take into account the individual's interest in not being a parent. *See Davis*, 842 S.W.2d at 604 ("Ordinarily, the party wishing to avoid procreation should prevail, assuming that the other party has a reasonable possibility of achieving parenthood by means other than use of the preembryos in question.").

149. **Answer (D) is the best answer**. *See Whitner v. South Carolina*, 492 S.E.2d 777 (1997) (upholding a statute criminalizing a mother's exposing her viable fetus to illegal drugs).

Answer (A) is incorrect. The statute is not precluded by *Roe v. Wade*, 410 U.S. 113 (1973), or by *Planned Parenthood of Southeastern Pennsylvania v. Casey*, 505 U.S. 833 (1992). *See Whitner v. South Carolina*, 492 S.E.2d 777, 783 (1997) (upholding similar statute in light of *Roe* and *Casey*).

Answer (B) is incorrect. The state does not have plenary power over all matters involving reproduction. *See Planned Parenthood of Southeastern Pennsylvania v. Casey*, 505 U.S. 833 (1992) (striking down section of Pennsylvania statute regulating abortion because it imposed an undue burden on the right to get an abortion).

Answer (C) is incorrect. Such a statute will likely be upheld. *See Whitner v. South Carolina*, 492 S.E.2d 777 (1997) (upholding similar statute in light of *Roe* and *Casey*).

150. This statue will be struck down as unconstitutional. A statute prohibiting abortion must provide exceptions if the life or health of the mother is at risk. *See Stenberg v. Carhart*, 530 U.S. 914, 930 (2000). Because this statute precludes all partial birth abortions even if this would be the safest method and any other method would significantly increase the risk to the woman carrying the fetus, the statute does not pass constitutional muster. The *Stenberg* Court made clear that "a State may promote but not endanger a woman's health when it regulates the methods of abortion." *See id.* at 931.

151. **Answer (B) is the best answer**. The court is likely to deny that adultery is protected and may well use the history and traditions test. *See Oliverson v. West Valley City*, 875 F.Supp. 1465 (D. Utah 1995). While the Court in *Lawrence v. Texas*, 123 S. Ct. 2472 (2003), struck down the state's sodomy law, it is unclear whether the Court would also strike down adultery laws. The Court might suggest that adultery is unprotected because it involves "abuse of an institution the law protects." *Id.* at 2484.

Answer (A) is incorrect. While the Court in *Eisenstadt v. Baird*, 405 U.S. 438 (1972) did suggest that singles and marrieds must be treated alike with respect to access to contraception, the case has not been construed to mean that adultery statutes are unconstitutional. *See, e.g., Oliverson v. West Valley City*, 875 F. Supp. 1465 (D. Utah 1995) (holding the adultery statute constitutional).

Answer (C) is incorrect. While the Court did discuss the "sacred precincts of marital bedrooms" in *Griswold v. Connecticut*, 381 U.S. 479, 485 (1965), the Court was not merely discussing where the relations took place but also the people who were having the relations, i.e., a married couple.

Answer (D) is incorrect. The couple is challenging the law on federal rather than state grounds. As a separate matter, state courts have rejected that adultery statutes violate federal or state constitutional guarantees. *See, e.g., City of Sherman v. Henry*, 928 S.W.2d 464 (Tex. 1996).

152. **Answer (C) is the best answer**. *See Sosna v. Iowa*, 419 U.S. 393 (1975) (upholding one-year residency requirement, suggesting that it merely imposed a delay of marriage and did not involve a deprivation of that right).

Answer (A) is incorrect. While the Court has recognized that the "the decision to marry is a fundamental right"), *see Turner v. Safley*, 482 U.S. 78, 95 (1987), that does not entail that residency requirements for divorce are unconstitutional.

Answer (B) is incorrect. The state does not have plenary power over the marital status of its domiciliaries, since some marital restrictions are unconstitutional. *See Loving v. Virginia*, 388 U.S. 1 (1967) (striking down anti-miscegenation laws as violating constitutional guarantees).

Answer (D) is incorrect. This is false. *See Sosna v. Iowa*, 419 U.S. 393 (1975) (upholding Iowa's one-year residency requirement).

153. **Answer (D) is the best answer**. *See Village of Belle Terre v. Borass*, 416 U.S. 1 (1974) (upholding a similar zoning statute on rational basis grounds).

Answer (A) is incorrect. A court is unlikely to find this unconstitutional, since the United States Supreme Court upheld a similar statute in *Village of Belle Terre v. Borass*, 416 U.S. 1 (1974).

Answer (B) is incorrect. While they will likely be unsuccessful, that is not merely because they could marry if they wanted to do so. The statute would apply to individuals who could not marry, *e.g.*, several individuals not related by blood who wanted to live in the same house, and the *Belle Terre* Court did not suggest that such a prohibition could only be applied to individuals who were choosing not to marry. *See Village of Belle Terre v. Borass*, 416 U.S. 1 (1974).

Answer (C) is incorrect. While such an attack might be successful as a matter of statutory interpretation, *see Braschi v. Stahl Assoc.*, 543 N.E.2d 49 (N.Y. 1989) (interpreting eviction statute to protect functional family), it would be unlikely to be successful as a federal constitutional matter. While the Court has been willing to extend protections to extended family, *see Moore v. City of East Cleveland*, 431 U.S. 494 (1977), the Court has not been willing to include functional families within that notion of extended family.

154. **Answer (C) is the best answer**. *See In re Baby Boy Doe*, 632 N.E.2d 326 (Ill. App. 1994) (holding in a case involving analogous circumstances that the mother has the right to make the relevant decision).

Answer (A) is incorrect. This is false. Jane may well be successful in avoiding the caesarian even if that decision increases the risk to her fetus. *See In re Baby Boy Doe*, 632 N.E.2d 326 (Ill. App. 1994). *But see Pemberto v. Tallahassee Memorial Regional Medical Center*, 66 F. Supp.2d 1247 (N. D. Fla. 1999).

Answer (B) is incorrect. Jane may well be successful in avoiding the caesarian even if that decision increases her own risk. *See In re Baby Boy Doe*, 632 N.E.2d 326 (Ill. App. 1994).

Answer (D) is incorrect. The fetus does not have the same right to life that she does. *Cf. Planned Parenthood of Southeastern Pennsylvania v. Casey*, 505 US 833 (1992) (statutes restricting abortion must have exceptions where the life or the health of the mother is at stake).

155. **Answer (B) is the best answer**. *See, e.g., State v. McKown*, 475 N.W.2d 63 (Minn. 1991) (state would have been able to prosecute parents whose child died as a result of their only permitting treatment via spiritual healing had there not been a statute which seemed to afford a good faith exception protecting the parents).

Answer (A) is incorrect. This is false. *See, e.g., People v. Rippberger*, 231 Cal. App.3d 1667 (Ct. App. 1991) (parents' conviction for death of child after only permitting spiritual treatment for acute bacterial meningitis did not violate First Amendment free exercise rights).

Answer (C) is incorrect. This is false. *Cf. Newmark v. Williams*, 588 A.2d 1108 (Del. 1991) (child not neglected when parents for religious reasons rejected cancer treatment having only 40% success rate).

Answer (D) is incorrect. This is false. *Cf. Newmark v. Williams*, 588 A.2d 1108, 1120 (Del. 1991) ("Parents must have the right at some point to reject medical treatment for their child.").

156. **Answer (D) is the best answer**. *See In re Wirsing*, 573 N.W.2d 51 (Mich. 1998) (sterilization would be permitted if it was in the best interests of the patient); *Matter of Moe*, 432 N.E.2d 712 (Mass. 1982) (sterilization permissible if it would have been chosen by incompetent as determined through substituted judgment procedure).

Answer (A) is incorrect. This standard will likely be viewed as too demanding. *See, e.g., Matter of Moe*, 432 N.E.2d 723 n.11 (Mass. 1982) (rejecting that a compelling state interest must be established before an incompetent's sterilization can be approved).

Answer (B) is incorrect. The procedure is to be performed for the sake of the individual himself or herself and not for the sake of the State. *See Matter of Moe*, 432 N.E.2d 723 (Mass. 1982) ("there is no State interest which could override the ward's refusal, or the court's substituted judgment of refusal, to consent to sterilization").

Answer (C) is incorrect. This focuses on the wrong party's interests. *See Matter of Susan B.*, 1996 WL 75343, *7 (Del. Ch.) (requiring a "demonstration that the proponents of sterilization are seeking it in good faith and that their primary concern is for the best interest of the incompetent person rather than their own or the public's convenience").

157. **Answer (C) is the best answer**. Under *Johnson v. Calvert*, 851 P.2d 776 (Cal. 1993), had Connie been unable to produce eggs but able to carry the child to term, she also would have been held to be the mother if that was the intention of the parties.

Answer (A) is incorrect. While it captures the *Baby M.* result, it does not capture the *Johnson* result. In *In re Baby M.*, 537 A.2d 1227 (N.J. 1988), the New Jersey Supreme Court held that surrogacy contracts are void. In *Johnson v. Calvert*, 851 P.2d 776 (Cal. 1993), the California Supreme Court upheld a surrogacy agreement. The two are reconcilable in that the former involved a genetic surrogacy agreement (where the surrogate has a genetic connection to the child because she provides the egg) whereas the latter involves a gestational surrogacy agreement (where fertilization occurs outside of the surrogate and she does not provide the egg). The *Johnson* court suggested that the intentions of the parties will govern where the woman providing gestational services is not the woman who is genetically related to the child. Given the *Johnson* result, Connie rather than Samantha would likely be held to be the mother. In California, genetic surrogacy arrangements are unenforceable. *See In re Marriage of Moschetta*, 25 Cal. App. 4th 1218 (Ct. App. 1994).

Answer (B) is incorrect. Connie rather than Samantha would likely be held to be the mother.

Answer (D) is incorrect. The *Johnson* court emphasized the intentions of the parties rather than who was genetically related to the child.

158. **Answer (D) is the best answer**. *See In re E.G.*, 549 N.E.2d 322 (Ill. 1989) (17-year-old found sufficiently mature to refuse treatment).

Answer (A) is incorrect. The state might have appointed a guardian if Julie had been found not sufficiently mature to have made the decision for herself. *See In re E.G.*, 549 N.E.2d 322, 325 (Ill. 1989) ("An infant [i.e., minor] child . . . can be compelled to accept life-saving medical treatment over the objections of her parents.").

Answer (B) is incorrect. This is false in that the state may refuse to appoint a guardian if the child is sufficiently mature to make these decisions for herself. *See In re E.G.*, 549 N.E.2d 322 (Ill. 1989).

Answer (C) is incorrect. The question at hand is whether Julie is sufficiently competent to make the decision. That will have to be decided by the court. *See In re E.G.*, 549 N.E.2d 322, 327 (Ill. 1989) ("The trial judge must determine whether a minor is mature enough to make health care choices on her own.").

159. **Answer (B) is the best answer**. This answer simply is not plausible. In *DeShaney v. Winnebago County Dept. of Social Services*, 489 U.S. 189 (1989), the Court held that the state was not liable for the failure to remove a child from the home when it was on notice that the child's father was abusing the child. The Court's holding that the state was not liable would not provide any incentive for the state to reduce the number of cases in which this kind of abuse would occur.

Answer (A) is incorrect. It is plausible to believe that counties would be less anxious to provide these services if they would be subject to potentially crushing liability for the failure to remove a child from an abusive home.

Answer (C) is incorrect. The imposition of liability for the failure to protect might well have induced the state to remove children from the home as soon as there was any hint of danger and also to refuse to return the child until the state could be very sure that the child was in no danger.

Answer (D) is incorrect. This in fact represented the position of the Court. *See DeShaney*, 489 U.S. at 201 ("While the State may have been aware of the dangers that Joshua faced in the free world, it played no part in their creation, nor did it do anything to render him any more vulnerable to them.").

160. **Answer (C) is the best answer**. Some states permit less severe penalties to be imposed for such crimes. *See, e.g.*, Ariz. Stat. sec. 13-1406.01 (permitting judge to classify the first offense of a sexual assault of a spouse as a misdemeanor); *Va. Stat.* 18.2-61(c) (permitting suspended sentence for sexual assault of a spouse under certain conditions).

Answer (A) is incorrect. *See People v. Liberta*, 474 N.E.2d 567, 574 (N.Y. 1984) ("right of privacy protects consensual acts, not violent sexual assaults").

Answer (B) is incorrect. *See, e.g.*, S. C. Stat. Ann. sec. 16-3-658 ("A person cannot be guilty of criminal sexual conduct under... [specified sections] if the victim is the legal spouse unless the couple is living apart and the offending spouse's conduct constitutes criminal sexual conduct in the first degree or second degree.").

Answer (D) is incorrect. This is false. The issue is not whether the refusal was "unreasonable" but whether the relations were nonconsensual.

161. **Answer (D) is the best answer**. The privilege will likely be held not to apply here. *See, e.g.*, Tenn. Stat. sec. 24-1-201(b) (marital privilege does not apply in case involving spousal abuse).

Answer (A) is incorrect. This is false. Even if the court were willing to protect more than verbal communication as protected expression, *see State v. Pelletier*, 818 A.2d 292, 298 (N.H. 2003) ("private, lawful, consensual sexual activity between a husband and wife constitutes privileged communications"), it is unlikely to apply in this case. *See, e.g.*, Tenn. Stat. sec. 24-1-201(b) (marital privilege does not apply in case involving spousal abuse).

Answer (B) is incorrect. While it may well be that the privilege applies to communications made during to the marriage even if the parties are no longer married, *see State v. Parent*, 836 So.2d 494, 504 (La. App. 2002) ("each spouse has a privilege during and after a marriage to refuse to disclose, and to prevent the other spouse from disclosing, confidential communications with the other spouse while they are husband and wife"), it is unlikely that the privilege would apply to this. *See Com. v. Kirkner*, 805 A.2d 514, 516 (Pa. 2002) (no marital privilege with respect to alleged spousal abuse).

Answer (C) is incorrect. While it is true that states differ with respect to which spouse owns the privilege, *compare* Tenn. Stat. sec. 24-1-201(b) ("In a civil proceeding, confidential communications between married persons are privileged and inadmissible if either spouse objects."), *with* Kan. Stat. Ann 60-428(a), that would likely be irrelevant here because the privilege would likely be held not to be implicated here. *See, e.g.*, Com. v. Kirkner, 805 A.2d 514, 516 (Pa. 2002).

162. While states are precluded from imposing an undue burden on a woman's right to choose to abort a fetus that has not yet reached viability, *see Planned Parenthood of Southeastern Pennsylvania v. Casey*, 505 U.S. 833, 846 (1992), this statute does not seem to impose such an undue burden both because it is expressly limited to viable fetuses and more importantly because it is not aimed at limiting a woman's right to choose. While a state might decide as a matter of public policy that it would be unwise to have such a statute, the constitutionality of the statute is likely to be upheld. *See Whitner v. South Carolina*, 492 S.E.2d 777 (1997) (upholding an analogous statute).

163. The test for whether a procedure can be performed on a child is whether it will promote that child's interests. Here, more discussion of how this would benefit Thomas must be offered. It may be that Thomas and Terry are very close and it would be devastating for Thomas to lose Terry. *Cf. Strunk v. Strunk*, 445 S.W.2d 145 (Ky. 1969) (authorizing transplant because loss of brother would be devastating to donor, who was an incompetent). Or, it may be that Thomas would suffer no long-term detriment were he to lose Terry, and the risks of surgery would outweigh the benefits to Thomas. *See Curran v. Bosze*, 566 N.E.2d 1319 (Ill. 1990) (bone marrow transplant could not be authorized because it would not be of sufficient benefit to potential donor, who was a minor).

164. John and Mary's challenge will be unsuccessful. In *Prince v. Massachusetts*, 321 U.S. 158 (1944), the Court made clear that "the custody, care and nurture of the child reside first in the parents, whose primary function and freedom include preparation for obligations the state can neither supply nor hinder." *Id.* at 166. However, in that same decision the Court established that while parents "may be free to become martyrs themselves, . . . it does not follow they are free, in identical circumstances, to make martyrs of their children before they have reached the age of full and legal discretion when they can make that choice for themselves." *Id.* at 170. As the Maryland Supreme Court explained in *Kirchner v. Caughey*, 606 A.2d 257, 261 (Md. 1992), "When the welfare of a child is threatened, however, the task of intervention cannot be avoided, and under some circumstances actions based upon the sincerely held religious beliefs of one parent or both parents must give way to the safety and welfare of the child."

165. **Answer (B) is the best answer**. See Zablocki v. Redhail, 434 U.S. 374, 388 (1978) ("When a statutory classification significantly interferes with the exercise of a fundamental right, it cannot be upheld unless it is supported by sufficiently important state interests and is closely tailored to effectuate only those interests.").

    Answer (A) is incorrect. This is false. *See Zablocki v. Redhail*, 434 U.S. 374, 386 (1978) ("reasonable regulations that do not significantly interfere with decisions to enter into the marital relationship may legitimately be imposed").

    Answer (C) is incorrect. This is false. The Fourteenth Amendment does not impose a national marriage law. The Court has never held that a marriage celebrated in one state must be recognized by all the states. *See, e.g., Loughran v. Loughran*, 292 U.S. 216, 223 (1934) (italics added) ("Marriages *not polygamous or incestuous, or otherwise declared void by statute*, will, if valid by the law of the state where entered into, be recognized as valid in every other jurisdiction.").

    Answer (D) is incorrect. This is false. States do not have great latitude with respect to the kinds of significant burdens that they can place on the right to marry. *See Zablocki v. Redhail*, 434 U.S. 374, 388 (1978).

166. **Answer (D) is the best answer**. *See Potter v. Murray City*, 585 F. Supp. 1126 (D. Utah 1984) (examining statute prohibiting plural marriage with strict scrutiny and upholding it).

    Answer (A) is incorrect. Were this the test then a state could simply say that marriage is defined as a union of two individuals of the same race and thereby preclude interracial marriage. However, *Loving v. Virginia*, 388 U.S. 1 (1967), establishes that states could not do that.

    Answer (B) is incorrect. While *Reynolds v. United States*, 98 U.S. 145 (1878), suggests that the Constitution does not preclude laws banning polygamy, it is also true that interracial marriage bans were also being upheld as constitutional at that time and the Court had not yet imposed close scrutiny on laws. *Loving* establishes that interracial bans are unconstitutional. One could not tell just from looking at *Reynolds* and *Loving* whether laws banning polygamy were constitutional.

    Answer (C) is incorrect. The Court in *Zablocki v. Redhail*, 434 U.S. 374 (1978), made clear that statutes significantly burdening marriage will be examined with close judicial scrutiny.

167. The state has a legitimate interest in assuring that children will receive the support that is due. However, to abridge the fundamental right to marry, the state must establish that it has very important interests and that the statute is sufficiently closely tailored to promote those interests. In *Zablocki v. Redhail*, 434 U.S. 374 (1978), the United States Supreme Court addressed whether a similar statute would pass constitutional muster, concluding that it did not. The same analysis would yield a similar result with respect to the Winnigan statute. Bob's challenge will likely be successful.

TOPIC 17: PARENTING RELATIONSHIPS — ANSWERS

168. **Answer (A) is the best answer**. John may well be viewed by the law as being a legal stranger to the child, and held to be neither the child's biological nor legal father. *See, e.g., Van v. Zahorik*, 597 N.W.2d 15 (Mich. 1999).

     Answer (B) is incorrect. This is inaccurate because more would have to be shown than that awarding him custody would promote the child's best interests. *See In re Guardianship of L.L.*, 745 N.E.2d 222, 228 (Ind. App. 2001) ("a generalized finding that a child's placement with a third party as opposed to a natural parent is in his or her 'best interests' is insufficient to rebut the parental preference presumption").

     Answer (C) is incorrect. Because adultery does not establish per se unfitness in most states, *see, e.g., Scott v. Scott*, 665 So.2d 760, 765 (La. App. 1995) ("One or several acts of adultery with the same person does not, per se, render a parent morally unfit who is otherwise suited for custody."), being unfaithful to one's non-marital partner would also be unlikely to establish per se unfitness.

     Answer (D) is incorrect. This is false. Were John to adopt a child, he would have all of the parental rights of a biological father. *See, e.g.*, Conn. Stat. 17(a)-1(11) (" 'Parent' means a biological or adoptive parent, except a parent whose parental rights have been terminated.").

169. **Answer (C) is the best answer**. *See In re Interest of R.C.*, 775 P.2d 27 (Colo. 1080); *McIntyre v. Crouch*, 780 P.2d 239 (Or. App. 1989).

     Answer (A) is incorrect. This is inaccurate. If Peter and Paula initially agreed that Peter would have parental rights, then he may be recognized as the father notwithstanding that conception occurred via artificial insemination. *See McIntyre v. Crouch*, 780 P.2d 239 (Or. App. 1989).

     Answer (B) is incorrect. This is inaccurate. Notwithstanding this biological connection, Peter's rights will depend upon the initial agreement that he had with Paula. *See In re Interest of R.C.*, 775 P.2d 27, 35 (Colo. 1989).

     Answer (D) is incorrect. This is false. Even if Paula does not want Peter to have parental rights, he may, depending upon their initial agreement and his subsequent attempts to support and establish a relation with Robert. *See In re Interest of R.C.*, 775 P.2d 27 (Colo. 1989).

170. **Answer (B) is the best answer**. *See Zerby v. Brown*, 160 N.W.2d 255, 258 (Minn. 1968) ("better practice in contested matters is to resolve the question of parental fitness before the adoption petition is heard . . . to avoid termination of parental rights on the basis of comparing the qualifications of natural and adoptive parents").

Answer (A) is incorrect. All else equal, efficiency is an advantage rather than a detriment. The difficulty is that a fit parent might lose his or her parental rights in the quest for efficiency.

Answer (C) is incorrect. It is not at all clear that this would be a difficulty. In an open adoption, the birth parent may have continued contact with the adoptive parents and their adoptive child. States differ about whether open adoption agreements are enforceable. *See, e.g., Birth Mother v. Adoptive Parents*, 59 P.3d 1233 (Nev. 2002) (holding that open adoption agreement is not enforceable in Nevada).

Answer (D) is incorrect. While it is true that a young child may be too immature to articulate a considered preference, that would be true whether these hearings were held jointly or separately and thus does not speak to the issue at hand.

171. **Answer (B) is the best answer.** *See In re Doe*, 978 P.2d 166, 176 n.11 (Haw. App. 1999) ("'open adoptions' have been characterized as arrangements in which the natural parents may retain either visitation rights or rights to information about their child after they have surrendered their parental rights").

Answer (A) is incorrect. While a biological parent may file a motion to set aside a judgment terminating parental rights before but not after an adoption has been finalized, *see, e.g.*, Conn. Stat. 452-719, that is not what is meant by an open adoption.

Answer (C) is incorrect. Because of privacy concerns, there is limited access to adoption information. *See, e.g.*, Ala. Stat. 26-10A-31 (specifying the people that would have access to that information).

Answer (D) is incorrect. This is inaccurate because an open adoption may nonetheless require that the biological parent's rights be terminated. *See People in Interest of B.S.*, 566 N.W.2d 446, 450 (S.D. 1997).

172. **Answer (A) is the best answer.** As a general matter, a parent cannot retain his or her parental rights if someone else is going to adopt his or her child. However, there is an exception to this rule, sometimes called the stepparent exception, which permits a stepparent to adopt his or her spouse's child without that spouse being required to give up his or her parental rights. *See, e.g.*, Ala. Code 1975 sec. 26-10A-27 (permitting stepparent adoptions).

Answer (B) is incorrect. As a general matter, a stepparent will not have a duty to support the children of his or her former spouse after they divorce unless the stepparent acted in some way to take on that obligation, e.g., by making a promise or by interfering with the non-custodial parent's attempt to support. *See, e.g., Miller v. Miller*, 478 A.2d 351, 355 (N.J. 1984) (discussing the conditions under which a stepparent might have a support obligation after divorce). However, this is not because an exception is being made for the stepparent but merely because as a general matter individuals do not have a responsibility to support a child with whom they have no legal connection.

Answer (C) is incorrect. While a stepparent may be a de facto parent, that status is by no means limited to stepparents and should not be construed as a status creating a special exception for stepparents. *See In re B.G.*, 11 Cal.3d 679, 692 n.18 (Cal. 1974) (discussing the "person who, on a day-to-day basis, assumes the role of parent, seeking to fulfill both the child's physical needs and his psychological need for affection and care").

Answer (D) is incorrect. The parent and stepparent are not placed on an equal footing with respect to parental decision-making. *See In re Shelby R.*, 804 A.2d 435, 441 (N. H. 2002) ("The stepparent's relationship with the stepchild may be a strong emotional attachment, but it has not been recognized as a constitutional interest on a par with the natural parent-child relationship.").

173. **Answer (C) is the best answer.** *See Matter of Adoption of Alyssa, L.B.*, 501 N.Y.S.2d 595, 596 (Sur. Ct. 1986) ("the usual reimbursable expenses of a natural mother are limited to those . . . on account of or incidental to the birth or care of the adoptive child, the pregnancy or care of the adoptive child's mother or the placement or adoption of the child and on account of or incidental to assistance in arrangements for such placement or adoption").

Answer (A) is incorrect. This is false. *See In re Baby Girl D.*, 517 A.2d 925, 927 (Pa. 1986) ("Traditionally, allowable expenses to adoptor parents have been limited to reasonable unreimbursed lying-in expenses, reasonable legal fees incident to the adoption proceedings and costs of the proceeding.").

Answer (B) is incorrect. This is also false. *See In re Baby Girl D.*, 517 A.2d 925 (Pa. 1986) (discussing the limited expenses that may be reimbursed).

Answer (D) is incorrect. This is false. Monies paid in addition to the costs would not be permitted. *See Matter of Adoption of Alyssa, L.B.*, 501 N.Y.S.2d 595 (Sur. Ct. 1986).

174. **Answer (B) is the best answer.** *See Geranifar v. Geranifar*, 688 A.2d 475, 477 (Md. App. 1997) ("Equitable adoption is sometimes called 'adoption by estoppel,' 'virtual adoption,' or 'de facto adoption.' By whatever name it is known, the doctrine in general involves the notion that if an individual who is legally competent to adopt a child enters into a contract to do so, and if the contract is supported by consideration in the form of part performance that falls short of completion of statutory adoption, then a court, applying equitable principles, may accord to the child the status of a formally adopted child for certain limited purposes.").

Answer (A) is incorrect. While it is hoped that the adoption would promote the best interests of all concerned, that is not the requirement. *See, e.g., Carter v. Knox County Office of Family and Children*, 761 N.E.2d 431, 436 (Ind. App. 2001) (discussing a judge's balancing the interest of the child against the interest of the mother when deciding that her parental rights should be terminated).

Answer (C) is incorrect. While as a matter of policy states will try to place children in a way that promotes their interests, *see State ex rel. Dept. of Social Services v. Roldan*, 67 P.3d 968, 969 (Or. App. 2003), that may mean keeping siblings together or instead separating them. In any event, this has nothing to do with equitable adoption. *See Geranifar v. Geranifar*, 688 A.2d 475, 477 (Md. App. 1997) (explaining equitable adoption).

Answer (D) is incorrect. This is false. A natural parent may withdraw his or her consent to an adoption upon a showing of fraud, duress or intimidation. *See Grafe v. Olds*, 556 So.2d 690, 694 (Miss. 1990).

175. **Answer (D) is the best answer**. Not only is this not required, but it might amount to a criminal offense. *See* Tex. Penal Code sec. 25.08 (Sale or Purchase of a Child).

Answer (A) is incorrect. This is one of the elements of an equitable adoption. *See Calista Corp. v. Mann*, 564 P.2d 53, 62 (Alaska 1977).

Answer (B) is incorrect. This is also one of the elements. *See Kupect v. Cooper*, 593 So.2d 1176, 1177 (Fla. App. 1992).

Answer (C) is incorrect. This is also required. *See Miller v. Paczier*, 591 So.2d 321, 322 (Fla. App. 1991).

176. **Answer (D) is the best answer**. *See In re Adoption of D.J.H.*, 18 Pa. D & C.3d 424,427 (Pa. Com. Pl. 1974) ("She [the grandmother] is not a party in interest to the adoption and whether she approved or disapproved of the adoption is irrelevant.").

Answer (A) is incorrect. This factor may be considered. *See Ross v. Dept. of Health and Rehabilitative Services*, 347 So.2d 753 (Fla. App. 1977) (upholding dismissal of adoption petition because of appellant's age, economic condition and marital status).

Answer (B) is incorrect. This factor may also be considered. *See Ross v. Dept. of Health and Rehabilitative Services*, 347 So.2d 753 (Fla. App. 1977).

Answer (C) is incorrect. This factor may also be considered. *See Ross v. Dept. of Health and Rehabilitative Services*, 347 So.2d 753 (Fla. App. 1977).

177. **Answer (C) is the best answer**. *See In re Bonfield*, 780 N.E.2d 241, 244 (Ohio 2002) ("Second parent adoption is a process by which a partner in a cohabiting and nonmarital relationship may adopt his or her partner's biological or adoptive child, without requiring the parent to relinquish any parental rights.").

Answer (A) is incorrect. While this would be the parent's second adoption, this might not be a second parent adoption. Indeed, here it is not clear whether someone else is also adopting the child. Many states permit single adults to adopt children. *See, e.g.*, Ala. Code 1975 sec. 26-10A-5(a)(2) ("No rule or regulation of the Department of Human Resources or any agency shall prevent an adoption by a single person solely because such person is single or shall prevent an adoption solely because such person is of a certain age").

Answer (B) is incorrect. First, the parent adopts the child rather than the other way around. Also, what is described here is a stepparent adoption rather than a second parent adoption. In the latter, the parent and his or her partner do not have a legally recognized relationship. The difference may be important. *See, e.g.*, Ga. Stat. sec. 19-8-5 ("[A] child who has any living parent or guardian may be adopted by a third party who is neither the stepparent nor relative of that child . . . only if each such living parent and each such guardian has voluntarily and in writing surrendered all of his rights to the child to that third person for the purpose of enabling that person to adopt the child.").

Answer (D) is incorrect. What is described here is simply an adoption or, perhaps, a second adoption, but not a second parent adoption.

178. **Answer (A) is the best answer**. *See In re Estate of Brittin*, 664 N.E.2d 687, 690 (Ill. App. 1996) ("The adoptee, regardless of his age upon adoption, attains the status of a natural child of the adopting parents.") A separate question is whether the adoption is for all purposes or only for purposes of inheritance. *Compare Gorman v. South Carolina Reinsurance Facility*, 511 S.E.2d 98, 101 (S.C. App. 1999) ("[T]he clear statutory mandate [is] that adult adoptions do not have the same legal consequences as child adoptions. The legislature chose to limit the legal consequences of adult adoptions to intestate succession."), *with In re Adoption of Swanson*, 623 A.2d 1095, 1099 (Del. 1993) ("Adult adoptions intended to foster a sexual relationship would be against public policy as violative of the incest statute.")

Answer (B) is incorrect. This is false. Adult adoptions involve an adoption of an adult and are not simply an adoption by an adult. *See e.g.*, Ohio Stat. sec. 3107.02(B) (specifying when adult adoptions may occur).

Answer (C) is incorrect. This is inaccurate as a general matter, although some states limit the conditions under which an adult may be adopted. *See* Ohio Stat. sec. 3107.02(B) ("An adult may be adopted under any of the following conditions:

(1) If the adult is totally and permanently disabled;

(2) If the adult is determined to be a mentally retarded person . . .;

(3) If the adult had established a child-foster caregiver or child-stepparent relationship with the petitioners as a minor, and the adult consents to the adoption.")

Answer (D) is incorrect. Adult adoption refers to a much broader category of adoptions than just this.

179. **Answer (C) is the best answer**. *See, e.g., In re Rayna M.*, 534 A.2d 897, 905 (Conn. App. 1987) ("Where a parent fails to visit a child, fails to display any love or affection for the child, has no personal interaction with the child, and no concern for the child's welfare, statutory abandonment has occurred.").

Answer (A) is incorrect. This requirement is too strong. Consistent contact, even if not frequent, may suffice. A parent might contact his or her child every month and be held not to have abandoned that child. *See In re Adoption of T.L.C.*, 46 P.3d 863 (Wyo. 2002).

Answer (B) is incorrect. While this is one type of abandonment, *see* Ala. Stat. sec. 13A-13-5(a) ("A man or woman commits the crime of abandonment of a child when, being a parent, guardian or other person legally charged with the care or custody of a child less than 18 years old, he or she deserts such child in any place with intent wholly to abandon it."), this is not the only type of action which would qualify as abandonment for these purposes.

Answer (D) is incorrect. The question is not merely one of subjective intent but in addition what the parent did. A parent may abandon the child by having no contact for an extended period even though never intending to permanently sever relations. *See In re Rayna M.*, 534 A.2d 897 (Conn. App. 1987).

180. **Answer (C) is the best answer**. While this is a matter of state law, a state may well adopt this approach. *See Tailor v. Becker*, 708 A.2d 626 (Del. Super. 1998).

Answer (A) is incorrect. This does not represent the law. *See, e.g., Tailor v. Becker*, 708 A.2d 626 (Del. Super. 1998) (stepparent awarded custody following death of custodial parent over objection of non-custodial parent).

Answer (B) is incorrect. This also does not represent the law. *See, e.g., In re A.R.A.*, 919 P.2d 388, 391 (Mont. 1996) ("where a surviving parent does not voluntarily relinquish custody, the best interest of the child test can be used only after a showing of dependency or abuse and neglect by the natural parent").

Answer (D) is incorrect. This standard may well not meet constitutional requirements. *See Greer v. Alexander*, 639 N.W.2d 39, 45 (Mich. App. 2001) (When "considering competing custody claims of a noncustodial natural parent and a third-person custodian, . . . it is not sufficient that the third person may have established by clear and convincing evidence that a marginal, though distinct, benefit would be gained if the children were maintained with him.").

181. **Answer (B) is the best answer**. *See Levesque v. Levesque*, 773 S.W.2d 220, 222 (Mo. App. 1989) ("the obligation to support a stepchild ordinarily ceases upon divorce").

Answer (A) is incorrect. This is false. *See, e.g.*, Mo. Stat. sec. 453.400(1) ("A stepparent shall support his or her stepchild to the same extent that a natural or adoptive parent is required to support his or her child so long as the stepchild is living in the same home as the stepparent.").

Answer (C) is incorrect. While he might well be required to support them during the marriage, he would likely not be required to support them after the marriage. *See Levesque v. Levesque*, 773 S.W.2d 220 (Mo. App. 1989).

Answer (D) is incorrect. This is false. *See Levesque v. Levesque*, 773 S.W.2d 220 (Mo. App. 1989).

182. **Answer (D) is the best answer**. *See Hackett v. Hackett*, 150 N.E.2d 431, 434 (Ohio App. 1958) (provisions in separation decree regarding religious education of children unenforceable).

Answer (A) is incorrect. *See, e.g., S.E.L. v. J.W.W.*, 541 N.Y.S.2d 675, 676 (Fam. Ct. 1989) ("the custodial parent has the right to determine a child's religious upbringing and training").

Answer (B) is incorrect. *See, e.g., S.E.L. v. J.W.W.*, 541 N.Y.S.2d 675 (Fam. Ct. 1989).

Answer (C) is incorrect. *See, e.g., S.E.L. v. J.W.W.*, 541 N.Y.S.2d 675 (Fam. Ct. 1989).

183. **Answer (C) is the best answer**. *See Zummo v. Zummo*, 574 A.2d 1130, 1141 (Pa. Super. 1990) ("We find that the requirement of a 'substantial threat' of 'physical or mental harm to the child' is applicable to proposed restrictions on a parent's post-divorce parental right regarding the religious upbringing of his or her children.").

 Answer (A) is incorrect. This is false. *See In re Marriage of Murga*, 163 Cal.App.3d 498, 504-05 (Ct. App. 1980) ("the courts have refused to restrain the noncustodial parent from exposing the minor child to his or her religious beliefs and practices, absent a clear, affirmative showing that these religious activities will be harmful to the child").

 Answer (B) is incorrect. This is false. The state will refuse to interfere unless the parent would thereby be harming the child. *See S.E.L. v. J.W.W.*, 541 N.Y.S.2d 675 (Fam. Ct. 1989).

 Answer (D) is incorrect. This is false. The court instead will decide in light of whether the children are being harmed. *See In re Marriage of Murga*, 163 Cal.App.3d 498, 504-05 (Ct. App. 1980).

184. Robert knew that Sarah was pregnant and offered no financial or emotional support during the pregnancy. Further, he waited until after the adoption was finalized before asserting his parental interests. He may well be unable to establish his parental rights. In some jurisdictions, he will be found to have at most inchoate parental rights which would not give him the right to challenge the adoption, *see Adoption of Michael H.*, 898 P.2d 891 (Cal. 1995) or that he abandoned her by doing nothing for so long after he had first heard about the pregnancy. *See* Ala. Code 1975 sec. 26-10A-9 (discussing abandonment prior to birth). As a separate matter, he might well be precluded from challenging this adoption because it had already been finalized. *See* Okla. Stat. Ti. 10 sec. 7505-7.2. Robert may well be unable to get his daughter back.

185. John may well be allowed to assert his parental rights. Matthew was not able to consent to the termination of John's parental rights. *See In re Clausen*, 502 N.W.2d 649 (Mich. 1993) (biological father's rights not compromised when a release was executed by someone falsely named as the child's father). If John asserts his rights in a timely fashion and he is held not to be an unfit parent or to have abandoned the child, *e.g.*, because he did nothing when he knew or should have known of her existence, he may well be recognized as her father.

TOPIC 18: TORT ACTIONS — ANSWERS

186. **Answer (C) is the best answer**. This captures what is essential to the cause of action. *See Pharr v. Beck*, 554 S.E.2d 851, 854 (N.C. App. 2001) ("A claim for alienation of affection requires proof of three elements: (1) there was a marriage with love and affection existing between the husband and wife; (2) that love and affection was alienated; and (3) the malicious acts of the defendant produced the loss of that love and affection.").

    Answer (A) is incorrect. This misstates what criminal conversation involves. *See Brown v. Hurley*, 477 S.E.2d 234, 237 (N.C. App. 1996) ("The elements of criminal conversation are the actual marriage between the spouses and sexual intercourse between defendant and the plaintiff's spouse during the coverture.").

    Answer (B) is incorrect. This answer also mischaracterizes the tort action. *See Brown v. Hurley*, 477 S.E.2d 234, 237 (N.C. App. 1996).

    Answer (D) is incorrect. This mischaracterizes the cause of action. Criminal conversation rather than alienation of affection involves sexual relations between one of the parties to the marriage and someone outside of the marriage. Sexual relations with a third party are neither a necessary nor a sufficient element of alienation of affections.

187. **Answer (D) is the best answer**. The states differ with respect to whether such a cause of action will be permitted. *Compare Giuliani v. Guiler*, 951 S.W.2d 318 (Ky. 1997) (cause of action recognized), *with Taylor v. Beard*, 104 S.W.3d 507 (Tenn. 2003) (declining to recognize cause of action for loss of parental consortium).

    Answer (A) is incorrect. This is false. Some states recognize that children have a cause of action for loss of consortium with their parents. *See, e.g., Giuliani v. Guiler*, 951 S.W.2d 318 (Ky. 1997).

    Answer (B) is incorrect. There is no requirement that such claims are only permitted when the parties have been having sexual relations, since parents are permitted to recover for the loss of services of their children. *See Gallimore v. Children's Hospital Medical Center*, 617 N.E.2d 1052 (Ohio 1993).

    Answer (C) is incorrect. This is false. While the consortium claim traditionally permits recovery for loss of a spouse's "companionship, security and love," *see Giuliani v. Guiler*, 951 S.W.2d 318, 320 (Ky. 1997), other relationships may also be the basis for a loss of consortium claim.

188. **Answer (D) is the best answer**. *Compare Heiman v. Parrish*, 942 P.2d 631 (Kan. 1997) (ring should be returned), *with Wion v. Henderson*, 494 N.E.2d 133, 134 (Ohio App. 1985) ("absent an agreement to the contrary an engagement ring need not be returned when the engagement is unjustifiably broken by the donor").

Answer (A) is incorrect. This is false. While a gift, the ring might be more felicitously characterized as a conditional gift which should be returned if the couple does not in fact marry. *See Heiman v. Parrish*, 942 P.2d 631, 634 (Kan. 1997) ("In the absence of a contrary expression of intent, it is logical that engagement rings should be considered, by their very nature, conditional gifts given in contemplation of marriage."). The court is likely to hold that Norman must return the ring. *Heiman v. Parrish*, 942 P.2d 631, 638 (Kan. 1997) ("Ordinarily, the ring should be returned to the donor, regardless of fault.").

Answer (B) is incorrect. This is false. Many jurisdictions would require that Norman return the ring even if neither party had been at fault. *See Heiman v. Parrish*, 942 P.2d 631 (Kan. 1997).

Answer (C) is incorrect. This is false. Norman should return the ring to Mary and she can decide what to do with it. *See Heiman v. Parrish*, 942 P.2d 631 (Kan. 1997).

189. **Answer (A) is the best answer**. *See Naccash v. Burger*, 290 S.E.2d 825 (Virginia 1982) (permitting wrongful birth action after negligent failure to detect the disease).

Answer (B) is incorrect. Live birth notwithstanding, many courts have accepted that a parent may nonetheless have suffered harm if denied the opportunity to decide whether to abort. *See Naccash v. Burger*, 290 S.E.2d 825, 830 (Va. 1982) ("[W]e hold that the erroneous Tay-Sachs report given Mrs. Burger deprived her, and, derivatively, her husband, of the opportunity to accept or reject the continuance of her pregnancy and the birth of her fatally defective child; this, in our opinion, was direct injury.").

Answer (C) is incorrect. Ursula should not be suing for wrongful life but instead for wrongful birth. *See Walter v. Rinck*, 604 N.E.2d 591, 593-94 (Ind. 1992) ("The phrase 'wrongful birth' applies to claims brought by the parents of a child born with birth defects alleging that due to negligent medical advice or testing they were precluded from an informed decision about whether to conceive a potentially handicapped child or, in the event of a pregnancy, to terminate it. When such action seeks damages on behalf of the child rather than the parents, the phrase 'wrongful life' instead of 'wrongful birth' is employed.").

Answer (D) is incorrect. *See James G. v. Caserta*, 332 S.E.2d 872, 875 (W. Va. 1985) (noting that an "overwhelming majority of other jurisdictions have recognized a cause of action for wrongful pregnancy or wrongful birth"); *Wilson v. Kuenzi*, 751 S.W.2d 741, 743 (Mo. 1988) (noting how few jurisdictions recognize wrongful life actions).

190. **Answer (B) is the best answer**. *See Wilson v. Kuenzi*, 751 S.W.2d 741, 743 (Mo. 1988).

Answer (A) is incorrect. *See James G. v. Caserta*, 332 S.E.2d 872, 875 (W. Va. 1985) (noting that an "overwhelming majority of other jurisdictions have recognized a cause of action for wrongful pregnancy or wrongful birth"); *Wilson v. Kuenzi*, 751 S.W.2d 741, 743 (Mo. 1988) (noting how few jurisdictions recognize wrongful life actions).

Answer (C) is incorrect. Many more states recognize wrongful birth than wrongful life and all of the states recognizing wrongful life also recognize wrongful birth. A separate issue would be raised if the parents were time-barred from raising their wrongful birth claim. *See Procanik v. Cillo*, 478 A.2d 755 (N.J. 1984).

Answer (D) is incorrect. Some jurisdictions have recognized a cause of action for wrongful life. *See Harbeson v. Parke-Davis Inc.*, 656 P.2d 483 (Wash. 1983); *Turpin v. Sortini*, 643 P.2d 954 (Cal. 1982); *Procanik v. Cillo*, 478 A.2d 755 (N.J. 1984)

191. **Answer (B) is the best answer**. *See, e.g., Weintraub v. Brown*, 470 N.Y.S.2d 634, 638 (App. Div. 1983) ("the birth of a healthy and normal child cannot, as a matter of law, constitute an injury to the child's parents").

Answer (A) is incorrect. The majority of jurisdictions are unwilling to award such damages in a wrongful conception case. *See Weintraub v. Brown*, 470 N.Y.S.2d 634, 641 (App. Div. 1983) ("the majority of the jurisdictions which have decided the issue, that denial of ordinary child rearing costs in wrongful pregnancy actions is to be preferred").

Answer (C) is incorrect. The conditions for a wrongful life claim are not present here. A wrongful life action is an action brought on behalf of the child because of the suffering the child will undergo as a result of the negligence of a medical professional. *See Siemieniec v. Lutheran Gen. Hosp.*, 512 N.E.2d 691, 695 (Ill. 1987) ("The essence of the child's claim is that the medical professional's breach of the applicable standard of care precluded an informed parental decision to avoid his conception or birth. But for this negligence, the child allegedly would not have been born to experience the pain and suffering attributable to his affliction.").

Answer (D) is incorrect. This is inaccurate. As a general matter, courts have held that it would be unreasonable to require a woman to undergo an abortion to mitigate damages. *See, e.g., Morris v. Sanchez*, 746 P.2d 184, 186 (Okla. 1987) ("the concept of requiring abortion or adoption under these circumstances is, as a matter of law, unreasonable").

192. **Answer (D) is the best answer**. *See Procanik v. Cillo*, 478 A.2d 755 (N.J. 1984) (wrongful life damages awarded in case involving similar circumstances).

Answer (A) is incorrect. This misconstrues what a wrongful life action is. A wrongful life action is a claim on behalf of the child that but for the medical professional's negligence, the child would not have been born and thus would not have had to undergo great suffering. *See Siemieniec v. Lutheran Gen. Hosp.*, 512 N.E.2d 691, 695 (Ill. 1987).

Answer (B) is incorrect. This is false. In those jurisdictions recognizing the cause of action, the doctor may be liable even if he could not have performed surgery in utero to correct the difficulty. *See Procanik v. Cillo*, 478 A.2d 755 (N.J. 1984).

Answer (C) is incorrect. This is false. In those jurisdictions recognizing the cause of action, the doctor will be liable even if he did not cause the disease if his negligence resulted in the child being born. *See Procanik v. Cillo*, 478 A.2d 755 (N.J. 1984).

193. **Answer (A) is the best answer**. The states vary with respect to whether they recognize parent-child immunity and, if so, the extent that they do. *See, e.g., Kirchner v. Crystal*, 474 N.E.2d 275 (Ohio 1984) (abolishing parent-child immunity); *Clark v. Estate of Rice ex rel. Rice*, 653 N.W.2d 166, 174 (Iowa 2002) ("immunity exists only for negligent acts involving the exercise of parental authority over a child or the exercise of parental discretion in providing care"); La. R.S. 9:571 ("The child who is not emancipated cannot sue: (1) Either parent during the continuance of their marriage, when the parents are not judicially separated; or (2) The parent who is entitled to his custody and control, when the marriage of the parents is dissolved, or the parents are judicially separated.").

    Answer (B) is incorrect. This is false. *See, e.g., Kirchner v. Crystal*, 474 N.E.2d 275 (Ohio 1984) (abolishing parent-child immunity)

    Answer (C) is incorrect. This is false. *See, e.g.*, La. Rev. Stat. 9:571 (unemancipated child may not sue his or her parents while they are still married).

    Answer (D) is incorrect. This is false. A child might be permitted to sue a parent for an intentional tort even if that child is not permitted to sue the parent for negligence. *See, e.g., Fields v. Southern Farm Bureau Cas. Ins. Co.*, 87 S.W.3d 224, 230 (Ark. 2002) ("Arkansas has already qualified the parental immunity rule and excepted intentional torts by a parent.").

194. **Answer (C) is the best answer**. Many states do not apply immunity in this context. *See Herzfield v. Herzfield*, 781 So.2d 1070, 1075 n.11 (Fla. 2001) (noting "a trend in state courts toward recognizing an exception to the immunity doctrine for unemancipated minor children injured by the intentional torts of a parent").

    Answer (A) is incorrect. This is false. A child might be permitted to sue a parent for an intentional tort even if that child is not permitted to sue the parent for negligence. *See, e.g., Fields v. Southern Farm Bureau Cas. Ins. Co.*, 87 S.W.3d 224, 230 (Ark. 2002).

    Answer (B) is incorrect. This is false. Henrietta and Herman would be subject to civil and criminal penalties. *See, e.g.*, W. Va. Stat. 61-8D-3(a) ("If any parent, guardian or custodian shall abuse a child and by such abuse cause such child bodily injury as such term is defined in section one, article eight-b of this chapter, then such parent, guardian or custodian shall be guilty of a felony.").

    Answer (D) is incorrect. This is false. The parental immunity doctrine involves civil rather than criminal matters. *See, e.g.*, La. Rev. Stat. 9:571 (children may not sue their parents while they are still married).

195. **Answer (B) is the best answer**. *See, e.g., Bellard v. South Central Bell Telephone Co.*, 702 So.2d 695 (La. App. 1997) (wife's damages may be reduced by percentage of fault attributed to husband driver).

Answer (A) is incorrect. As a general matter, this is inaccurate. *See, e.g., Noone v. Fink*, 721 P.2d 1275, 1276 (Mont. 1986) (because interspousal tort immunity has been abrogated, husband may be responsible for contribution).

Answer (C) is incorrect. This is false, at least as a general rule, since insurance companies may be permitted to include spousal exclusion policies, even though such policies might well deplete the family purse. *See Porter v. Farmer Ins. Co. of Idaho*, 627 P.2d 311, 315 (Idaho 1981) (spousal immunity abrogation notwithstanding, public policy does not prohibit an insurance policy exclusion of spousal coverage).

Answer (D) is incorrect. This is false. Because this is a comparative rather than a contributory negligence state, the wife will be entitled to some recovery.

196. **Answer (C) is the best answer**. *See Wells v. Hickman*, 657 N.E.2d 172, 176 (Ind. App. 1995) ("[H]ere are four common law exceptions to the general rule that a parent is not liable for the tortious acts of her child: (1) where the parent entrusts the child with an instrumentality which, because of the child's lack of age, judgment, or experience, may become a source of danger to others; (2) where the child committing the tort is acting as the servant or agent of its parents; (3) where the parent consents, directs, or sanctions the wrongdoing; and (4) where the parent fails to exercise control over the minor child although the parent knows or with due care should know that injury to another is possible.").

    Answer (A) is incorrect. This is false. *See, e.g., Robertson v. Wentz*, 187 Cal.App.3d 1281, 1288-89 (Ct. App. 1986) (The parent has "a duty to exercise reasonable care so to control his minor child as to prevent it from intentionally harming others or from so conducting itself as to create an unreasonable risk of bodily harm to them, if the parent (a) knows or has reason to know that he has the ability to control his child, and (b) knows or should know of the necessity and opportunity for exercising such control.").

    Answer (B) is incorrect. While a statute might make parents strictly liable for up to a certain amount for certain harms perpetrated by the children, *see Wells v. Hickman*, 657 N.E.2d 172, 176 (Ind. App. 1995) ("the statute makes a parent strictly liable for the knowing, intentional or reckless tortious acts of the parent's minor child."), this does not make the parents responsible for any and all harms caused by the child.

    Answer (D) is incorrect. This is false. *See Wells v. Hickman*, 657 N.E.2d 172 (Ind. App. 1995) (parents may be liable for their child's tortious acts under certain circumstances).

197. **Answer (D) is the best answer**. *See Meracle v. Children's Services Society of Wisconsin*, 437 N.W.2d 532, 537 (Wis. 1989) ("we only allow recovery for the *extraordinary* medical expenses which will be incurred by the Meracles as a result of the negligent misrepresentation").

    Answer (A) is incorrect. Courts can impose liability for a fraudulent misrepresentation in the adoption context without thereby making the agency a guarantor of a happy and healthy child. *See Burr v. Bd. County Commissioners of Stark County*,

491 N.E.2d 1101, 1109 (Ohio 1986) (imposing liability but in no way implying "that adoption agencies are guarantors of their placements").

Answer (B) is incorrect. This is inaccurate. The court might well suggest that the usual costs associated with raising a child were expected by the parents and thus should not be imposed on the agency. *See Gibbs v. Ernst*, 647 A.2d 882, 891 (Pa. 1994) (noting that "the parents must show that any negligently communicated information is causally related to their damages").

Answer (C) is incorrect. This is not the appropriate test. While the agency would not *know* what would happen, it could nonetheless give the parents the available information to let them make an informed adoption decision. *See Gibbs v. Ernst*, 647 A.2d 882, 893 (Pa. 1994) ("the creation of a duty in this instance will further the interests of parents by providing them with as much factual and valid information as possible about the child they are to adopt without placing an undue burden on adoption agencies, as they are required only to make reasonable efforts to disclose fully and accurately the medical history they have already obtained").

198. **Answer (A) is the best answer**. *See, e.g., In re Matter of Adoption of T.B.*, 622 N.E.2d 921, 925 (Ind. 1993) ("In order to set aside the order of adoption based on fraud, there must be a material misrepresentation of past or existing fact made with knowledge or reckless disregard for the falsity of the statement, and the misrepresentation must be relied upon to the detriment of the relying party.").

Answer (B) is incorrect. However, states have statutes specifying the period after the final adoption has been granted during which the adoption can be contested. *See, e.g.*, Tenn. Stat. sec. 36-1-122(b)(2) ("In no event, for any reason, shall an adoption be overturned by any court or collaterally attacked by any person or entity after one (1) year from the date of entry of the final order of adoption by a court of competent jurisdiction.").

Answer (C) is incorrect. This is a faulty analysis precisely because a child rather than a product is concerned. *See, e.g., In re Teleka*, 780 N.E.2d 304, 311 (Ill. 2002) (noting that "[p]ublic policy considerations require that adoptions be accorded a certain degree of stability and finality").

Answer (D) is incorrect. This is inaccurate. Depending upon the state, the adoption might be set aside. *See In re Matter of Adoption of T.B.*, 622 N.E.2d 921, 925 (Ind. 1993).

199. **Answer (C) is the best answer**. *See, e.g., Plante v. Engel*, 469 A.2d 1299 (N.H. 1983) (the custodial parent will have a cause of action in these circumstances).

Answer (A) is incorrect. This is false. *See Plante v. Engel*, 469 A.2d 1299, 1302 (N.H. 1983) ("where a parent has been awarded custody of a child by court decree and the noncustodial parent abducts the child, an action will lie in favor of the custodial parent upon an allegation of damages").

Answer (B) is incorrect. This is false. Some states will permit such an action against the non-custodial parent. *See Plante v. Engel*, 469 A.2d 1299 (N.H. 1983).

Answer (D) is incorrect. This is false. *See Plante v. Engel*, 469 A.2d 1299 (N.H. 1983).

200. **Answer (D) is the best answer**. *See Cosner v. Ridinger*, 882 P.2d 1243, 1246 (Wyo. 1994) (jurisdictions tend not to permit this kind of action by the non-custodial parent).

Answer (A) is incorrect. This is false, both because Jim is not likely to be given custody when he does not want it and because he may well be unsuccessful in his quest for damages. Many jurisdictions will not award damages in this kind of case. *See Cosner v. Ridinger*, 882 P.2d 1243, 1246 (Wyo. 1994) ("The jurisdictions recognizing this tort [of intentional interference with custodial relationship] have limited the cause of action to the custodial parent and have not extended it to a non-custodial parent who is somehow deprived of visitation privileges.").

Answer (B) is incorrect. While it is correct that the state would likely not modify custody, it also will likely not award damages. *See Cosner v. Ridinger*, 882 P.2d 1243, 1246 (Wyo. 1994). Even if he had sought custody, he might well not have been awarded it. *See Sweeney v. Sweeney*, 654 N.W.2d 407, 410 (N.D. 2002) ("When a request for a change of custody is predicated upon the custodial parent's frustration of the noncustodial parent's visitation rights, the court must act with restraint and caution.").

Answer (C) is incorrect. This is false, since many jurisdictions recognize such an action for the custodial but not the non-custodial parent. *See Cosner v. Ridinger*, 882 P.2d 1243, 1246 (Wyo. 1994).

201. To be successful in a suit for alienation of affections, Horace must show that Gertrude's feelings for him changed as a result of Matthew's actions. *See Nunn v. Allen*, 574 S.E.2d 35 (N.C. App. 2002) (action requires establishing that love and affection were alienated). Given that Horace and Gertrude had already separated, this might be difficult, although it would not be impossible. To establish criminal conversation, Horace must establish that Matthew had sexual relations with Gertrude while Horace and Gertrude were still married, even if separated. *See Johnson v. Pearce*, 557 S.E.2d 189 (N.C. App. 2001) (action can be maintained for post-separation sexual relations). Horace may well be successful on the criminal conversation claim even if he cannot establish that Gertrude's feelings for him were diminished once she started having relations with Matthew.

202. States vary greatly with respect to whether they will allow children to sue their parents for negligent supervision. Some have abrogated parental immunity entirely, *see Elam v. Elam*, 268 S.E.2d 109 (S.C. 1980), whereas others impose it in the circumstances at issue here, *see Clark v. Estate of Rice ex rel. Rice*, 653 N.W.2d 166, 174 (Iowa 2002) (parental "immunity exists only for negligent acts involving the exercise of parental authority over a child or the exercise of parental discretion in providing care"). It is simply unclear whether this suit will be permitted under state law. Had there been some indication that a parent was intentionally harming his or her child, the doctrine might well not apply, *see Fields v. Southern Farm Bureau Cas. Ins. Co.*, 87 S.W.3d 224, 228 (Ark. 2002) (noting that the doctrine does not

apply to protect intentional torts). However, here, there is no suggestion of intentional harm. If the jurisdiction recognizes parental immunity, the doctrine may well preclude this kind of suit.

203. As a general matter, an individual suing for intentional infliction of emotional distress must show that extreme and outrageous conduct which was performed intentionally (or with a reckless disregard for the harm it would cause) caused plaintiff's severe emotional distress. *See Sverdick v. Koch*, 721 A.2d 849, 862 (R.I. 1998). Jurisdictions vary with respect to whether this kind of action will be permitted in this context, at least in part, because they vary with respect to whether permitting such suits would violate public policy. *Compare Day v. Heller*, 653 N.W.2d 475 (Neb. 2002) (an intentional infliction of emotional distress claim against a mother for her misrepresentation of biological fatherhood is contrary to public policy), *with G.A.W. III v. D.M.W.*, 596 N.W.2d 284 (Minn. App. 1999) (Former husband could bring interspousal tort action against former wife, seeking recovery under theories of fraud, misrepresentation, or infliction of emotional distress, based upon former wife's misrepresentation of paternity of children born during marriage.). Thus, even were a jury to find that the criteria had been met, the jurisdiction might nonetheless preclude the action as a matter of public policy.

204. Even if the jurisdiction no longer recognizes spousal immunity, it may nonetheless preclude this kind of action. *See Day v. Heller*, 653 N.W.2d 475 (Neb. 2002) (notwithstanding that interspousal tort immunity had been abolished, this type of action was a violation of public policy). Further, even if they recognize spousal immunity, *e.g.*, on the theory that it is better for family unity not to permit such an action, that may not speak to whether suits would be permitted in this context, since the marriage may well not remain intact in any event. *See Henriksen v. Cameron*, 622 A.2d 1135 (Me. 1993) (doctrine of spousal immunity does not bar all actions between current or former spouses for intentional infliction of emotional distress). Finally, it should be noted that some jurisdictions will permit suits for intentional infliction of emotional distress even within the context of marriage if the behavior is sufficiently extreme and outrageous. *See McCulloh v. Drake*, 24 P.3d 1162 (Wyo. 2001). Thus, whether the jurisdiction has abrogated spousal immunity is likely not a good predictor of whether it will allow this kind of action.

205. The paradigmatic action by a bystander for negligent infliction of emotional distress involves a close relative who was present at the scene and witnessed the accident and who suffered severe emotional harm evidenced by physical symptoms as a result of the accident. *See Marchetti v. Parsons*, 638 A.2d 1047 (R.I. 1994). In some jurisdictions., these different requirements will be relaxed. Here, because she suffered greatly as a result of the accident which she witnessed at the scene, the requirements have been met if Yolanda is considered a close family member of Xerxes. Some jurisdictions would not so consider her because she has no legal ties to Xerxes. *See Elden v. Sheldon*, 758 P.2d 582 (Cal. 1988) (precluding recovery by individual who witnessed the death of the woman with whom he was living but to whom he was unmarried). Others will consider other elements in addition to the legal relationship, and thus might permit such a suit even if the relationship is not recognized in law. *See, e.g., Graves v. Estabrook*, 818 A.2d 1255 (N. H. 2003)

(permitting recovery by fiancée who witnessed auto accident resulting in his death). Here, whether a cause of action will lie may well depend upon whether the jurisdiction will allow only those in a person's legally recognized family to sue or instead will allow those in the person's functional family to sue.

TOPIC 19: PROFESSIONAL RESPONSIBILITY

ANSWERS

206. **Answer (D) is the best answer.** *See In re Braun*, 227 A.2d 506 (N.J. 1967) (suggesting that once an attorney has met with a husband and wife in circumstances like these, he should decline to represent either).

     Answer (A) is incorrect. This is not a good answer. While solicitation is prohibited, Arthur Attorney still would have acted unethically had he agreed to represent her after she had called him. *See In re Braun*, 227 A.2d 506, 507 (N.J. 1967) ("after respondent discussed the marital and financial problems of complainant in April 1965, it was highly improper for him to agree to substitute himself as attorney for complainant's wife in her divorce action").

     Answer (B) is incorrect. Even had he not accepted payment from Bob, Arthur would have been precluded from representing Betty. *See In re Braun*, 227 A.2d 506, 507 (N.J. 1967).

     Answer (C) is incorrect. Even had he agreed to represent Bob rather than Betty, he still would have acted unprofessionally once he talked to both of the parties with the aim of inducing them to reconcile. *See In re Braun*, 227 A.2d 506, 507 (N.J. 1967) ("[A]fter respondent had attempted to counsel both husband and wife with a view to reconciliation at the meeting of June 1964, he could not thereafter with propriety represent either in a divorce action.").

207. **Answer (D) is the best answer.** *See Walden v. Hoke*, 429 S.E.2d 504 (W. Va. 1993) (dual representation improper in these circumstances, even with informed consent); *Ishmael v. Millington*, 241 Cal. App. 2d 520 (Ct. App. 1966) (dual representation permissible with full disclosure and informed consent).

     Answer (A) is incorrect. Whether this is permissible depends on the jurisdiction and not simply on whether the parties are satisfied. *See Walden v. Hoke*, 429 S.E.2d 504, 509 (W. Va. 1993) ("it is improper for a lawyer to represent both the husband and the wife at any stage of the separation and divorce proceeding, even with full disclosure and informed consent").

     Answer (B) is incorrect. Some jurisdictions will permit this representation. *See Ishmael v. Millington*, 241 Cal. App. 2d 520, 526 (Ct. App. 1966) ("Minimum standards of professional ethics usually permit him [the attorney] to represent dual interests where full consent and full disclosure occur.").

     Answer (C) is incorrect. This is false. *See Walden v. Hoke*, 429 S.E.2d 504 (W. Va. 1993)

208. **Answer (C) is the best answer.** *See Meyers v. Handlon*, 479 N.E.2d 106 (Ind. App. 1985) (contingency fee contract in this context unenforceable); *Ballesteros v. Jones*, 985 S.W.2d 485 (Tex. App. 1998) (contingency fee contract valid and enforceable).

Answer (A) is incorrect. Whether contingency fee contracts in domestic relations matters are enforceable varies by jurisdiction. *See Meyers v. Handlon*, 479 N.E.2d 106 (Ind. App. 1985) (refusing to enforce such a contract).

Answer (B) is incorrect. This is false. *See, e.g., Ballesteros v. Jones*, 985 S.W.2d 485, 497 (Tex. App. 1998) (discussing rare circumstances in which contingency fee arrangements in divorce matters are permissible).

Answer (D) is incorrect. This is false. Some states will enforce such agreements and others will not.

209. Jurisdictions vary with respect to what obligations exist in different situations. While the duties of a scribe may be less robust than those of an attorney who should be zealously representing her clients' interests, *see Chem-Age Industries, Inc. v. Glover*, 652 N.W.2d 756, 774-75 (S.D. 2002) (suggesting that the duties of an attorney are more robust than those of someone merely acting as a scrivener), an attorney may well be thought to have a duty not to remain silent when she discovers fraud–she may have a duty to withdraw. *See, e.g., Matter of Marriage of Eltzroth*, 679 P.2d 1369, 1372-73 & n.7 (Or. App. 1984) (suggesting that an attorney would have a duty to withdraw in certain circumstances, even if only acting as a scrivener). Here, Lucy should probably withdraw, even if she has less robust duties because she is only acting as a scribe.

TOPIC 20: FEDERAL-STATE POWER DISTRIBUTION — ANSWERS

210. **Answer (A) is the best answer**. *See Ankenbrandt v. Richards*, 504 U.S. 689, 703 (1992) (explaining the domestic relations exception).

 Answer (B) is incorrect. This is false. The United States Supreme Court discussed the right to marry in *Loving v. Virginia*, 388 U.S. 1 (1967).

 Answer (C) is incorrect. This is false. Even couples who have contracted a common law marriage must divorce to end their marriage. *See Ram v. Ramharack*, 571 N.Y.S.2d 190, 192 (Super. 1991) ("Once a relationship satisfies the three requirements for a common-law marriage, the parties are considered to be married until divorced.").

 Answer (D) is incorrect. There is no such rule. Courts have taken into consideration that an individual proposed an open marriage when determining custody, *see Mazurek v. Mazurek*, 575 S.W.2d 227 (Mo. App. 1978), or that the person had sexual relations with a non-spouse (even with the other spouse's permission) when determining parental fitness. *See Madson v. Madson*, 313 N.W.2d 42 (S.D. 1981)

211. **Answer (C) is the best answer**. *See Hisquierdo v. Hisquierdo*, 439 U.S. 572, 581 (1979) (offering this standard).

 Answer (A) is incorrect. Precisely because "domestic relations law is primarily an area of state concern," *see Boggs v. Boggs*, 520 U.S. 833, 850 (1997), Congress is not given great discretion in this area. *See also United States v. Morrison*, 529 U.S. 598, 615-16 (2000) (refusing to construe the commerce power very broadly, at least in part, because that might thereby permit Congress to regulate family law).

 Answer (B) is incorrect. This is false as well because there are situations in which Congress will be permitted to preempt state regulation of family law. *See Hisquierdo v. Hisquierdo*, 439 U.S. 572, 581 (1979) ("State family and family-property law must do major damage to clear and substantial federal interests before the Supremacy Clause will demand that state law be overridden.").

 Answer (D) is incorrect. Notwithstanding that there is no federal domestic relations law as such, Congress has passed a number of statutes which affect the family, e.g., the Parental Kidnaping Prevention Act, and thus the issue may arise.

PRACTICE FINAL EXAM: ANSWERS

PRACTICE FINAL EXAM

ANSWERS

212. **Answer (D) is the best answer.** *See Greene v. Williams*, 9 Cal.App.3d 559 (Ct. App. 1970) (voidable minor marriage in effect until declared void by a court).

    Answer (A) is incorrect. This is false. Because the marriage is treated as voidable by Marrylania, it will be recognized until declared void by a court. *See Greene v. Williams*, 9 Cal.App.3d 559 (Ct. App. 1970) (voidable minor marriage in effect until declared void by a court).

    Answer (B) is incorrect. This is false. The parents will not be able to challenge the marriage now that Alfred has died. *See Greene v. Williams*, 88 Cal.Rptr. 261 (Ct. App. 1970) (parent cannot annul minor child's marriage after death of child merely because the child married without parental consent).

    Answer (C) is incorrect. This is false. They will be considered married whether or not they had consummated the marriage. *See Greene v. Williams*, 9 Cal.App.3d 559 (Ct. App. 1970).

213. Because Arkanado treats minor marriages as voidable rather than void, the marriage will be treated as valid if the couple ratifies the marriage once they have attained majority. Because they were living together when they each were eighteen, the marriage will have been ratified and will be treated as valid. *See Medlin v. Medlin*, 981 P.2d 1087 (Ariz. App. 1999) (minor marriage ratified when couple lives together after minor reaches majority). Terry will not be able to have the marriage annulled on the basis that they married before they were of age to do so.

214. **Answer (C) is the best answer.** Some states would preclude their marriage because they are siblings by adoption. *See, e.g.*, Minn. Stat. sec. 517.03(2) (refusing to distinguish between whole blood, half blood, and adoption with respect to prohibition against sibling marriages); Ore. Rev. Stat. sec. 106.020(2) (same); S. D. Stat. sec. 25-1-6 (same).

    Answer (A) is incorrect. This answer is false. In most jurisdictions, individuals eighteen years of age and older can marry without the need for parental or judicial permission. *See, e.g.*, W. V. Code 48-2-301(a) (age of consent is eighteen); Okla. Stat. Ann. Ti. 43 sec. 3 (same); Wis. Stat. Ann. 765.02(1) (same).

    Answer (B) is incorrect. This is false. Family approval will not somehow make an incestuous marriage valid which the jurisdiction treats as void. Certain marriages will simply be treated as void. *See, e.g.*, Cal. Fam. sec. 2200 ("Marriages between parents and children, ancestors and descendants of every degree, and between brothers and sisters of the half as well as the whole blood, and between uncles and nieces or aunts and nephews, are incestuous, and void from the beginning, whether the relationship is legitimate or illegitimate.").

Answer (D) is incorrect. Some states would in fact preclude their marriage, notwithstanding that they are not related by blood.

215. The jurisdictions vary greatly with respect to whether they will recognize marriages between first cousins. Some jurisdictions treat such marriages as valid. See Mass. Gen. Laws Ann. Stat. 207 sec. 1 & 2 (no prohibition against marriages involving cousins). Others treat them as void, *see In re Mortenson's Estate*, 316 P.2d 1106 (Ariz. 1957) (marriage between first cousins void), and still others will recognize them if they are celebrated in a state which permits them. *See Mazzolini v. Mazzolini*, 155 N.E.2d 206 (Ohio 1958); *In re Miller's Estate*, 214 N.W. 428 (Mich. 1927). The question here is whether Restrictsylvania law treats first cousin marriages like Ohio does. If so, the marriage would be recognized because it is valid where celebrated, Sarah would be recognized as Rodney's spouse, and she would receive the benefits. However, if the state treats them like Arizona treats them, the marriage would be treated as void, Sarah would not be recognized as Rodney's spouse, and she would not receive the benefits.

216. **Answer (A) is the best answer.** If they understood what they were doing, then the marriage will be treated as valid. *See Christoph v. Sims*, 234 S.W.2d 901, 904 (Tex. Civ. App. 1950) ("A party claiming he was intoxicated at the time of marriage cannot escape liability unless he was incapable at the time of understanding his acts; he must be so drunk that he did not understand what he was doing and the nature of the transaction."). Even if they did not understand what they were doing, the marriage will be recognized if the jurisdiction treats such marriages as voidable rather than void, *see Dean v. Dean*, 146 A.2d 861 (Md. 1958), because it was not challenged during the lives of the parties.

Answer (B) is incorrect. This is false. If they knew understood what they were doing, the marriage will be treated as valid. *See Christoph v. Sims*, 234 S.W.2d 901, 904 (Tex. Civ. App. 1950).

Answer (C) is incorrect. Even were the marriage between Norman and Olga invalid because they were incompetent to contract it, this would not entail that the other marriage would also be invalid, if the other couple had not had so much to drink that they did not understand the nature of what they were doing when contracting the marriage. *See Christoph v. Sims*, 234 S.W.2d 901 (Tex. Civ. App. 1950).

Answer (D) is incorrect. This is false. *See Franklin v. Franklin*, 28 N.E. 681, 682 (Mass. 1891) ("The consummation of a marriage by coition is not necessary to its validity.")

217. **Answer (C) is the best answer.** Postnuptial agreements can be invalidated when one of the parties has misrepresented the nature and value of the assets. *See Gabaig*

v. Gabaig, 717 P.2d 835 (Alaska 1986); *In re Marriage of Richardson*, 606 N.E.2d 56 (Ill. App. 1992).

Answer (A) is incorrect. This is not the best answer, notwithstanding that Miriam is unlikely to be able to have the agreement invalidated based on duress. *See Davis v. Miller*, 7 P.3d 1223, 1231 (Kan. 2000) (individual making agreement under stress of attempting to save the marriage nonetheless entered the agreement voluntarily). If she can establish fraud or misrepresentation, then she will be able to have the agreement invalidated notwithstanding the lack of duress.

Answer (B) is incorrect. While Miriam may have felt pressured to sign, this does not constitute duress and will not provide the basis for invalidating the agreement. *See Davis v. Miller*, 7 P.3d 1223, 1231 (Kan. 2000).

Answer (D) is incorrect. This is inaccurate. Miriam's consultation with an attorney will not immunize Ken's material misrepresentations. *See, e.g., In re Marriage of Richardson*, 606 N.E.2d 56 (Ill. App. 1992) (postnuptial agreement unconscionable notwithstanding an attorney's having suggested that his client should sign it).

218. **Answer (C) is the best answer.** Such an agreement may well be held to be unconscionable and hence unenforceable. *See Girard v. Girard*, 1998 WL 345541 (Conn. Super.) *See also Blue v. Blue*, 60 S.W.3d 585, 589 (Ky. App. 2001) ("An agreement is unconscionable and must be set aside if the court determines that it is manifestly unfair and unreasonable.").

Answer (A) is incorrect. An agreement presented a day before the wedding day may well be enforceable depending upon its content. *See Donovan v. Donovan*, 51 Va. Cir. Ct. 34 (Va. Cir. Ct. 1999) (agreement signed day before wedding was not signed under duress but, instead, voluntarily).

Answer (B) is incorrect. While Samuel is correct that a prenuptial agreement presented and signed a day before the wedding may well be held to have been signed voluntarily, *see Donovan v. Donovan*, 51 Va. Cir. Ct. 34 (Va. Cir. Ct. 1999), this does not end the matter. The agreement still must be examined to see whether its content is unconscionable. *See Fick v. Fick*, 851 P.2d 445, 449 (Nev. 1993) ("a prenuptial agreement is unenforceable if it was unconscionable at execution, involuntarily signed, or the parties did not fully disclose their assets and obligations *before* the agreement's execution").

Answer (D) is incorrect. It would in effect change the criterion for enforcement so that the agreement would be enforceable if it was either voluntary or not unconscionable. However, both criteria must be met for the agreement to be enforceable. *See Fick v. Fick*, 851 P.2d 445, 449 (Nev. 1993).

219. **Answer (C) is the best answer.** *Compare Edwardson v. Edwardson*, 798 S.W.2d 941, 945 (Ky. 1990) (agreement must not be unconscionable at time of enforcement), *with Simeone v. Simeone*, 581 A.2d 162, 166 (Pa. 1990) (unconscionability assessed at time of agreement's inception).

Answer (A) is incorrect. Some states require not only that the prenuptial agreement not be unconscionable at the time that it is made but also that the facts and circumstances not have changes so that its enforcement would be unfair and unreasonable. *See Scherer v. Scherer*, 292 S.E.2d 662, 666 (Ga. 1982). *See also Edwardson v. Edwardson*, 798 S.W.2d 941, 945 (Ky. 1990) ("the agreement must not be unconscionable at the time enforcement is sought"); DeMatteo v. DeMatteo, 762 N.E.2d 797, 813 (Mass. 2002) (circumstances justifying non-enforcement of prenuptial provision "include, for example, the unanticipated mental or physical deterioration of the contesting party").

Answer (B) is incorrect. Some states only consider whether the agreement was reasonable when it was signed. *See Simeone v. Simeone*, 581 A.2d 162, 166 (Pa. 1990) ("parties viewed an agreement as reasonable at the time of its inception, as evidenced by their having signed the agreement, they should be foreclosed from later trying to evade its terms by asserting that it was not in fact reasonable") and *id.* ("If parties choose not to address such matters [e.g., the possibility of illness] in their prenuptial agreements, they must be regarded as having contracted to bear the risk of events that alter the value of their bargains.").

Answer (D) is incorrect. While it is true that some states have abrogated the common law doctrine of necessaries, *see North Ottawa Community Hosp. v. Krief*, 578 N.W.2d 267 (Mich. 1998), and some states have expanded it, *see Kilbourne v. Hanzelik*, 648 S.W.2d 932 (Tenn. 1983), that will not be the basis for determining whether the premarital agreement would be enforceable. Michigan will consider whether the agreement would be unfair or unreasonable at the time of its enforcement, *see Butcher v. Butcher*, 2003 WL 327715, *1 (Mich. App), whereas Tennessee focuses on the time that the agreement is made. *See Randolph v. Randolph*, 937 S.W.2d 815, 819 (Tenn. 1996).

220. Custody provisions in prenuptial agreements are against public policy and unenforceable because they have been made without consideration of which parent's having custody would promote the best interests of the child. *See Edwardson v. Edwardson*, 798 S.W2d 941, 946 (Ky. 1990). Such agreements can discuss property division and support and those provisions will not be invalidated merely because the applicable laws would have dictated a different result. See DeMatteo v. DeMatteo, 762 N.E.2d 797, 812 (Mass. 2002) ("a valid antenuptial agreement is not unenforceable at the time of divorce merely because its enforcement results in property division or an award of support that a judge might not order under [the applicable law] or because it is one sided"). Here, the terms are described as very favorable—it simply is not clear whether they are unconscionable. If not unconscionable, they may well be enforced. Courts have found that a prenuptial agreement's having unenforceable provisions need not invalidate the entire agreement, because the invalid provisions may well be severable. *See Reese v. Reese*, 984 P.2d 987, 995 (Utah 1999).

221. **Answer (C) is the best answer.** *In re Marriage of Barnes*, 755 N.E.2D 522, 527 (Ill. App. 2001) (conditioning marriage upon execution of premarital agreement does not constitute coercion).

Answer (A) is incorrect. This is false. If coercion is established the agreement is unenforceable. *See Huck v. Huck*, 734 P.2d 417, 419 (Utah 1986) ("in general, prenuptial agreements concerning the disposition of property owned by the parties at the time of their marriage are valid so long as there is no fraud, coercion, or material nondisclosure").

Answer (B) is incorrect. This is false. *See In re Marriage of Barnes*, 755 N.E.2d 522, 527 (Ill. App. 2001) ("We disagree with Sandra's assertion that conditioning marriage upon the execution of a premarital agreement constitutes coercion. Acts or threats cannot constitute duress unless they are legally or morally wrong.".

Answer (D) is incorrect. This is false. *See In re Marriage of Barnes*, 755 N.E.2D 522, 527 (Ill. App. 2001).

222. **Answer (D) is the best answer.** *See Wolfe v. Wolfe*, 389 N.E.2d 1143 (Ill. 1979) (annulment granted on very similar facts because the fraud went to the essentials of the marriage).

Answer (A) is incorrect. This is false. A marriage can be annulled even after consummation if the fraud goes to an essential of marriage. *See Wolfe v. Wolfe*, 389 N.E.2d 1143 (Ill. 1979).

Answer (B) is incorrect. The marriage will be annulled only if the deception goes to the essentials of marriage. *See Wolfe v. Wolfe*, 389 N.E.2d 1143 (Ill. 1979).

Answer (C) is incorrect. While length of the marriage might be a factor militating against its annulment, the couple's having been married for three years may well not be viewed as a bar to an annulment. *See Wolfe v. Wolfe*, 389 N.E.2d 1143 (Ill. 1979) (marriage annulled after nine years and one child having been born of the marriage).

223. **Answer (C) is the best answer.** *See B.H. v. K.D.*, 506 N.W.2d 368 (N.D. 1993) (putative father precluded from establishing his paternity of a child born after the child's mother had married another).

Answer (A) is incorrect. This is false. *See B.H. v. K.D.*, 506 N.W.2d 368 (N.D. 1993) (putative father precluded from challenging paternity of child conceived before but born into marriage).

Answer (B) is incorrect. This is false. The nonmarital father's rights will be afforded protection when the child is not born into a marriage. *See, e.g., In re A.J.F.*, 764 So.2d 47 (La. 2000) (adoption not permitted because unwed father's rights not respected).

Answer (D) is incorrect. This is false both because he might have been precluded from establishing parental rights even had he acted in a more timely manner, *see B.H. v. K.D.*, 506 N.W.2d 368 (N.D. 1993), and because John did not do as much to protect his rights and his child as he might have. By failing to act promptly to find Carol and to try to provide support for her and the child, John may have made it less likely that his parental rights would be recognized. *See Michael M. v. Giovanna F.*, 7 Cal. Rptr. 2d 460 (Cal. App. 1992) (timely action by unwed biological father helped preserve his paternal rights); *In re Adoption of M.D.K.*, 58 P.3d 745 (Kan. App. 2002) (father loses parental rights because he failed to offer support without reasonable cause during last six months of pregnancy).

224. **Answer (C) is the best answer.** *See Van v. Zahorik*, 597 N.W.2d 15, 20 (Mich. 1999) ("[W]e adopt the doctrine of equitable parent and find that a husband who is not the biological father of a child born or conceived during the marriage may be considered the natural father of that child where (1) the husband and the child mutually acknowledge a relationship as father and child, or the mother of the child has cooperated in the development of such a relationship over a period of time prior to the filing of the complaint for divorce, (2) the husband desires to have the rights afforded to a parent, and (3) the husband is willing to take on the responsibility of paying child support.").

    Answer (A) is incorrect. This is a red herring. While parents should aspire to be fair to their children, there is no special term of art in the law that refers to parents who make an extra effort to be fair to their children.

    Answer (B) is incorrect. While there is such a doctrine as equitable adoption, *see Lankford v. Wright*, 489 S.E.2d 604, 606 (N.C. 1997) ("Equitable adoption is a remedy to protect the interest of a person who was supposed to have been adopted as a child but whose adoptive parents failed to undertake the legal steps necessary to formally accomplish the adoption."), equitable parentage refers to a different way that parent-child relations can be established.

    Answer (D) is incorrect. While guardians may and sometimes must be appointed to protect the interests of children, *see D.J.L. v. Bolivar County Dep't of Human Services ex rel. McDaniel*, 824 So.2d 617, 622 (Miss. 2002) (discussing mandatory appointment of guardian *ad litem* in parental rights termination proceedings), "equitable parent" is not a synonym for guardian *ad litem*.

225. **Answer (D) is the best answer.** *See In re Interest of R.C.*, 775 P.2d 27 (Colo. 1989) (paternal rights of known sperm donor would be recognized if that had been the intentions of the parties).

    Answer (A) is incorrect. This is false. As the United States Supreme Court made clear in *Lehr v. Robertson*, 463 U.S. 248, 260 (1983), "rights do not spring full-blown from the biological connection between parent and child."

    Answer (B) is incorrect. This is false. Here, Beverly had been divorced for several months before she became pregnant. Had the child been born within 300 days of her divorce, however, her ex-husband might have been presumed by the law to be the father. *See Leger v. Leger*, 829 So.2d 1101 (La. App. 2002).

    Answer (C) is incorrect. This is false. Had Carl and Beverly agreed that they would each be the parent of Juanita, Beverly's desire to raise her alone now would not preclude Carl from establishing paternal rights. *See McIntyre v. Crouch*, 780 P.2d 239 (Or. App. 1989).

226. Even if Edward is not the biological father of the twins, he may nonetheless be awarded custody if that would in fact promote their best interests. If Donna knew that Herbert was the twins' father but she nonetheless implicitly or expressly suggested that Edward was, she might be estopped from challenging Edward's paternity. *See Randy A.J. v. Norma I.J.*, 655 N.W.2d 195 (Wis. App. 2002) (affirming trial court's estoppel of wife's asserting that her ex-husband was not the father of children born into the marriage). Further, Edward might be declared the twins' equitable father if the twins acknowledge him as their father, Donna promoted the relationship between Edward and the twins, and Edward wants the rights and responsibilities of fatherhood. *See Van v. Zahorik*, 597 N.W.2d 15, 20 (Mich. 1999). In that event, he would have the same rights as he would have had he been their biological father and could be awarded custody if doing so would promote the best interests of the twins. See Randy A.J. v. Norma I.J., 655 N.W.2d 195 (Wis. App. 2002).

227. **Answer (B) is the best answer.** *See Harris v. Harris*, 621 N.W.2d 491, 501 (Neb. 2001) (Defining dissipation of marital assets as "one spouse's use of marital property for a selfish purpose unrelated to the marriage at the time when the marriage is undergoing an irretrievable breakdown.").

    Answer (A) is incorrect. This is false. This expenditure is unlike other expenditures because it has been spent for selfish purposes once it was clear that the marriage was over. *See Harris v. Harris*, 621 N.W.2d 491, 501 (Neb. 2001) (defining dissipation of marital assets).

    Answer (C) is incorrect. This is inaccurate, since many courts suggest that it is quite fair to adopt this remedy when dissipation of marital assets has occurred. *See Barth v. Barth*, 593 N.W.2d 359, 363 (N.D. 1999) ("Where a party transfers marital assets, resulting in dissipation of marital assets, inclusion of the value of the transferred assets in the dissipating party's share of the marital property distributed is an appropriate method of reaching an equitable property division in light of [that party's] economic fault.").

    Answer (D) is incorrect. This is not a good answer because it ignores, among other things, when these purchases occurred. The car was bought when there was no indication that the marriage was in trouble, whereas the extravagant dinner was bought when it was clear that the marriage was over. *See In re Marriage of O'Neill*, 563 N.E.2d 494, 498-99 (Ill. 1990) (dissipation refers to the "use of marital property for the sole benefit of one of the spouses for a purpose unrelated to the marriage at a time that the marriage is undergoing an irreconcilable breakdown").

228. **Answer (D) is the best answer.** *See Johnson v. Dar Denne*, 296 P. 1105, 1106 (Wash. 1931) (jewelry bought with marital funds treated as gift); *Compton v. Compton*, 902 P.2d 805 (Alaska 1995) (car purchased with separate funds to replace wife's car and used as family car was marital asset).

Answer (A) is incorrect. While the necklace could be a marital asset, it is more likely to be treated as a gift from William to Ethel in which case it would be Ethel's separate property. *See Johnson v. Dar Denne*, 296 P. 1105, 1106 (Wash. 1931) ("jewelry or articles of personal adornment, acquired after marriage with community funds, but worn and used solely by the wife, will be held to be the separate property of the wife by gift from the husband upon comparatively slight evidence"). Notwithstanding the use of separate funds to buy the car, it might well be treated as a marital asset because it was titled in both their names, was used primarily by Ethel and as a family car. *See Compton v. Compton*, 902 P.2d 805 (Alaska 1995) (family car purchased with separate funds treated as marital asset).

Answer (B) is incorrect. This is false. Funds coming from salary during the marriage would be marital rather than separate. *See Steiner v. Steiner*, 746 So.2d 1149, 1150 (Fla. App. 1999) ("Marital assets are those acquired during the marriage, created or produced by the work efforts, services, or earnings of one or both spouses.") The car may well be treated as marital. *See Compton v. Compton*, 902 P.2d 805 (Alaska 1995).

Answer (C) is incorrect. While the car may well be treated as marital, *see Compton v. Compton*, 902 P.2d 805 (Alaska 1995), the necklace is more likely to be treated as separate property. *See Semasek v. Semasek*, 502 A.2d 109 (Pa. 1985) (diamond rings treated as separate property).

229. The court might take several approaches with respect to the house. First, in order for the character of the house to be affected, the contributions of marital assets to separate property must be significant. Here, because they have paid off the mortgage and made improvements to the home all with marital funds, it may well be held that the contributions were sufficiently significant to justify Lisa's receipt of some of the increased value of the house. *See In re Marriage of Olson*, 451 N.E.2d 825, 829 (Ill. 1983) ("The commingling of marital and nonmarital assets, and the contribution of marital assets to nonmarital property must be sufficiently significant to raise a presumption of a gift of the property to the marital estate."). Where there is a significant contribution by the non-owning spouse, that individual may well be entitled to a share of the increased value of the house over the period of the marriage. *See Cohen v. Cohen*, 937 S.W.2d 823, 833 (Tenn. 1996) ("[E]quity in separate property that accrues during the marriage is subject to division as marital property if the non-owner spouse makes a substantial contribution to the increase in the value."). Since there was no evidence of intent to contribute the house to the marital estate and thereby transmute its character, *see Barta v. Barta*, 2002 WL 1293030 (Alaska) ("Separate property acquired prior to marriage transmutes into marital property where that is the intent of the owner and there is an act or acts which demonstrate that intent."), the property may well continue to be treated as separate but Lisa will be entitled to a share of the increased value. Depending upon the records kept and whether tracing would be possible, the court might say that commingling the marital funds with the separate property made the home marital because the home's separate identity had not been maintained. *See In re Marriage of Sokolowski*, 597 N.E.2d 675, 681 (Ill. App. 1992) ("when marital and

non-marital property are commingled resulting in a loss of identity of the contributing estates, the commingled property shall be deemed transmuted to marital property").

230. **Answer (B) is the best answer.** *See Young v. Hector*, 740 So.2d 1153, 1157 (Fla. App. 1998) (making clear that the primary caretaker is the primary caregiver rather than the primary wage-earner).

Answer (A) is incorrect. The primary caretaker presumption refers to the parent who has been the primary caregiver rather than the primary wage-earner. *See Young v. Hector*, 740 So.2d 1153, 1157 (Fla. App. 1998) ("A trial court's decision as to which parent should be awarded primary residential custody of the children should attempt to preserve and continue the caretaking roles that the parties had established.").

Answer (C) is incorrect. *See Young v. Hector*, 740 So.2d 1153, 1157 (Fla. App. 1998). The presumption is not a synonym for the parent whose having custody would promote the child's best interests but instead helps to determine which parent that would be.

Answer (D) is incorrect. *See Young v. Hector*, 740 So.2d 1153, 1157 (Fla. App. 1998). The presumption does not speak to which parent feels more emotionally attached to the child, although it may turn out that the parent with the primary caretaking duties is more attached.

231. **Answer (D) is the best answer.** *See Thornhill v. Midwest Physician Center of Orland Park*, 787 N.E.2d 247, 254 (Ill. App. 2003). If the plaintiff could not establish that they would have aborted had they had the relevant information in a timely way, then they will not be able to establish that they were harmed by not having been apprised more promptly of their child's condition.

Answer (A) is incorrect. This is inaccurate both because this is not a wrongful life suit, *see Walter v. Rinck*, 604 N.E.2d 591, 593-94 (Ind. 1992) ("The phrase 'wrongful birth' applies to claims brought by the parents of a child born with birth defects alleging that due to negligent medical advice or testing they were precluded from an informed decision about whether to conceive a potentially handicapped child or, in the event of a pregnancy, to terminate it. When such action seeks damages on behalf of the child rather than the parents, the phrase 'wrongful life' instead of 'wrongful birth' is employed."), and because these causes of action, where recognized, can be brought even if the doctor's negligence did not cause the existence of the condition but, instead, deprived the parents of the opportunity to abort.

Answer (B) is incorrect. While they are correct to bring a wrongful birth rather than a wrongful life suit, *see Walter v. Rinck*, 604 N.E.2d 591, 593-94 (Ind. 1992), they would not need to establish that Carolyn would have been better off never having lived at all, since that claim characterizes a wrongful life rather than a wrongful birth suit. *See Garrison v. Medical Center of Delaware Inc.*, 581 A.2d 288, 289 n.1 (Del. 1989).

Answer (C) is incorrect. This is inaccurate. They would not be bringing a wrongful pregnancy claim. Further, were they to have brought such a claim, they would not have needed to have an amniocentesis performed, since a wrongful pregnancy claim asserts that an unexpected child was born as a result of a faulty sterilization procedure or contraceptive device. *See Chaffee v. Seslar*, 786 N.E.2d 705, 710 n.3 (Ind. 2003).

232. If the court does not have personal jurisdiction over Avrum, it cannot distribute marital property that is not located in the state. *See Abernathy v. Abernathy*, 482 S.E.2d 265, 267 (Ga. 1997). Courts have split about whether property which is part of the marital state can be distributed in an ex parte divorce when that property is within the state. *Compare Dawson-Austin v. Austin*, 968 S.W.2d 319 (Tex. 1998) (no jurisdiction to divide up property located in state), *with Abernathy v. Abernathy*, 482 S.E.2d 265 (Ga. 1997) (awarding husband divorce from nonresident wife and the property located in the state). Here, the court will not have jurisdiction to divide up property not located in the state and may have jurisdiction to divide up property which is in the state.

233. Mary may well have her request for a reduction in support denied because her decrease in income was caused by her desire to have her child support payments reduced. She may well be viewed as acting in bad faith and thus not entitled to a reduction. *See Schroader v. Schroader*, 463 S.E.2d 790, 794 (N.C. App. 1995) ("If a trial court finds that a party was acting in bad faith by deliberately depressing her income or otherwise disregarding the obligation to pay child support, the party's earning capacity may be the basis for the award."). However, if the decrease in her compensation had been involuntary, then her request would likely have been granted. *See McGee v. McGee*, 453 S.E.2d 531 (N.C. App. 1995) (substantial involuntary decrease in non-custodial parent's income justifies modification of support payment).

234. **Answer (C) is the best answer.** *See New Hanover County v. Kilbourne*, 578 S.E.2d 610, 614 (N.C. App. 2003) (under Uniform Interstate Family Support Act, a foreign support order, once registered, may not be vacated or modified unless the parties consent or unless all parties have permanently left the issuing state).

Answer (A) is incorrect. While this accurately captures the rule regarding support obligations, *see McGee v. McGee*, 453 S.E.2d 531 (N.C. App. 1995) (substantial involuntary decrease in non-custodial parent's income justifies modification of support payment), this is not the best answer because it ignores the relevant jurisdictional issues. *See New Hanover County v. Kilbourne*, 578 S.E.2d 610, 614 (N.C. App. 2003).

Answer (B) is incorrect. Even if one brackets the jurisdictional issue, it may well be that even a very capable Miguel will not be able to get a job offering similar compensation, despite his best efforts, and it thus might not be appropriate to impute that level of income to him. *See State ex rel. Human Services Dept. v. Kelley*, 64 P.2d 537 (N.M. App. 2003).

Answer (D) is incorrect. People as a general matter know that there is some possibility that they will lose their jobs. This would mean that people who lost their jobs through no fault of their own would nonetheless not be able to have support reduced. This is too strict a rule. *See In re Marriage of Lavelle,* 565 N.E.2d 291, 293 (Ill. App. 990) (well settled that child support payments should be reduced when substantial economic reversal due to involuntary change to or loss of employment).

235. **Answer (C) is the best answer.** *See Ruth F. v. Robert B.,* 690 A.2d 1171 (Pa. Super. 1997) (father estopped from challenging paternity where he is on notice that he was not the father and nonetheless accepted child as his own).

Answer (A) is incorrect. This is false. *See Anderson v. Anderson,* 845 So.2d 870 (Fla. 2003) (former husband required to pay support for child notwithstanding blood test establishing that he was not the biological father).

Answer (B) is incorrect. This is false. Under different facts, if Robert could have rebutted the presumption of paternity, he might well not have been forced to pay child support. *See Williams v. Williams,* 843 So.2d 720 (Miss. 2003).

Answer (D) is incorrect. This is false because he might not be ordered to pay support, *see Williams v. Williams,* 843 So.2d 720 (Miss. 2003), and because child support may be ordered even if the father does not visit the child. *See Hester v. Hester,* 663 P.2d 727 (Okla. 1983) (child support not contingent on exercise of visitation privileges).

236. **Answer (D) is the best answer.** *Compare Kirchner v. Crystal,* 474 N.E.2d 275 (Ohio 1984) (no immunity), *with Clark v. Estate of Rice ex rel. Rice,* 653 N.W.2d 166 (Iowa 2002) (immunity for negligent supervision).

Answer (A) is incorrect. The issue here is whether parental immunity has been abolished, not whether interspousal immunity has been abolished. *See, e.g., Unah By and Through Unah v. Martin,* 676 P.2d 1366 (Okla. 1984) (analyzing whether parental immunity should bar suit by child through one parent against the other parent).

Answer (B) is incorrect. Some states have abolished parental immunity entirely while others have only partially abrogated it and have retained it for cases involving negligent supervision. *Compare Kirchner v. Crystal,* 474 N.E.2d 275 (Ohio 1984) (abolishing parent-child immunity), *with Clark v. Estate of Rice ex rel. Rice,* 653 N.W.2d 166, 174 (Iowa 2002) ("immunity exists only for negligent acts involving the exercise of parental authority over a child or the exercise of parental discretion in providing care"). Only if this jurisdiction were among the latter would this suit be barred.

Answer (C) is incorrect. This is false. *See, e.g., Clark v. Estate of Rice ex rel. Rice,* 653 N.W.2d 166, 174 (Iowa 2002) (immunity for negligent acts involving parental authority); La. Rev. Stat. 9:571 (children may not sue their parents while they are still married).

237. **Answer (D) is the best answer.** *See, e.g., Stevens v. Stevens*, 492 N.E.2d 131, 135 (Ohio 1986) ("[A] professional degree or license is not marital property and the present value of the projected future earnings of the degreed spouse is not a marital asset subject to division upon divorce. Although not an asset, the future value of a professional degree or license acquired by one of the parties during the marriage is an element to be considered in reaching an equitable award of alimony.").

Answer (A) is incorrect. This is false. Even if the law degree is not considered property, the enhanced earning capacity could be considered when dividing up the marital estate. See Roberts v. Roberts, 670 N.E.2d 72 (Ind. App. 1996). Further, the law degree might be treated as a marital asset subject to distribution. See Postema v. Postema, 471 N.W.2d 912 (Mich. App. 1991).

Answer (B) is incorrect. This is false. *See Roberts v. Roberts*, 670 N.E.2d 72 (Ind. App. 1996) (refusing to treat law degree as marital asset). Further, courts vary greatly with respect to how the non-degreed spouse should be compensated. *See, e.g., Mahoney v. Mahoney*, 453 A.2d 527 (N.J. 1982) (while a professional degree is not property, the non-degree holder can be reimbursed for funds contributed to acquisition of degree).

Answer (C) is incorrect. This is false, because not all jurisdictions have adopted this approach. *See Mahoney v. Mahoney*, 453 A.2d 527 (N.J. 1982).

238. **Answer (C) is the best answer.** Here, because they have made improvements to the home with marital funds, it may well be held that the contributions were sufficiently significant to justify Cynthia's receiving some of the increased value of the house. *See In re Marriage of Olson*, 451 N.E.2d 825, 829 (Ill. 1983) ("The commingling of marital and nonmarital assets, and the contribution of marital assets to nonmarital property must be sufficiently significant to raise a presumption of a gift of the property to the marital estate."). Since there was no evidence of intent to contribute the house to the marital estate and thereby transmute its character, *see Barta v. Barta*, 2002 WL 1293030 (Alaska) ("Separate property acquired prior to marriage transmutes into marital property where that is the intent of the owner and there is an act or acts which demonstrate that intent."), the property may well continue to be treated as separate but Cynthia will be entitled to a share of the increased value.

Yet, it should not be forgotten that Cynthia contributed separate funds (her inheritance) to the improvement of the house. Depending upon her intent when doing so, that might justify her receipt of a credit for those funds or, perhaps, treating the house as part of the marital estate. *See In re Marriage of Sokolowski*, 597 N.E.2d 675, 681 (Ill. App. 1992) ("when marital and non-marital property are commingled resulting in a loss of identity of the contributing estates, the commingled property shall be deemed transmuted to marital property").

Answer (A) is incorrect. Because funds from the marital estate were used to pay the mortgage and make improvements, the increase in value of the house during the marriage may well be treated as part of the marital estate. Where there is a significant contribution by the non-owning spouse, that individual may well be entitled to a share of the increased value of the house over the period of the marriage. *See Cohen v. Cohen*, 937 S.W.2d 823, 833 (Tenn. 1996) ("equity in separate property that accrues during the marriage is subject to division as marital property if the non-owner spouse makes a substantial contribution to the increase in the value"). It would be unlikely that Cynthia's contributions would be treated as a gift, absent some indication of her intent to do so.

Answer (B) is incorrect. Because funds were contributed from the marital estate for improvements, the increase in value of the house might well be viewed as marital. *See Cohen v. Cohen*, 937 S.W.2d 823, 833 (Tenn. 1996).

Answer (D) is incorrect. Merely because marital funds were used to maintain the house would not justify treating it as marital. *See Caruso v. Caruso*, 814 So.2d 498 (Fla. App. 2002) (house bought by husband with separate funds did not become part of marital estate merely because marital funds were used to maintain it).

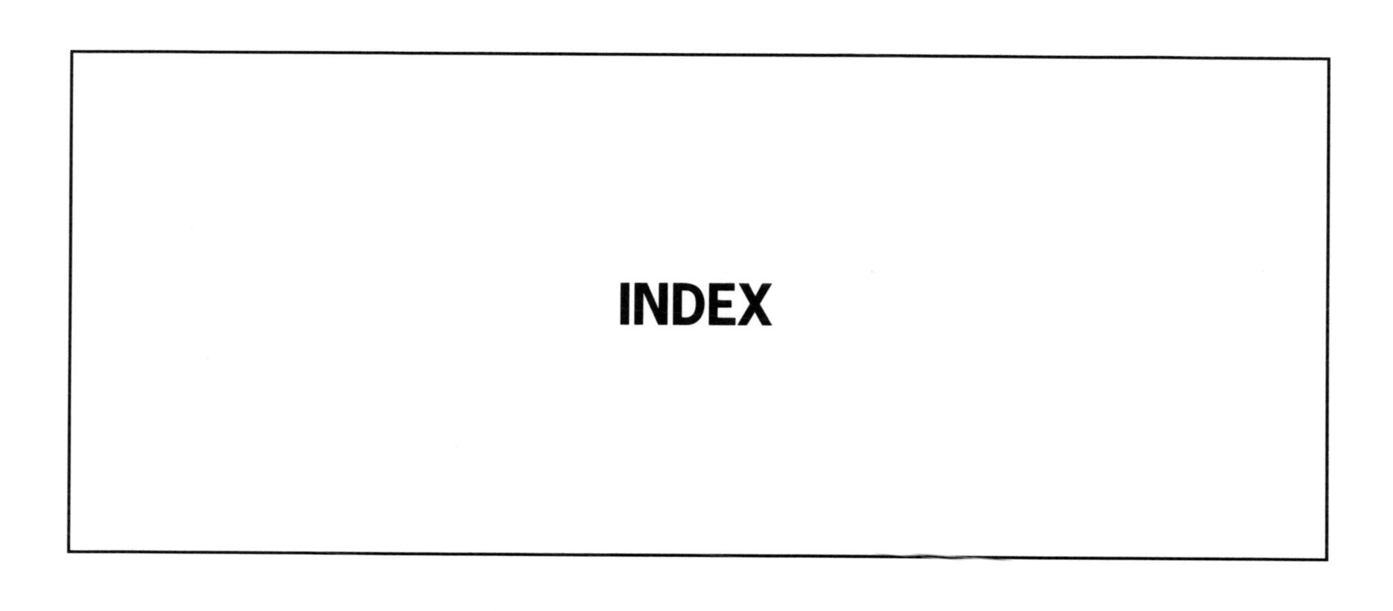

INDEX

INDEX